Early Marriage Records (1819-1850) and Will Records (1820-1870) of Cooper County Missouri

By:
Elizabeth Prather Ellsberry

Southern Historical Press, Inc.
Greenville, South Carolina

This volume was reproduced from
An 1959 edition located in the
Publisher's private Library

All rights reserved. No part of this publication may be reproduced,
stored in a retrieval system, transmitted in any form, posted
on to the web in any form or by any means without
the prior written permission of the publisher.

Please direct all correspondence and orders to:

www.southernhistoricalpress.com
or
SOUTHERN HISTORICAL PRESS, Inc.
PO Box 1267
375 West Broad Street
Greenville, SC   29601
southernhistoricalpress@gmail.com

Originally published: Chillicoths, MO 1959
New material © 2019
By: Southern Historical Press, Inc.
ISBN #0-89308-894-3
All rights Reserved.
Printed in the United States of America

TO

MISS NANON CARR
6109 the Paseo
Kansas City, Missouri
and
MRS. HALE HOUTS
230 West 61st Street
Kansas City, Missouri
For Their Moral Support
and
MRS. MARGARET GRAY BLANTON
200 East 66th Street
New York City, N. Y.
For Suggesting Cooper County

SPECIAL NOTE

This reproduction of this book was made from an original copy. Every effort has been made to make and enhance this reprint to quality of the original.

PREFACE

Page 639-726 History of Howard and Cooper Counties, Missouri 1883

Cooper county was originated on the 17 day of December, 1818, and comprised all that part of what had been Howard county, lying south of the Missouri River.

The county was named in honor of Colonel Benjamin Cooper.

At the time of its organization, it included the territory now embraced in the whole of the counties of Cooper, Saline, Lafayette, Jackson, Cass, Henry, Johnson, Pettis, Morgan, Moniteau, and Cole; and parts of the counties of Bates, St. Clair, Benton, Camden, and Miller.

On 9 April 1821, the will of Thomas McMahan, deceased, was probated, it being the first will proven before the court.

During the year 1821, John V. Sharp a soldier who had served in the revolutionary war...

The first early settlers of Boonville township were Stephen and Hannah Cole, who settled there in 1810. The settlers who arrived previous to the year 1815, were Gilliad Rupe, Muke Box, Delany Dowlin, William Savage, James Savage, John Savage, and Walter Burress, and in 1815, Umphrey and William Gibson. Those who settled between the years 1815 and 1820 were: William McFarland, John S. and Jesse McFarland, George, Samuel, and Alexander McFarland, William Mitchell, James Bruffee, Robert P. Clark, Joseph and William Dillard, Littleberry Hendricks, William Bartlett, Jesse Ashcraft, Russell Edgar, John M. Bartlett, Abram Gibson, Thomas Twentyman, James Dillard, Jacob Newman, William Potter, Frederick Houx, William Poston, George Potter, Benjamin L. Clark, John J. Clark, Kyra Dunn, K. McKenzie, Marcus Williams, James, Robert, and Alexander Givens, Jacob Chism, John B. Lucas, Charles B. Mitchell, Nicholas McCarty, Lewis Edgar, John B. Seat, Jacob McFarland, James McCarty, William Ross, Abiel Leonard, James W. Bernard, James McFarland, Ephraim Ellison, John Roberts, Thomas Mitchell, Reuben George, Fleming G. Mitchell, Jesse Thomas, Asa Morgan, Peter B. Harris, James Chambers, Benjamin F. Hickox, William H. Curtis, William W. Adams, John D. Thomas, William Lillard, James M. Anderson, Peyton R. Hayden, John S. Brickey, Peyton Thomas, David Adams, Luke Williams, John Potter, Andrew Reavis, David Reavis, Jonathan Reavis, Jesse Homan, John H. Moore, Green B. Seat, W. D. Wilson, Thomas Rogers, Mrs. Mary Reavis, William Chambers, James Chambers, and Justinian Williams.

Mr. John Kelly and Mrs. Tibitha Kelly were in the township frequently between 1818-1820.

William McFarland, the first sheriff of Cooper county, was born in Buncombe county, North Carolina, in the year 1778.

Benjamin F. Hickox was born in New York.

Justinian Williams was born in Bath County, Virginia and while young emigrated to Kentucky and there married.

Marcus Williams, the first mayor of the city of Boonville, was born in Bath County, Virginia, and while young emigrated to Kentucky.

Boonville was laid out by Asa Morgan and Charles Lewis in 1817.

William Christie and John G. Heath temporarily settled in Blackwater township in 1808. James Broch, the first permanent settler, arrived in 1816, Enoch Hambrich came in 1817; David Shellcram, in 1818; George Chapman, the father of Mrs. Caleb Jones, came in 1818; Nathaniel T. Allison, Sr. in 1831; Fleming Marshall and Robert Clark in 1832; Nathaniel Bridgewater, in 1835 and Edmund M. Cobb and Larkin T. Dix, in 1838.

John Glover was the first settler in Clark's Fork Township in the year 1813. The next settlers were Zephemiah Bell and John C. Rochester. The last named gentleman was a grandson of the founder of the city of Rochester, New York. He married Callie Kelly, the daughter of James Kelly, who was an honored soldier of the revolution.

Among the early settlers of Clear Creek Township were James Taylor, who had three sons: William, John, and James. He emigrated from the state of Georgia. Jordon O'Bryan, a son in law of James Taylor, was also an early settler. He was born in North Carolina, moved to Kentucky and came to Cooper county in 1817. In 1830 he removed to Saline township. Charles R. Berry, the father of Finis E. Berry, Isaac Ellis, and Hugh and Alexander Brown, are among the oldest citizens.

The first settlers of Kelly Township in 1818 were: John Kelly, William Stephens, James D. Campbell, James Kelly, William J. Kelly, Caperton Kelly, William Jennings, General Charles Woods, Philip E. Davis, Rice Challis, Hugh Morris, Jesse White, Hartley White, Jeptha Billingsley, Joshua Dellis, and William Swearengen.

James Kelly a revolutionary soldier died in 1840. The Kellys came from Tennessee and James D. Campbell, Kentucky. William Jennings emigrated from Georgia to Cooper in 1819.

Joshua Reavis settled in the year 1823. He, together with his sons, Lewis, William T., Jackson, and Johnston.

Lamine Township was first settled in 1812. The first settlers were David Jones, a revolutionary soldier, Thomas and James McMahan, Stephen, Samuel, and Jesse Turley.

Among the first settlers of Moniteau township were Thomas B. Smiley, Seth Joseph, Waid, and Stephen Howard, William Coal, James Stinson, Hawking and David Burress, Charles Hickox, Samuel McFarland, Carroll George, James Snodgrass, Martin George Mathew Burress, Jesse Martin, Alexander Woods, William Landers, Jesse Bowles, James Donelson, William A. Stillson, Samuel Snodgrass, James W. Maxey, Job Martin, James Jones, David Jones Augustus K. and John B. Longan, Patrick Mahan, Valentine Martin and John Jones.

T. Abbott to Martha Hickox 15 November 1847 256

Francis Achllie to Eliza Jane Mack 14 June 1846 211

Adaline H. Adams to Peter Shelby 25 Feb. 1839 92
Andrew Adams to Sarah Flournoy 16 Dec. 1847 249
Eli Adams to Mary Jane Robertson 24 Jan. 1833 164
Eli T. Adams to Martha Ann Davis 5 Sept. 1839 102
Emiline Adams to Pike M. Bradley 15 Dec. 1842 151
Ignatius Adams to Julian Taylor 26 Feb. 1833 3
John Adams to Margretome Loller 15 Jan. 1846 203
Joshua D. Adams to Amanda M. Tucker 9 Oct. 1838 87
Margaret Adams to Robert Tucker 10 Jan. 1839 91
Maria Adams to William H. Stephens 9 Nov. 1847 242
Martha Adams to Robert O'Bryan 22 Feb. 1848 255
Mathew Adams to Lucinda Johnson 23 Oct. 1827 86
Mrs. Nancy Adams to James Handlin 28 May 1840 110
Robert I. Adams to Jemima Amanda Catoon 19 Sept. 1850 33
Thomas Adams to Phebe Dillard 22 Dec. 1842 152
Turner Adams to Rebecca Eller 26 Jan. 1834 14
Washington Adams to Eliza Brown 27 Feb. 1840 105

Major Adier to Elizabeth Weever 8 July 1827 79

William Adkerson to Selinda Allison 8 June 1847 234

Page 115 B
Will of John Ainslie
    At Edinburgh the first day of August 1844 in presence of the Lord of Council Sepron appeared James Moncreiff, Esq. advocate procater for John Ainslie after desiring and gave Disposition and settlement under written desiring the same might be registered in Their Lordships Books....
    I John Ainslie of Maxpoff Esquire Advocate being do resolve to execute a settlement of my affairs to the place after my death and for the love and affection which I have to Mrs. Borron or Ainslie my wife...
    To my children...
Written 2 March 1835
Witnesses: William Jennions Tailor, Wavertree Nook, and Thomas Broughton Shoemaker
Recorded: 15 November 1844

Elizabeth Alexander to Harrison Corum 25 Aug. 1848 264
Mary Ann Alexander to Joseph W. Stinson 15 May 1845 191
Penelope Alexander to Phillip W. Thompson 21 Feb. 1850 29

James M. Allcorn, Jr., of Howard County, Mo. to Cinthy F.
    Wear 14 Feb. 1833 163
James M. Allcorn to Nancy Ellen McFarland 5 Feb. 1846 203

Page 86 A
Will of David Allee
    To Lucy and Betsey Combs...
    To my children--Beuford Allee, Nicholas Allee, John Allee, William Allee, David Allee, Anna Scott, Winey Burdsong, Jarusha Hill, Charity Howard, and the heirs of Betsey Scott: Anna Adams, William Scott, David Scott, John Scott, Kemp Scott, Polly Luster, Charity Scott, and Betsey Scott, children of my daughter Betsey Scott, dec....
Written: 3 January 1835
Witnesses: Moses Martin and C. P. Arbuckle
Recorded: 16 February 1835
Charity Allee to Kesiah Howard 1 April 1825 53
Nancy Allee to John Russell 2 September 1830 125

Page 207 2A
Will of David H. Allen
    To my mother, Mary Allen...
    To my wife, Melinda...
Written: 9 September 1857
Witnesses: John S. Martin, Washington Martin, and Jefferson C. Martin
Recorded: 17 September 1857
Mrs. Barbary Ann Allen to Reuben V. Harvey 7 May 1836 51
James Allen to Martha Ann Hill 15 March 1843 159
Jane Allen to Joseph Gooden 14 March 1820 12
John Allen to Letta Vaughan 27 Feb. 1849
Moses Allen to Nancy Wright 30 April 183   79
Samuel Allen to Sarah Benson 11 Sept. 1827 83
Thomas Allen to Ealenor George 30 June 1831 135

Thomas Alley to Jerrumah Evans 7 Feb. 1832 142

Page 444 2A
Will of Greenberry Allison
    To my son, John...
    To my daughter, Lucinda Chany...
    To Susan Allison, widow of my son, Lovet Allison...
    To my grand children: Joseph W. Allison and Henderson A. Allison, sons of James Allison, dec. ...
    To my grand daughter, Mary E. DeWitt, sister of said Joseph W. and Henderson A. Allison...
    My son, John Allison, Executor
Written 7 February 1871
Recorded 15 March 1871
Page 167 B
Will of Hugh Allison
    To my sons: Jesse Allison, Thomas W. Allison, and Nathaniel T. Allison...
(Continued)

To my three grandchildren: Shelton Allison, Cincinattus Allison, and Lucinda Allison children of John L. and Mary Allison, dec. ...
To my grandchildren who are the children of James and Lucinda Pearce...
My sons Thomas W. and Nathaniel T. Allison, Exe.
Written: 22 Oct. 1844
Witnesses: Henry Slotzhour, J. F. Summers, and L. A. Summers
Recorded: 20 August 1846
Page 342 2A
Will of William Allison
To my three daughters: Eliza Jane Stephens, Mary Adaline Allison, and Sarah Catherine Crocket...
To my sons: Stephen Cole Allison, William Robert Allison, Charles Holbert Allison, John Richard Allison, David Crocket Allison, Samuel Aquillap Allison, Peyton Alexander Allison, and Benjamin Franklin Allison...
My sons Charles H. and John Richard Allison, Exe.
Written: 28 January 1864
Witnesses: S. C. Stephens, A. M. Crockett, and G. W. Stephens
Recorded: 18 February 1864
Eliza Jane Allison to Levin Stephens 19 May 1846 209
Elizabeth Allison to John Charbers 10 Nov. 1826 59
Green P. Allison to Katherine Truce 10 Jan. 1841 122
Hugh Allison to Sarah Robard 30 Jan. 1844 166
Katherine Allison to James Cole 16 Jan. 1842 138
John Allison to Frances Parrish 1 March 1848 252
John K. Allison to Mary Richardson _ Jan. 1832 144
Josafiene Allison to William Y. Clalomb 2 April 1846 205
Lucinda Allison to Henry Chaney 29 Nov. 1832 162
Lucy Allison to Vincent Johnson 2 Oct. 1823 46
Margaret Allison to James H. White 17 July 1830 91
Mary Allison to James Harvey 11 Jan. 1835 24
Mary Ann Allison to Louis F. Evans 7 July 1847 238
Rebecca Allison to Thomas Jones 1 Sept. 1844 180
Robert Allison to Mary Jane Cole 21 Jan. 1842 140
Samenda Allison to John P. Lilly 11 Sept. 1843 160
Selinda Allison to William Adkerson 8 June 1847 234
William Allison to Elizabeth Ford 14 Oct. 1841 134

Page 282 A2
Will of Jacob Allstadt
  To Aaron McVarney...
  To the heirs of William and Elizabeth Rider...
  To Rachel Ann Rider...
  Richard E. Ransom of Kentucky, Exe.
Written 29 April 1856
Witnesses: George S. Cockrell and Thomas M. Harris
Recorded: 16 July 1860

Page 56 2A
Will of Jesse W. Amick
    To my wife, Lucy Ann...
    to Atkinson M. Lee, of Howard Co., Mo. ...
    To my children: Mary Pope, Martha Manah, and Jesse Angeline Amick...
    My wife and Atkinson M. Lee, Exe.
Written: 16 August 1851.
Witnesses: I. Hobbs, Samuel Roe, and Phillip Amick
Recorded: 18 October 1851
Eli D. Amick to Susan R. Mann   11 Jan. 1849   8
John W. Amick to Mary L. Bower   25 Dec. 1846   224
Malvina Amick to William Kirkendoll   28 Feb. 1833   2
Nancy Amick to Rev. Minor Neal   18 Aug. 1842   145

James Amos to Mary S. Rankin   27 April 1848   256

Adaline Anderson to John Jackson   23 March 1834   18
Angeline Anderson to Robert Hornbeck   24 May 1846   212
Margaret J. Anderson to Anthony Welch   21 May 1843   158
Nancy C. Anderson to Robert March   6 Nov. 1836   56
William Anderson, Saline Co., Mo. to Malinda Scott   18 April 1830   119
William Anderson to Mrs. Catharine Ann Thompson   18 Sept. 1842   148
William Anderson to Mary McClanahan   12 Dec. 1845   214

James E. Ansell to Lucinda Bridgewater   2 Jan. 1844   168

John Anthony, Morgan Co., Mo. to Macoline B. Wear   20 Nov. 1845   201

Page 229 2A
Will of Francis Apperson
    To my daughters: Mary Jones and Milly York...
    To my sons: Gilbert Apperson and William Apperson...
Written: 27 March 1857
Witnesses: Thomas Harris, Stanton Harris, and Thomas A. Harris
Recorded: 15 December 1858
Elizabeth Apperson to Gabriel Cotton   26 Sept. 1828   93
Elizabeth Apperson to William H. Todd   19 Sept. 1850   36
Gilbert Apperson to Martha Berkley   16 March 1837   67
Millie Apperson to William York   23 December 1847   247
William Apperson to Damsin Bazzoll   21 Jan. 1841   131

John Arbuckle to Louisa Jones   22 Dec. 1833   12
Silas P. Arbuckle to Dianna Evans   7 Sept. 1831   138

Elizabeth Arhart to Samuel Dennis   26 Feb. 1831   129

Sarah Jane Armstrong to William Stephens   25 Oct. 1849   20

___ Arnold to Nancy Morris   26 Nov. 1833   19

Frederick Arrent, Andrew Co., Mo. to Hannah B. Taylor
14 June 1846   211

Page 152 A2
Will of Martha Ashley, County of Powhatan, state of Virginia
    I desire all my property in the state of Missouri be sold to pay my just debts after which I desire the remainder to be divided among: Leroy Hopkins, William Hopkins, Martha A. Hopkins, Samuel B. Hopkins, and Elizabeth B. Hopkins...
    To Joanna Jackson...
    Leroy Hopkins, Exe.
Written: 9 February 1854
Witnesses: Wiley Jackson, Thomas Forsee, and D. Saprode
Recorded: 24 July 1850

Amos Ashcraft, Howard Co., Mo. to Sarah D. Wood, daughter of
    General Woods   11 March 1841   130
Elizabeth Ashcraft to Americus Elliott   28 April 1848   25
John E. Ashcraft to Susan N. Woods   19 Sept. 1844   180

James Atkins to Elizabeth Martin   9 Jan. 1840   105

William Aton to Mary Drinkwater   14 Aug. 1836   59

Sophia Aull to George Hain   27 April 1845   197

Robert S. Austin to Emilee M. Wright   20 Dec. 1848   5

Samuel Awford to Mary Allison   13 Oct. 1840   118

Page 207 A2
Will of Jaron Babbitt
    To my father, Loren Babbitt of Utah Territory...
    Arvin Allen Avery, Exe.
Written: __ June 1857
Witnesses: Harrison Avery and Mitchell Zimmerman
Recorded: 29 July 1857

Lydia Margaret Pace to John Dehart, of Howard Co., Mo.
24 Feb. 1842   140

Robert B. Bacon to Amanda Hayden   1 Sept. 1840   114
Thomas Bacon to Frances Kirton   5 Jan. 1845   184

John R. Bagwell to Harriett E. Wilson   9 Sept. 1847   255
Woodson Bagwell to Mary Rector   14 April 1847   238

Harmon Bailey to Polly Fisher 16 Jan. 1828 87
Millie Bailey to Isaac N. Ellis 1 Nov. 1849 27
Susan E. Bailey to C. B. Daly 18 July 1849 16
William Bailey to Susannah Belsher 2 Aug. 1840 113

James H. Baker to Lucy Ann Taliafur 14 March 1848 259
John Baker to Jane Turley 5 Nov. 1846 219
Katy Baker to Daniel Millsap 25 May 1826 64
Mary Jane Baker to William B. Foster 27 July 1848 264
William Baker to Elizabeth Frazier 20 March 1832 132
Wilson C. Baker to Mary C. W. Billingsley 1 Oct. 1844 178

Miss Baler to William Miller 3 Nov. 1843 165

Obadiah F. Ballard to Sarah Ann Dempsey 12 June 1843 156

Daniel Bankston, Morgan Co., Mo. to Hannah Westbrook
    3 March 1842 142
Holman F. Bankson to Polly Bowles 17 Dec. 1829 117
Pleasant Bankston to Mariah Smith 21 Nov. 1833 9
Rebecca Bankson to Samuel Berk 28 July 1822 34
Sarah Bankston to James Farris 15 Jan. 1826 57

Rebecca C. Bannion to Tabin Johnson 28 Aug. 1833 4

Elias Barker to Sarah Dennis 20 July 1829 105

Andrew T. Barnes to Dorothy Ann Vaughn 2 Sept. 1845 193
Andrew Barnes to Susanna Bradley 29 July 1849 18
Emily Barnes to Young E. Miller 31 Aug. 1831 138
Ira Barnes to Nancy Calvert 31 May 1842 144
Ira E. Barnes to Catharine Vaughn 12 April 1846 206
Malissa Barnes to James D. Jordan 16 April 1839 95
Mary Jane Barnes to Joseph Furs 18 Jan. 1846 204
Talton T. Barnes to Jane R. Patterson 24 December 1839 104
Victerena Barnes to Zechariah Hinchle 18 Jan. 1846 204

Phillip Barner to Mary Ann Roberson 21 Feb. 1839 94

Elizabeth Jane Barnett to Larkin Erwin 21 Oct. 1841 138
Nancy Barnett to Obediah Ballard 3 Dec. 1850 38
Sarah Barnett to George Dempsey 13 Aug. 1840 128

Sarah Barnhart to Mark G. Hardin 4 July 1847 232

Henrietta Bartlett to Peter Wilson 13 Dec. 1849 23
Luther C. Bartlett to Lutetia Bartoe 27 June 1850 31

Isaac Barton to Jane Wilson 17 March 1840 107
Kimber Barton to Margaret Lockhart 7 Nov. 1821 37

Thomas Baskerville to Mary Susan Graham 11 Jan. 1849 257

Eleanor Bass to Samuel Hornback 21 Nov. 1833 12
Nancy Bass to Henry S. Sarters 12 June 1835 29
Nancy Bass to Henry S. Sarters 12 June 1835 29
Polly Bass to William Hatfield 14 October 1832 160

Virginia Bastable to James O'Brian 26 June 1846 212

William C. Batchelor to Nancy Samuel 22 March 1838 78

Sarah Jane Bath to Benjamin Bowles 29 June 1834 22

Sarah A. Baulton to William A. Pollock 6 Aug. 1843 161

Jacob Bauthman to Mary Parks 13 June 1833 10

Page 257 A2
Will of Henry Bausfield, Jr.
    To my mother, Polly...
    To my father, Henry...
    To my sisters: Elizabeth O'Brien and Fannie Bausfield
    James F. Conner and John L. O'Brien, Exe.
Written: 17 January 1860
Witnesses: Joseph Chambers and John Crawford
Recorded: 30 January 1860

Abraham Baxter to Elizabeth Hoozer 26 Dec. 1843 169
Benjamin Baxter to Mary M. Martin 20 Sept. 1848 3
Edmond Baxter to Anna White 27 Dec. 1849 25
Surilda Baxter to John A. Stephens 6 Feb. 1845 186
John Backster to Patsy Mullins 16 July 1820 16

Damson Bazzell to William Apperson 21 Jan. 1841 131
Mary Bazzell to Absalom McClanahan 8 Feb. 1844 167

James F. Bear to Sophia E. Rochester 14 April 1842 143

Louisa Beaty to Luke Williams 14 July 1833 12
Infamy Beaty to William Campbell Given 10 May 1827 82
Mary Beaty to Stephen M. Fine 24 Sept. 1835 33
Silvitia Beaty to Henry Woolery, Jr. 31 Dec. 1829 116

John Bebybee to Louisa Parks 30 Aug. 1839 100

Page 305 A2
Will of John Jeffrey Beck, County of Santa Fe Territory of N.Mex.
    To my bethrothed wife Ellen Lea Shoemaker of Ft. Union,
N. Mex. County of Toas...
Written: 11 August 1858
Witnesses: Abraham Rencher, George H. Estes, and Joab Houghton
Recorded: 2 October 1861

Page 286 A2
Will of Preston Beck, Jr., a resident of the County of Santa Fe and Territory of New Mexico
    To my brother Simpson Beck, dec. ...
    To my nephew, James P. Beck and my niece Elizabeth C. Beck, children of my brother, Lewis Beck...
    To my nephew, William P. Beck and my nieces Anna D. Beck and Elizabeth Beck, children of my brother, Simpson Beck, dec.
    To my brother John Jeffrey Beck...
    To my cousin, Preston H. Lee...
    To my nieces Mary Ann Cracroft and Elizabeth Cracroft children of my sister Mary Beck...
    John Jeffrey Beck, Exe.
Written 1 April 1854
Witnesses: R. H. Tompkins, J. M. Giddings, and H. N. Smith
Recorded: 30 October 1860
Parmelia Beck to Alfred McDaniel 2 Jan. 1849 6
Simpson Beck to Miss J. A. Sterret 18 July 1843 165

Margaret Becker to Leonard Cline 18 Aug. 1843 174
William M. Becker to Eliza Bridgewater 6 Feb. 1845 184

Nancy Beckett to James Johnson 1 July 1827 81
Polly Beckett to Jacob Quick 1 Jan. 1828 86

Page 375 A2
Will of Adam Bell
    To my wife Catharine Sophie...
    To my daughters: Mina, wife of Casper Hinges and Catherine Bell...
    To my sons: Phillip Bell, August Bell, Hiram Bell, Charles Bell, and William Bell...
    My wife Catherine, Exe.
Written 8 Dec. 1865
Witnesses: William Sombart and A. Hosp
Recorded: 28 September 1866
Andrew J. Bell to Susan Campbell 19 Aug. 1835 37
Benjamin Bell to Brunett Walton 3 Oct. 1844 210
Dorinda Bell to John Fort 19 Oct. 1828 97
Emily Bell to William Parker 20 Aug. 1835 36
James Bell to Mary Thomas 29 May 1823 42
James Bell to Elizabeth McNeel 13 Jan. 1826 60
John Bell to Martha E. Stone 12 Nov. 1840 117
Robert C. Bell to Rox Ann Williams 8 Oct. 1843 164
Robert C. Bell to Elizabeth Elliott 27 July 1845 194
Thornton Pagdet Bell to Mary Susan Menifee 25 March 1847 234
Valentine Bell to Margaret Houx 2 Dec. 1830 126
William G. Bell to Louisa E. Calhoun 21 Oct. 1841 138

Susannah Belsher to William Bailey 2 Aug. 1840 113

Betsey Bennett to Abraham Potter 10 Nov. 1842 150
Nancy Bennett to Robert Miller 10 Jan. 1850 26
Polly Bennett to Samuel Harmon 21 Aug. 1838 86

Sarah Benson to Samuel Allen 11 Sept. 1827 83

Henry Berger to Polly Titsworth 23 June 1833 12
Joseph Berger to Elizabeth Forshsye 22 Aug. 1832 154
Nancy Berger to Robert Harris 19 Sept. 1838 94

Samuel Berk to Rebecca Bankson 28 July 1822 34

Benjamin F. Berkley to Mary Jane Wells 21 June 1849 14
Benoni Berkly to Sarah Williams 10 Oct. 1838 89
Martha Berkley to Gilbert Apperson 16 March 1837 67
Sarah Berkley to Anderson W. Reavis 4 Aug. 1836 53

Frances B. Bernard to James M. Major 24 March 1840 117
Mary N. Bernard to John A. S. Major 15 Dec. 1841 139

Page 43 B
Will of James Berry
      To the children of my daughter Eliza L. Weeden, dec. whose names are: Sally Ann Weeden, Artinosa Rebecca Weeden, Henry James Weeden, and Eliza Ellen Weeden...
      To my sons: Young E. W. Berry, Charles R. Berry, James Smith Berry, William M. Berry, and Finis E. Berry...
      William M. and Finis E., Exe.
Written: 28 December 1837
Witnesses: F. R. Hayden, C. M. Smith, A. Porter, and Alex Hanna
Recorded 25 Nov. 1842
Page 121 B
Will of William M. Berry
      To my wife, Malecy Eveline...
      To my three children: James Clifton Statiann and Ibez Ann Beverly Hampton...
      To my brother, Finis E. Berry...
      My brother in law Beverly T. Hampton, Exe.
Written 24 October 1844
Witnesses: Thomas J. Shanklin and James L. Wear
Recorded: 15 November 1844
Caroline Berry to William Scott 7 Dec. 1843 164
Charles R. Berry to Betsey Ewing 16 Dec. 1824 50
Eliza Berry to Benjamin Weeden 3 Jan. 1828 90
Finis E. Berry to Sarah Jane Corum at the dwelling of her father
      Hiram Corum 27 Nov. 1842 152
James S. Berry to Martha Kirkpatrick 1 Jan. 1822 29
John M. Berry to Josephine D. Jones 30 Dec. 1845 197
Martha Berry to John C. McAtha 24 Dec. 1849 25
Thomas C. Berry to Martha Meredith 10 Dec. 1849 63
William M. Berry to Malissa E. Lampton 29 Nov. 1836 62

Nancy Berryman to James Broils 24 March 1838 78

Sally Ann Betts to Dewitt Clinton Mack 2 Dec. 1847 244

Page 219 A2
Will of William E. Bidstrup
    To my sons: Herman Bidstrup, Jesse Bidstrup, and William T. Bidstrup...
    To my daughters: Louisa Harlan, Ellen Bidstrup, Sarah Bidstrup, and Julia Bidstrup...
Written: 20 March 1858
Witnesses: Jesse Thomas, Polly Ann Thomas, Benjamin B. Brerton, and Jane Drew Brerton
Recorded: 15 October 1858
Herman E. Bidstrup to Sarah Thomas 12 Dec. 1823 45
Columbia L. Bidstrup to Robert Harlan 18 March 1847 229

Elizabeth Biggs to Hiram Dial 13 Sept. 1830 125
Jesse Biggs to Maria Ramsey 29 Aug. 1830 123

Page 30 A
Will of John Bigham
    To my wife Jane...
    To my children...
    To my oldest daughter, Elizabeth
    To my oldest son John
    To my niece Tiney McGee...
Written 28 March 1826
Wittnesses: David McGee and Nathaniel T. Allison
Recorded: 2 May 1826
Henry V. Bigham to Saminda A. McLahan 31 March 1850 30
Mrs. Jane Bigham to Jonathan R. Stanley 30 Nov. 1828 95
John Bighum to Alminia Ann Cathey 16 Oct. 1837 72
Polly Bigham to William Dodine 24 May 1827 78
William Bighum to Patience Clark 13 Oct. 1821 25

Hannah Billingsly to George Carter 1 Aug. 1848 62
Mary C. W. Billingsley to Wilson C. Baker 1 Oct. 1844 178
Tabitha Billingsley to James Turner 4 Jan. 1822 32

Betsey Birdsong to Joshua Vaughn 2 Aug. 1827 79
James Birdsong to Mary Parks 1 Aug. 1839 103

Mary Biscoss to Henry Nabring 5 Aug. 1844 173

Benton C. Blades to Eleanor J. Turbin 18 May 1848 259

Huston Blakely to Vireaney Moon 10 Oct. 1839 100

William Blanchard to Emiline Jones 25 May 1839 96

James Blankenship to Eliza Donaghe 21 Dec. 1831 142

Rode Blasengame to Nathaniel Morrison 12 Dec. 1828 99

Nancy Jane Boatman to William M. Warden at the dwelling of
U. E. Ruby 2 Feb. 1843 157
Peter S. Boatman to Nancy Ann Smithers 8 March 1849 12

Mary Boatright to Edward Kelly 8 March 1844 172

William Bodine to Polly Bigham 24 May 1827 78

Nicholas Bolbrath to Lofeth Brenneizen 18 Jan. 1849 6

Obediah Bollard to Nancy Barnett 3 Dec. 1850 38

Lucy Bolvin to Robert E. Downing 2 June 1841 131B

Minerva Bone to Levy Tailor 20 Jan. 1831 126
Nancy Bone to Thomas Shornwell 6 Jan. 1835 30

Benjamin Boolin to Sopia Dood 30 Jan. 1831 134
Elizabeth Boolin to David McGee 14 July 1825 54

Page 312 A2
Will of Martha Boon
    To my son in law William T. Heard...
    To my daughter Ann Elizabeth, wife of William T. Heard...
    William T. Heard, Exe.
Written: 11 December 1851
Witnesses: Barton L. Wilson and Andrew Gibson
Recorded: 22 March 1862

Eliza Ellen Borron to Robert Forest Ainslie 2 Oct. 1837 72

Peter Borner to Ketty Ann Mahan 5 Dec. 1827 85

George W. Bosley to Martha Norris 18 July 1836 59

James W. Boswell to Nancy D. Jones 4 March 1846 214

Page 21 A2
Will of William S. Boulware
    To my daughters: Sally Ann Boulware and Lucinda Frances
Roe Boulware...
    To Harriett Gray Boulware my youngest child and daughter..
    To my daughters: Lucy Conner Boulware, wife of Robert
E. Downing, Matilda Terrell Boulware, to Mildred Elizabeth
Boulware, now wife of John Miller, to Emily Huscoe Boulware,
To Sally Ann Boulware...
Continued-

To my son William Fleming Boulware...
My son, William F. and my sons in law Robert E. Downing and John Miller, Exe.
Written: 22 March 1848
Witnesses: Enoch Moss and George W. Phillips
Recorded: 8 February 1849

Egley Ann Boulton to Harvey McDaniel 19 Oct. 1835 43

Elizabeth Bowen to James F. Newbold 18 March 1841 125

Page 279 2A
Will of Mahlon Bowers
    To my wife, Elizabeth
Written: 19 April 1866
Witnesses: J. W. Draffen and J. L. Stephens
Recorded: 1 December 1866
Mary L. Bowers to John W. Amick 25 Dec. 1846 224

Benjamin Bowles to Sarah Jane Bath 29 June 1834 22
Catherine Bowles to Ashley L. Reavis 20 Oct. 1835 36
Eliza Boles to Nancy Hurt 26 Oct. 1843 161
Jane Bowls to Noddy Calvert 13 Nov. 1823 44
Jane Ann Boules to Alfred A. Yancy 14 Jan. 1845 182
Joseph A. Bowles to Catherine Parks 1 Aug. 1850 32
Maranda Poles to Washington Franklin Levens 3 March 1842 140
Mary Bowles to John Curnell 16 May 1847 230
Minor Boles to Mary Drinkwater 16 July 1846 215
Peter T. Bowls to Elizabeth Henderson 26 Sept. 1822 38
Polly Bowles to Holman F. Bankson 17 Dec. 1829 117
Reuben Bowles to Margaret Elizabeth Stevens __ __ 1840 114

Mary Bowlin to Jonathan Mickel 19 Aug. 1835 36

Joseph N. Bowman to Nancy Calvert 21 Sept. 1846 222
Mahaley Bomen to David E. N. Craig 22 Nov. 1845 203
Polly Bowman to Abraham Dyler 3 Feb. 1831 127
Ransom P. Bowman to Harriet Reavis 4 Aug. 1836 63

Henry Bowsfield to Polly Embree 28 April 1823 43

Page 99 A
Will of Robert Boyd
    To my wife, Nancy...
    To my sons: Simeon A. Boyd, Joshua N. L. Boyd, John N. Boyd, Joseph C. Boyd, William A. Boyd, and Robert B. Boyd...
    To my daughters: Nancy Green, Matilda H. Rains and Sally P. Scritchfield...
Written: 30 September 1835
Witnesses: Joshua H. Berry and John Clayton
Recorded: 1 December 1835

Emily Boyd to Jonathan C. Odle 21 May 1832 151
John Boyd to Vina Goodno 21 Aug. 1833 12
Joseph Boyd to Betsy Ann Hasty 6 Feb. 1836 47
Joshua L. Boyd to Lucinda Margaret Goodard 27 April 1844 174
Levisa Boyd to George Novel 14 May 1839 96
Mathew Boyd to Lucy Cary 2 Dec. 1821 25
Nancy Boyd to John Green 6 May 1819 3
Permalia Boyd to Garlan Lee Scrietchfield 22 Aug. 1833 9
Robert Boyd to Lucinda Schrichfield 18 Sept. 1828 97
Ruth Boyd to Milan Kirk 26 July 1835 30
Simon Boyd to Armanda Wardcastle 24 Sept. 1839 108
Syrinda Boyd to Andrew P. McKee 15 Dec. 1836 55

James Boiles to Polly Miller 28 Dec. 1836 57
Miss M. A. L. Boyles to J. D. Heiranymous 22 Oct. 1846 220
Marlin W. Boyles to Mary Ann Taylor 10 Dec. 1840 128
Rhody Boyles to George K. Hughes 30 Nov. 1838 89
Sarah Boyles to Evi Marley 5 March 1833 3

Eliza Burrus to Robert Steel 30 Aug. 1848 264

Emily Bradley to Edward Wright 20 July 1842 147
Josephine Bradley to Roland Hughes 27 Nov. 1841 137
Pike M. Bradley to Emaline Adams 15 Dec. 1842 151
Pike H. Bradley to Jail W. Tittsworth 5 Sept. 1849 18
R. L. S. Bradley to Nancy E. Read 22 June 1848 260
Sally Bradley to Joseph Wells 20 March 1820 13
Susannah Bradley to Andrew Barnes 29 July 1849 18

Jamah Draindfield to Gail Collins 11 July 1845 192

Emily Branaum to Abraham Woolery 7 Sept. 1845 198
Lonurbille Branium to William U. Gibson 1 Oct. 1849 20
Richard Brannum to Lucy Jane Rice 23 Nov. 1837 76

Page 262 A2
Will of John Brand, city of Lexington State of Kentucky
    To my wife Elizabeth...
    To my granddaughter, Elizabeth, dau. of my son, William M. Brand...
    To my sons: George W. Brand and Alexander H. Brand...
    To my daughter, Eliza Macalister
    To the children of my deceased son, John Brand towit Elizabeth Mary Brand and John Brand...
    To my grand daughters: Elizabeth, Mary, Harriett, Catharine, and Emily...
Written 22 December 1845
Witnesses: John Tilford and M. T. Scott
Recorded: 13 March 1860

Page 303 2A
Will of William M. Brand, City of Lexington, State of Kentucky, County of Fayette
    To my wife Harriet W. ...
    To my father, John Brand...
    To my brother, George W. ...
    To my brother in law, Edward Macalester...
    To my sons: William H. Brand, Horace Brand, George C. Brand, and John Brand...
    To my daughters: Elizabeth H., Mary A., Harriett W., Emily A., and Catherine M.
    My wife, Harriet W., my father, John Brand, my son, William H. Brand, my brother, George W., and my brother in law, Edward Macalester, Exe.
Written: 10 Feb. 1845
Witnesses: Ben Warfield and E. Warfield'
Recorded: 28 August 1861

Mrs. Susan Branson to Jessie Apperson 2 Oct. 1850 33

Jottha D. Brashear to Mary Ellen Cou 15 Feb. 1849 7

C. Brenhuisen to Charles Frey 14 Aug. 1849 17

Lefeth Brenneizen to Nicholas Bolbrath 18 Jan. 1849 6

Thomas L. Brice to Mary L. Taylor 14 Jan. 1846 197

Amanda B. Bridgewater to James Thornton 21 Nov. 1844 181
Eliza Bridgewater to William C. Becker 6 Feb. 1845 183
Lucinda Bridgewater to James W. Ansell 2 Jan. 1844 168
Nancy Bridgewater to Carter Dicks 17 Oct. 1839 102
Sarah Bridgewater to Muckleberry Southerland 5 March 1835 26
William Bridgewater to Martha Dicks 7 Nov. 1839 104

Augusta C. W. Briglieb to Chr. A. Cunso 12 April 1844 175

James Briles to Nancy Mize 7 Oct. 1849 24

James W. Brindin to Sarah Neal 26 May 1840 111

Frances Briscoe to William Briscoe 17 July 1823 42
Frances W. Briscoe to Joseph P. Reaves 3 Jan. 1839 91
Joel K. Briscoe to Barnett Miller 30 Oct. 1837 73
Margaret Briscoe to John Keyron Given 10 Oct. 1828 96
Mary Briscoe to Thomas N. Hill 8 March 1848 254
Patsy Briscoe to Jackson Elliott 10 Sept. 1840 114
Peggy Briscoe to Russell Smallwood _ June 1820 116
Sarah Briscoe to Samuel Cole 24 April 1823 43
Susannah Briscoe to William Taylor 26 July 1826 63
William Briscoe to Frances Briscoe 17 July 1823 42

Abner Brisendien to Susannah J. Epperson 30 July 1849 16

Hew Britton to Mary Stover 23 Dec. 1821 28

Catherine P. Bronaugh to Jacob H. Tucker 21 Nov. 1848 4
Maria E. Bronaugh to Douglas A. Tucker 14 May 1846 209

Page 431 A2
Will of John Brown
    To my son, James H. ...
    To my daughters: Mary E. Boyce, Louisa M. Browning, and Sarah E. Knight...
Written: 15 January 1870
Witnesses: Green Steele and David K. Steele
Recorded: 18 April 1870
Ann Brown to Reuben B. Harris 22 June 1820 6
Cecero Brown to Elizabeth Jeffries 28 Sept. 1819 14
Eliza Brown to Washington Adams 27 Feb. 1840 105
Elizabeth Brown to Lewis Manes 1 Jan. 1839 90
Hugh Brown to Celia Taylor 7 Feb. 1836 50
Jane Brown to Joseph Rennison 28 Jan. 1847 230
Martha Ann Brown to George W. Conner 24 Feb. 1846 202
Michael Brown to Jane Martin 21 Oct. 1830 124
Parmelia Jane Brown to Sikugus Smiley 30 May 1848 262
Polly Brown to Joshua Lakey 20 Aug. 1819 9
Soloman Brown to Ann Edgar 21 March 1821 19
William R. Brown to Ann J. Robinson 26 Oct. 1831 140

Christian Brownfield to Harriet Firk 1 Oct. 1846 220
John Brownfield to Mary Potter at the home of John Potter
    19 Dec. 1840 120

Charles Brownlee to Frances McCorkle 5 Oct. 1848 4
Elizabeth Brownlee to William Taylor 14 Oct. 1847 248

Elizabeth Broiles to Andrew J. McClanahan 21 Jan. 1841 126
James Broils to Nancy Berryman 24 March 1838 78
James Broyles to Parthena Robeson 22 Sept. 1839 99

Lidy Brils to William Rickman 8 May 1842 144

Emilee Bruce to James Jeffreys 11 Oct. 1849 21
Elizabeth Bruce to R. Kirkpatrick 9 Sept. 1847 240
Marilda A. Bruce to John W. Lampton 20 Feb. 1838 79

Charles M. Brucking to F. A. Huffman 20 May 1845 190

Ann E. Bruffee to William H. Cook 17 April 1847 233
Eliza Bruffee to Henry W. Crowther 19 July 1832 151
Continued

George W. Bruffee to Martha W. Harper   17 March 1842   141
Emilee Bruffee to John Williams   25 May 1837   68
Katherine Bruffee to Hamilton Finney   28 Nov. 1847   245
Mary Bruffee to Wesley Johnston   17 March 1831   130

William Bryant to Betsey Sloan   17 Aug. 1824   50

Page 106 B
Will of James Buchanan, M. D., of the Borough of Allegany in the County of Allegany, Commonwealth of Pennsylvania
    To my wife, Mrs. Janet Stark or Buchanan
Written: 16 February 1838
Witnesses: James W. Buchanan and Charles T. Gilliland
Recorded: 11 November 1844
Page 134 A2
Will of James Buchanan, Jr.
    To my brother, Robert, a resident of Louisville in the state of Kentucky,.
    Andrew Buchanan, a resident of Louisville in the state of Kentucky to be my executor.
Written 14 August 1850
Witnesses: J. Hayes, Charles C. Orr, and John Ferguson, Jr.
Recorded: 7 November 1854
Mrs. Jessie Buchanan at the residence of the late Dr. James Buchanan to Dr. George Wylde Mann   28 May 1848   261

Page 29 A2
Will of Sarah T. Buckner
    My friend, Col. James Quarles, my exe.
Written: 16 April 1847
Witnesses: John Calhoun, Charles F. Lewis, and Alfred Harris
Recorded: 10 November 1849
Judy Ann Buckner to James Thompson   16 Jan. 1840   106

Elizabeth Jane Bull to Thomas N. Korton   21 Dec. 1845   201
John W. Bull to Ellen Korton   12 July 1846   213

Nathaniel Bullard to Mrs. Sally Langly   21 Oct. 1819   7

Frances Burch to John Gilmore   22 July 1826   91
Harvey Burch to Sally Smith   9 March 1826   59
Nancy Burch to James Scott Gilmore   28 April 1826   62
Nancy Burch to Jesse Greer   5 July 1832   162

Rebecca Burchel to John P. Dix   23 July 1846   216

William Burgan to Rhoda Ann Gibson   9 Sept. 1827   81

Lavanna Burger to William Son   7 Dec. 1826   66
Patsy Burger to Hisekial Harraman   30 Dec. 1830   133
Salina Burgher to Andrew I. Snodgrass   22 July 1834   22
Sarah Burger to Evins Cary   4 April 1822   31

Lemember Gurgess to Phillip Shoemaker 18 July 1850 31

John Burk to Ellen Neal 18 July 1847 237

Jesse G. Burkeley to Cornelia Woolsey 9 Nov. 1826 68

Mansfield Burnard to Martha Robertson 4 Aug. 1842 146
William Burnard to Abigail Harper 4 Aug. 1825 52

Chesley Burnett to Elizabeth Burns 13 Dec. 1832 158
Chesley Burnett to Sarah Burns 13 Jan. 1847 230
Nancy A. Burnitt to Mr. H. George 8 Aug. 1850 33

Elizabeth Burns to Chesley Burnett 13 Dec. 1832 158
Frances Burns to James Gilbreth 5 March 1846 203
James N. Burns to Margaret Forsythe 22 May 1834 20
Mary Burns to Benjamin Hearn 22 May 1845 189
Sarah Burns to Chesley Burnett 13 Jan. 1847 230

Charlotte Burriss to William Martin 21 Dec. 1843 169
James Burrus to Justian Davis 1 June 1848 263
James M. Burris, Morgan Co., Mo. to Ann Nancy King 1 Sept. 1842 149
Polly Burris to William H. Stanly 13 Aug. 1838 88
Sarah Burris to Henry Harris 1 Aug. 1847 239
William Burrus to Sarah Ann Harvey 20 Dec. 1843 169

Sarah Burress to Presley Wood 13 April 1843 155

Abraham Byler to Polly Bowman 3 Feb. 1831 127
Abram Byler to Mrs. Penelope Howard 5 March 1844 168
David Byler to Nancy Lilly 13 March 1832 149
Joab Byler to Eliza Gilbreath 17 Jan. 1829 103
Jacob Byler to Louiza Stephens 20 Jan. 1831 126
Joseph Byler to Mary Wilson 10 Aug. 1835 31
Polly Ann Byler to Peter Ferrill 5 April 1832 149
Thomas Byler to Jane Gilbreath 9 April 1829 108

Sarah Cahanberger to Nathaniel Hardeson 2 March 1848 253

Jacob Calahan to Nancy Smith 4 Dec. 1843 167

Benjamin P. Caldwell to Mary A. Powell 2 March 1847 228
Elizabeth P. Caldwell to Levin Cropper 16 Jan. 1845 182
Francis Marvin Caldwell to Augustina Henretta Stahl
     19 April 1842 141
Lydia Caldwell to Milton Miller 6 Jan. 1831 129
Mary J. Caldwell to William Eager 4 Nov. 1847 250
Sarah A. Caldwell to William Henshaw 24 Aug. 1843 161

Elizabeth R. Calhoun to Alfred Harris 6 Dec. 1847 253
Louisa E. Calhoun to William G. Bell 21 Oct. 1841 138

Agnes Callaway to James Tankerly 23 May 1838 81
Charles Calloway to Elizabeth Ware 15 April 1846 214
John Calloway to Catharine Ware 21 Dec. 1842 167
Sarah Maria Calloway to John T. Ware 20 Oct. 1843 162
Sydney C. Calloway to Robert Douglas Paxton 10 Nov. 1842 148
Susan Callaway to John Keeger 3 Oct. 1842 145

Rice Callas to Sarah Kelly 1 Dec. 1822 40

Page 119 A
Will of John Calvert, Senior
    To my wife, Dorcas...
    To my sons: Leonard Calvert and William Calvert...
    To my daughters: Ursula Carson, Nancy Dixon, and Elizabeth Taylor
    Thomas Plemons, Exe.
Written: 9 Sept. 1839
Witnesses: J. S. Buster, Vincent Cropper, and Alfred Calvert
Recorded: 5 December 1839
Page 162 B
Will of John Calvert
    To my wife, Emma...
    To my brother, Leonard Calvert...
    To my minor children: Anne, Mary Jane, Nancy, William, and Carson...
    Leonard Calvert Exe.
Written: 20 April 1846
Witnesses: C. A. Carson and Benjamin P. Caldwell
Cynthia Calvert to Moses A. Hawkins 28 Aug. 1844 178
Elias Calvert to Kesiah Hughes 25 April 1839 96
Elizabeth Calvert to John Taylor 12 April 1832 148
Elizabeth Ann Calvert to Silvester Kellogg 5 April 1832 145
John Calvert to Elizabeth Dale 25 July 1842 144
Leonard Calvert to Rocksey Morley 4 Dec. 1829 103
Martha Calvert to Charles A. Carson 14 Oct. 1845 194
Nancy Calvert to George Dickson 18 Nov. 1828 117
Nancy Calvert to Joseph R. Bowman 21 Sept. 1846 221
Nancy Calvert to Ira Barnes 31 May 1842 144
Noddy Calvert to Jane Bowls 13 Nov. 1823 44
Peter Calvert to Patsy Vaughn 26 Nov. 1835 40
Polly Calvert to Thomas Plemon 28 Sept. 1829 113
Rebehak Calvert to Thomas Pate 4 April 1824 45
Sarah Calvert to Andrew Sharp 3 Sept. 1835 33
William Calvert, Jr. to Martha Mitchell 26 July 1837 73
William W. Calvert to Priscilla Tittsworth 31 Dec. 1839 105
William W. Calvert to Clarinda Seat 3 Oct. 1849 19

Page 115 A
Will of Joseph Campbell
    To my sister, Kissiah...
    To my daughter, Mary Ann...
    My kinsman, William Campbell is to take care of my daughter.
    I leave as the persons I desire to share my estate the following persons: Russell Campbell, Kissiah Campbell, Nancy Turner, William Campbell, Bradley Campbell, and Smith Campbell
Written: 6 January 1838
Witnesses: Jesse Driskell and Thomas Pate
Recorded: 9 August 1839

Bradley Campbell to Meckey Hall 21 July 1829 109
Elizabeth Campbell to James Colwell 12 March 1846 205
Ellena Campbell to Archibald Weatherford, 22 Oct. 1845 196
Frances M. Campbell to Thomas W. F. Price 24 Nov. 1841 139
George W. Campbell to Louisa G. Pollock 21 Feb. 1839 93
John Campbell to Emely Smith 14 June 1846 93
Joseph Campbell to Lucy Ann Cox 7 Sept. 1845 196
Joshua Campbell to Sidney R. Ewing 6 Feb. 1823 41
Manerva Campbell to Alexander Ross 24 March 1835 28
Mariah Campbell to Levi Wood 6 Oct. 1833 9
Mary Campbell to Asa McClain 7 Jan. 1847 227
Mary Ann Campbell to Granderson Stone 21 Dec. 1848 7
Nancy Campbell to John Turner 11 Feb. 1819 1
Nancy Jane Campbell to Riley Millsap 22 Nov. 1836 58
Rhoda Campbell to Jefferson Maxwell 22 Nov. 1836 60
Kitty Campbell to Wesley Stoffle 29 March 1849 9
Susan Campbell to Andrew J. Bell 19 Aug. 1835 37
William Campbell to Lufany Baity Given 10 May 1821 82
William J. Campbell to Louiza Rowles, daughter of William and
    Sarah Rowles 4 Jan. 1844 169

Ambrose Canada to Mary McDonel 25 Jan. 1827 69
Lucinda Canada to John Trotter Given 10 May 1827 82

Michael Capp to Elizabeth Rinel 1 Sept. 1844 178

Nancy Card to James L. Ketton 1 March 1833 167

Page 365 A2
Will of Robert D. Carlos
    To my wife, Sarah Elizabeth
Written: 24 Oct. 1865
Witnesses: William N. McClanahan and H. H. Hudson
Recorded: 18 January 1866
Lafayette Carlos to Lucy Ann Leville 13 June 1850 36

Page 324 A2
Will of William H. Carnal
    To my wife, Margaret...
    To my children: Eliza, William, Reuben, Edward, Alexander, Kenneth, Betsy, John, and Laura Carnal...
Written: 3 January 1863
Witnesses: James H. Baker and Robert Seaton
Recorded: 29 January 1863

Andrew H. Carpenter to Mary Ann Gilbert 28 Oct. 1847 248
Catherine Carpenter to Hugh F. Galbreath 1 Oct. 1846 222
Fanny Carpenter to James Davis 25 Nov. 1828 88
Henry Carpenter to Emely Galbreath 27 Aug. 1846 217
John J. Carpenter to Lucinda McFarland 12 April 1840 111
Susan Mary Carpenter to James C. Short 27 Oct. 1844 179
Polly Carpenter to William Miller 14 July 1827 80
Robert Carpenter to Lucy Jane Goode 21 Sept. 1847 240
Sarah Carpenter to Alfred Huff 15 May 1845 190
Susan Carpenter to Jeremiah Cooper 2 Aug. 1838 85

Page 124 A2
Will of Washington M. Carr, Londoun Co., Virginia
    To Isaac Vandventer, $4000.; to Manie Vandventer, brother of Isaac Vandventer, $4000.; to Gabriel Vandventer, brother of Isaac Vandventer $2000.; to Armistead T. Vandventer, brother of Isaac Vandventer, $2000.; to Washington Vandventer, brother of Isaac Vandventer, $2000.
    To Mary Clarke, wife of Addison Clarke, $2000.
    To Eliza Ann Braden, wife of Rodney Braden, $2000.
    To Josephus Carr, son of William Carr, $2000.
    To William Carr, son of William Carr, $2000.
    To David Carr, $2000.
    To his brother, John Henry Carr, $500.
    To William Clogett, $1000 and $500 to be kept in trust for his education
    To Mary Macpherson, wife of Samuel Macpherson, $500.
    My friend, Isaac Vandventer, Exe.
Written: 9 September 1846
Witnesses: John Janney and Charles Miller
Recorded: 2 March 1854

Eliza Carrell to William Mitchel 24 Dec. 1829 117
John Carrall to Susannah Hughes 3 Aug. 1837 70
Robert Carroll to Emilee Gale 7 April 1845 234

Charles A. Carson to Martha Calvert 14 Oct. 1845 194
Mary A. Carson to Henry N. Ruby 15 Oct. 1839 101

Page 10 A
Will of James Carter

In the name of God Amen I James Carter of Cooper County being in sound and perfect mind but considering the uncertainity of this mortal life due hereby make and publish this my last will and testament in manner and form following that is to say:

Item 1 I give and bequeath to my beloved wife Patience Carter my waggon and gears one sorrel mare, all my household furniture, five head of sheep, as likewise all my farming utensils.

Item 2 I also give and bequeath unto my loving wife Patience all my cattle amounting to 20 head and all increase that spring from them until such time as she and my children shall have crossed the Sabine River at which time they shall all be sold and equally divided between all my children and herself.

Item 3 I give and bequeath unto the above Patience Carter all debts due in demand of every kind that are due to me at my decease.

Item 4 I give and bequeath unto the above named Patience all my hogs and do hereby devise and appoint that within six months after my decease they shall be sold to defray the expense of herself and children to and cross the Sabine River.

Item 5 I give and bequeath to my second son Elijah one black mare to be taken---after crossing the Sabine River---and not before.

Item 6 I give and bequeath unto my third son Manuel my black mare sorrel colt to be taken---after crossing the Sabine River---and not before.

Item 7 I give and bequeath unto my daughter Polly my sorrell mare black horse colt to be taken after crossing the Sabine River----and not before.

Item 8 I give and bequeath unto my daughter Betsey my sorrell horse to be taken after crossing the Sabine River--- but not before.

Item 9 I give and bequeath unto my daughter Nancy my old bay mare and in case of the death of the bay mare her value shall be paid by each one of the within named children and my wife Patience at any rate---after crossing the Sabine River. She is to have as good a horse as any of the rest of the children to be contributed to her by them equally.

I do hereby will and appoint and decree that if the above named Patience Carter marries again all the property shall be divided among the children that I have bequeathed her.

I do like wise appoint and decree that if Patience Carter refuses to go and cross the Sabine River with her children and family in such case my daughter Betsey shall in addition to what is bequeathed her have all and everything that is bequeathed to my wife Patience.

I do likewise will and appoint and decree that if my daughter Betsey marries previous and before she crosses the

Sabine River, she shall forfeit all and everything that is above given and bequeathed to her.
 To my son Elijah in his case of any forfeiture give her one horse to the value of $100.
 I do likewise will and appoint that my son Ezekial shall be supported equally by my wife and children.
 Edmund J. Carter shall be a guardian for all his brothers and sisters and my children each and severally.
 I appoint my wife Patience Carter, Exe.
Written 4 April 1821
Witness F. F. Cleveland and James Carter
Recorded: 19 May 1821
Caty Carter to Peter Fisher   23 Dec. 1821   28
George Carter, Moniteau Co., Mo. to Hannah Billingsly
      1 Aug. 1848   262

Fenepe D. Carthea to Elizabeth McGauchlin   28 Oct. 1845   200

Page 16 A
Will of William Cartner
    To my wife...
    To my oldest son, James...
    To my two sons: William Cartner and Joseph Cartner...
    To my son, Thomas...
    To my daughters: Mary Cartner, Jane Cartner, and Lucy Cartner
Written: 6 August 1823
Witnesses: George Crawford, William George, and Henry Bausfield
Recorded: 4 November 1823
Page 100 A2
Will of William Cartner
    To my wife, Kesiah...
    To my children: Mary, Charles, Julian, John, Sarah Frances, and Elizabeth...
    My wife, Kesiah, Exe.
Written: 20 April 1853
Witnesses: William P. Speoduc Mack and Samuel J. Tutt
Recorded: 17 May 1853
James Cartner to Mary Penison   14 Jan. 1830   120
Jane Cartner to John Nanson   11 June 1822   32
Jane Cartner to Stephen Yarnall   5 Oct. 1848   5
Lucy Cartner to Thomas H. Pearson   4 Aug. 1831   135
William Cartner to Kesiah Robinson   28 July 1842   147
William Cartner, Jr. to Martha Goodno   1 March 1848   253

Mary Carver to Benjamin G. Pollock   18 Nov. 1841   130

Alford Carey to Sarah Ann Wood   3 April 1849   10
Evins Cary to Sarah Burger   4 April 1822   31
Lucy Cary to Mathew Boyd   2 Dec. 1821   25
Nancy Ann Carry to William J. Underwood   27 Aug. 1848   1

Jane Cashady to James Faris 26 April 1838 81
Louiza Casady to Alexander Roe 13 Aug. 1832 154

Conrad Cash to Carry Blutchour 20 March 1841 127

Pemberton Cason to Zilphy Stephens 22 July 1825 72

Ann Casteel to A. Farley ___ 1840 120
Elizabeth Casteel to Jeremiah Howerton 11 Dec. 1833 15
Jane Casteel to Jefferson Howerton 24 April 1838 79
Priscilla Casteel to Larkin Dewitt 12 July 1840 114

Joseph Castolo to Nancy Hurley 24 May 1826 64

Jemima Amanda Catoon to Robert I. Adams, 19 Sept. 1850 33
Martha E. Caton to Henry B. Harvey 8 Nov. 1840 116

Alminda Ann Cathey to John Digham 16 Oct. 1837 72
Andrew Cathey to Jane Ross 22 June 1832 150
James Cathey to Nancy McClenehan 12 Jan. 1822 26
Nancy Cathey to Jasper Moon 11 Sept. 1831 137
Polly Cathey to Alexander S. Miller 1 March 1829 100
Rebecca Cathey to Joseph Jolly 8 Dec. 1836 59

Elizabeth Catron to William Young 30 Nov. 1819 8
Phany Catren to John Roberson 12 June 1820 20

William Caughman to Mary Jane Eubanks 31 Aug. 1850 32

Emilee Cerrary to A. B. Woolery 14 March 1849 8

Alfred Chadwick to Delia Gillespie 24 June 1845 190

James B. Chalmers to Margaret Evans 14 Feb. 1833 164

Page 97 B
Will of William Chambers
    To my sons: William Chambers, John Chambers, and Samuel Chambers...
    To my daughters: Elizabeth Chambers, Hannah Carpenter, widow of Robert Carpenter, dec., Martha George, wife of Lewis George, and Abigail Chambers...
    To my sons: Joseph Chambers and James Chambers...
    To my son in law, Peter Carpenter...
Written: 19 October 1842   My friend, Jeremiah Rice, Exe.
Witnesses: Ferry Rockwell, William H. Trigg, and Robert Stuart
Recorded: 15 November 1844
John Chambers to Elizabeth Allison 10 Nov. 1826 59

Page 373 A2
Will of Sarah Ann Chandler, wife of Leroy Chandler
    To my daughter, Mary Lewis Tucker, wife of Oren D. Tucker..
    To my sons: James H. Chandler, Timothy Chandler, and Charles Quarles Chandler...
    To my brother, James Quarles...
    To my sons in law: Dr. Carr who married my daughter, Elvisa; George Augustus Goodman who married my daughter, Margaret; Henry McPherson, who married my daughter, Maria Louise; and Thomas L. Tucker who married my daughter, Sarah Ann.
    To my single daughters: Susan Henry Chandler and Florence Matilda Chandler...
    To my sons: John T. Chandler, Robert Leroy Chandler, and Kelly Ragland Chandler...
    My sons, John T. and James H., Exe.,
Written: 22 October 1865
Recorded: 9 August 1866
Witnesses: J. R. Bowman and Lewis Eager

Frances Eliza Chandler to John W. Conner   6 June 1838   83
Lucy P. Chandler to James R. Payne   6 Dec. 1837   76

Henry Chaney to Lucinda Allison   29 Nov. 1832   162
John Chaney to Ann Hall   16 Jan. 1833   162

Rebeckah Chapman to James Collins   28 Feb. 1820   23
Samuel Chapman to Sarah Langley   7 Feb. 1822   33

John H. Chinn to Sarah Ann Jones   6 April 1840   112

Polly Chisholm to Thomas Letchworth   5 April 1821   20

Howard Chism to Emilee Cline   16 May 1850   31
Mickel Chism to Diadian Smith   4 Feb. 1830   118

Amanda Church to Henry Mave, Saline Co., Mo.   30 April 1846   208

William Y. Clalomb to Josafiene Allison   2 April 1846   205

Page 327 A2
Will of Harriett Clark
    To my daughter, Marion, wife of R. L. Bradley...
    R. L. Bradley, Exe.
Written 13 October 1862
Witnesses: James L. Bell and John Rootcap
Recorded: 16 March 1863
Page 3 B
Will of Robert F. Clark
    To my wife, Susan...
Continued--

To my daughters: Melinda D. Clark, Sarah Jane Clark, and Elizabeth T. Wilson...
To my sons: Robert P. Clark, Stephen T. Clark, and Bennett C. Clark...
My son, Bennett C. and my wife, Susan, Exe.
Written: 13 August 1841
Witnesses: Washington Adams and James Thompson
Recorded: 27 August 1841
Bennett C. Clark to Margaret H. Hutchinson 9 Sept. 1841 133
Christiana Clark to Samuel Parks 7 Feb. 1833 3
Isaac Clark to Mrs. Zulica Hillsap 29 Dec. 1836 57
John F. Clark to Nancy Tomlin 9 Nov. 1843 164
Patience Clark to William Digum 18 Oct. 1821 25
Rebecca Clark to Adam Simonton 12 Dec. 1839 105
Renfrelour Clark to Nancy Tarwater 27 Jan. 1820 8
Susan Clark to Benjamin Sutherland 18 Feb. 1841 126
Robert F. Clark to Susan Terrill 27 Aug. 1835 35

Page 365 A2
Will of Richard Clawson
To my children: William Clawson, Eliza Jane Clawson, John Clawson, Amanda Clawson, and Ann Clawson...
Written: 10 October 1865
Witnesses: A. J. Wright, James Douglass, and G. W. Maccubbin
Recorded: 12 December 1865

Johnson Clay to Rebecky Collet 4 May 1820 15
William Clay to Sally Colbert 14 June 1822 45

Luncinda Claypole to Lindsey Green 23 Dec. 1843 174

Ann Clayton to Robert Wardcastle 19 March 1845 214
John M. Clayton to Elizabeth Lam 24 Dec. 1844 183
John Clayton to Mrs. Elcy Maxwell 11 June 1849 16
Martha Clayton to John Gilbreath 18 Feb. 1840 106

Daniel Cline to Elizabeth Ellison 15 May 1834 21
Eliza J. Cline to Hiram H. Homan 13 Jan. 1842 140
Emilee Cline to Howard Chism 16 May 1850 31
Jacob Cline to Margaret Hiel 12 Sept. 1842 147
Joseph Cline to Susan C. Potts 16 April 1846 212
Leonard Cline to Margaret Becker 18 Aug. 1843 174
Matthias Cline to Martha Ann Kirkpatrick 7 March 1841 127
Orbany C. Cline to Samuel Wear 20 Dec. 1848 11
Orleanny C. Cline to Samuel Wear 20 Dec. 1848 4
William D. Cline to Caralee Hogan 14 Oct. 1847 249

Elizabeth Cobbs to Albert Calloway Maddox 25 Nov. 1841 139
Thomas W. Cobbs to Elizabeth Cramer 22 Dec. 1842 143

Ann B. Cockrell to William B. Dingle 20 Aug. 1833 7
Catherine Cockrell to Urban E. Rubey 18 Feb. 1830 113
Elizabeth Cockrill to John Taylor 27 June 1844 172
Peter B. Cocrille to Sally Steel Given 25 Dec. 1828 100

Andrew Coffman to Mary McClanahan 9 July 1826 63
Samuel Coffman to Sally Ann Weave 18 May 1848 261
Susan Coffman to Samuel F. Jones 9 Dec. 1847 245

Sally Colbert to William Clay 14 June 1822 45
William Colbert to Amanda Susan Oglesby 23 April 1843 150

Page 58 B
Will of Holbert Cole
    To my children...
    To my son, William L.
    My brothers, Samuel Cole and William T. Cole, Exe.
Written: 24 Nov. 1843
Witnesses: A. F. Read, Abraham Woolery, N. Leonard, and Phillip W. Shoemaker
Recorded: 9 February 1844
Angeline Cole to James M. Hill 5 Jan. 1848 250
Eleanor Cole to James M. C. Eller 6 April 1832 145
Holbert Cole to Ann Ron 28 Dec. 1819 22
James Cole to Nancy Dickson 25 Jan. 1836 43
James Cole to Katherine Allison 16 Jan. 1842 138
James Cole to Sophia Evans 21 Oct. 1847 243
Jane Cole to Charles Davis 14 April 1822 35
John J. Cole to Malinda Woolery 27 Dec. 1850 36
Mark Cole to Mary Ann Woods 27 May 1834 21
Martha Cole to Arthur Patrick 4 Dec. 1827 71
Mary Jane Cole to Robert Allison 21 Jan. 1842 140
Mary Jane Cole to James M. Lowry 21 March 1847 231
Nancy Cole to Samuel Harris 22 Sept. 1839 101
Nancy D. Cole to William E. Keyton 29 June 1826 63
Peter Cole to Lucinda Shoemaker 6 March 1845 183
Polly Cole to James McCarty 9 May 1832 147
Samuel Cole to Sarah Briscoe 24 April 1823 43
Thomas Cole to Malissa Martin 19 Jan. 1849 9
William Cole to Nancy Woods Given 10 Oct. 1828 95
William J. Cole, Howard Co., Mo. to Elizabeth Jolly
    7 June 1838 83
William T. Cole to Janey Sullivan 11 Feb. 1840 108

Anthony Coleby to Elizabeth L. Howerton 21 April 1841 113

Page 46 A2
Will of Charles E. Coleman, a native of Fairfax Co., Virginia
    to my sister, Susan C. Coleman...
Continued

       To my four brothers: John T. Coleman, George G. Coleman, James S. Coleman, and Richard Coleman...
       My mother, Sarah Coleman, Exe.
Written: 4 December 1850
Witnesses: Robert Brent, I. K. Lacy, and Samuel Roe
Recorded: 27 January 1851
Virginia Coleman to John Fenton 2 Jan. 1847 223

Rebecky Collet to Johnson Clay 4 May 1820 15

Mahala Collier to William A. Reed 22 Jan. 1833 163

Andrew Collins to Malvina L. Smith 25 Feb. 1845 184
Gail Collins to Jamah Draindfield 11 July 1845 192
Eliza Collins to James M. Egdar 5 Nov. 1837 77
James Collins to Rebeckah Chapman 28 Feb. 1820 23
John G. Collins to Jail C. Woods 5 March 1849 13
Lucy M. Collins to Alexander H. Thompson 7 May 1844 170
Mary E. Collins to Mathew Robinson 7 Jan. 1846 212
Peter W. Collins to Louisa Houx 14 Sept. 1841 136
Sally Ann Collins to Presley Manion, Van Buren Co., Mo.
       6 May 1845 187
Susan Collins to Elias Patrick 19 Jan. 1837 61

David Colter to Eliza Stone 13 April 1820 5

James Colwell to Elizabeth Campbell 12 March 1846 205

Page 226 A2
Will of John Combs
       To my wife, Mary Bullock Combs...
       To my sons: Christopher Combs and Joseph Combs...
       My wife and sons, Exe.
Written: 25 May 1857
Witness: Robert C. Combs, Linn County, Mo.
Recorded: 27 October 1858
Christopher Combs to Mary Harris 10 March 1847 233
Robert C. Combs to Martha B. Hunt 25 Feb. 1834 172
Stephen Combs to Synthey Wright 27 July 1822 35

Gersham Compton to Jane Davis 27 Feb. 1820 11
Warner Compton to Mary Ann How 13 April 1848 255 the former
       of Saline Co., Mo.

Page 91 A
Will of George Condra
       To my wife Rebecca, land granted me by an act of Congress.
       to my daughters: Mary, Elizabeth, Nancy, Sarah, Catherine and Rebecca Jane...
       To my sons: John W. and William Jordan..
Continued--

Rebecca and my son, Greenberry, Exe.
Written: 7 September 1852
Witnesses: Robert Pogue, Alexander Givens, and J. Bennett
Recorded: 15 February 1853

Joel J. Conn to Celevland Pain 23 June 1835 31

Page 25 A
Will of Martin Conner
    To my children: Dennis Conner, Sally Conner, Martha Conner, and Mary Conner...
    To my wife...
Written: 8 July 1825
Witnesses: Isaac Allen, William Travis, and Frances Travis
Recorded: 12 November 1825
Allen Conner to Elizabeth Snodgrass 24 July 1827 83
Betsey Conner to Charles Force 7 Sept. 1819 4
Eliza A. Conner to Henry Elliott 11 July 1844 176
George W. Conner to Martha Ann Brown 24 Feb. 1846 202
James F. Conner to Frances Eliza Chandler 6 June 1838 83
Jane Conner to David Wadley 27 Jan. 1825 51
Mariah H. Conner to Edmond P. Elliott 14 Aug. 1843 158
Mary Conner to William McDaniel 8 Feb. 1835 46
Sarah Conner to William Goodman 21 March 1830 121
Sarah Conner to John Rea 22 Feb. 1842 140
Starling Conner to Mary Cotton 12 Aug. 1829 107
Susannah Conner to Anderson W. Reavis 5 March 1844 171
Thomas Conner to Julia Ann Jelly 27 Dec. 1849 6
William Conner to Delila Wolf 19 July 1830 122

George Conrad to Mary Ann Elliott 23 May 1850 31

Calvin Cook to Green Harmon 13 Nov. 1849 26
Mary Ann Cook to Henry Harmon 27 Oct. 1842 150
William H. Cook to Ann E. Truffee 17 April 1847 233
Wilson Cook to Caroline Harmon 31 Oct. 1844 179

William Cool to Rodah Smiley 12 May 1822 35

Benjamin Cooper, Howard Co., Mo. to Phebe H. Sloan 18 March 1831 131
Dudley Cooper to Sarah E. Wallace 1 May 1850 31
Jeremiah Cooper to Susan Carpenter 2 Aug. 1838 85
Nathan Cooper to Hannah Jones 30 Jan. 1834 14

Page 72 A2
Will of Thomas M. Cordry
    To my wife, Martha Jane...
    To my son, Prentis Elliott Cordry...
    William S., guardian of my son, Prentis...
Continued--

James Cordry, Senior and my wife, Exe.
Written: 17 July 1852
Witnesses: John D. Cordry, Lewis M. Hutchinson, and William C. Ewing
Recorded: 29 July 1852
Cathren E. Cordry to Joanathan W. Wear 12 Jan. 1843 151
Frances Cordry to George Hutchinson 4 July 1843 160
Green Rayburn Cordry to Eliza Jane Steel 11 Aug. 1839 105
James Cordry to Ann Eliza Robison 15 Jan. 1850 28
John D. Cordry to Mary E. Wear 4 July 1838 84
Mary Ann Cordry to George D. Wear 27 Sept. 1838 87
Stacy Ann Cordry to Daniel Varner 1 Feb. 1844 156
Col. Thomas M. Cordry to Martha Jane Elliott 23 Sept. 1841 132
William L. Cordray to Mary Wear 29 March 1837 79

Page 73 A
Will of Hubber Corum
    To my wife, Sidney S. ...
    My brother, Henry, Exe.
Written 16 April 1830
Witnesses: Anthony F. Read and Nancy Woolery
Recorded: 10 June 1833
Alpha Ann Corum to Samuel Brisco 9 April 1846 205
Elizabeth R. Corum to Robert C. Moore 19 Oct. 1843 166
Felix Corum to Mary Robinson 25 Feb. 1836 51
Harden Corum to Agnes Cramer 14 June 1827 80
Heli Corum to Eveline Lowrey 23 July 1824 47
Harrison Corum to Juliana Tevis 27 Jan. 1835 42
Harrison Corum to Elizabeth Alexander 25 Aug. 1848 264
Lucretia P. Corum to William C. Ewing 3 Feb. 1845 188
Margaret Lydia Corum to Joseph L. Stephens 12 Nov. 1850 37
Mary Jane Corum to Francis Simpson 6 Oct. 1840 115
Sarah Jane Corum to Finis E. Berry at the dwelling of her
    father, Hiram Corum 28 Nov. 1842 152
Thompson B. Corum to Rachel Riggs 7 Oct. 1834 23

Gabriel Cotton to Elizabeth Apperson 28 Sept. 1828 93
Gabriel Cotton, Morgan Co., Mo. to Margaret Geyer, daughter of
    John Geyer 14 Oct. 1835 34
Mary Cotton to Starling Conner 12 Aug. 1829 106

Mary Ellen Cou to Jettha D. Brashear 15 Feb. 1849 7

Sarah Coudor to James McGee 5 Feb. 1850 26

Samuel S. Coulburn to Rhoda Ross 8 Oct. 1846 222

Andrew Couts to Martha J. Harlow 28 April 1847 231

Cornelius Cowen, Cole Co., Mo. to Elizabeth Miller 22 March
    1827 75

Henry Cowen to Honor Howard 8 July 1819 3
John E. Cowan to Sarah Ann Ward 1 May 1845 186

Joshua Cox to Esthur Kelly 7 April 1823 42
Lucy Ann Cox to Joseph Campbell 7 Sept. 1845 196
William Cox to Lousanna Williams 30 Nov. 1834 25

Lydia M. Coy to Edward Robinson 20 Feb. 1827 76

David E. N. Craig to Mahaley Bomen 22 Nov. 1845 203

Page 55 A
Will of George Cramer
    To my wife, Polly...
    To my sons: William S., Thomas J., Jonathan J., and George...
    To my daughters: Harriett Amanda Cramer, Susan Martin, Mary Barlow, Agnes A. Corum, and Karnly Cramer...
    My wife, Polly, Exe.
Written: 4 December 1832
Witnesses: Joseph Yarnal, William Yarnal, and John Yarnall
Recorded: 31 December 1832
Agnes Cramer to Harden Corum 14 June 1827 80
Andrew Cramer to Nancy Shackleford 27 Oct. 1850 36
Caroline Cramer to Joseph Cunningham 12 May 1831 134
Elizabeth Cramer to Thomas W. Cobbs 22 Dec. 1842 153
Harriet Amanda Cramer to James H. Glasgow 12 Oct. 1836 64
Lucinda Cramer to William Petitt 8 Sept. 1839 100
Nancy Cramer to Richard B. Sanford 9 March 1848 254
Rebecca Cramer to Charles Herndon 12 Nov. 1835 41
Sudwill A. Cramer to Elizabeth Shackleford 16 Feb. 1843 153
William Cramer to Catharine Houx 75 1 Feb. 1827

John Cranston to Nancy Donneldson 26 March 1835 27

John J. Cravens to Anna Hines 24 June 1849 15

Page 74 A2
Will of George Crawford
    To my sons: John Crawford and William H. Crawford
    To my daughter, Mary E.
    To my friend, James Baker
    Should my son, John die then his wife Eliza Jane will be entitled to his proportion
Written: 28 July 1852
Witnesses: A. S. Shortridge and James H. Baker
Recorded: 12 August 1852
Christina Crawford to James Deckard 12 Sept. 1819 4
Cinthy Jane Crawford to John M. Savage 2 April 1830 120
Elender B. Crawford to Frederick E. Houx 26 March 1835 31

Eliza Crawford to Huston McFarland 7 Jan. 1835 28
Elizabeth J. Crawford to John Haas 26 Nov. 1840 118
James L. Crawford to Ann T. McCarty 17 March 1836 48
John Crawford to Eliza J. Greenhalt 28 April 1849 11
Polly Crawford to John Deckard 5 Sept. 1832 153
Zelah Crawford to Houston McFarland 25 Oct. 1841 134

Perry Crews to Margaret McCorch 22 March 1849 14

Page 62 A2
Will of Lovin Cropper
    To my children who may suit themselves in regard to the estates disposal
    John Fluke and Joseph Stephens, Exc.
Written: 4 Feb. 1852
Witnesses: Urer Morley, Adam Vivion, Synard Calvert, and Robert W. Gale
Recorded: 12 February 1852
Cynthia Cropper to Adam Simonton 30 Oct. 1828 93
Lovin Cropper to Elizabeth P. Caldwell 16 Jan. 1845 23
Mary Cropper to Dodge Stephens 4 Sept. 1834 23
William H. Cropper to Nancy J. Hutchinson 17 Jan. 1850 28

Francis Crouse to Mary Roamspeacher 7 Jan. 1844 166

Louisa Crowder to Caleb Martin 28 Nov. 1833 17

Henry W. Crowther to Eliza Bruffoe 19 July 1832 151

Demonas Cruse to Lorenzo D. Pulley 22 April 1834 19

Page 222 A2
Will of Joseph C. Culp, Senior
    To my 3rd son, Thomas H. ...
    To my wife, Frances G. ...
    To my daughters: Martha J. Culp, Sarah W. Culp, Josiah C. Culp, and Lucy Ann Howard...
    To my sons: Paul S., George, James M., John M., Albert S., and William M. Culp...
Written: 3 April 1857
Witnesses: E. W. Clark and William H. Bernard
Recorded: 20 September 1858

Chr. A. Cunto to Augusta C. F. Briglub 12 April 1844 175

Joseph Cunningham to Caroline Cramer 12 May 1831 134

Elizabeth Dale to John Calvert 25 July 1842 144
C. B. Daly to Susan E. Bailey 18 July 1849 16

William N. Dandridge to Catherine M. Reaves 1 May 1845 188

James Daniel to Rebecca Erwin 5 Oct. 1848 2

Andrew T. Dashner to Elizabeth A. Ford 15 Oct. 1846 221

Fahot Dauker to Maria Watterson 9 Dec. 1849 23

James A. Davenport to Nancy Herndon 27 April 1840 112

Tititha C. Davidson to Reuben Donnington 19 July 1838 84

Page 20 A
Will of Traverse Davis
    To my wife, Fanny...
    To my two youngest sons: Traverse Davis and Henry Harrison Davis; to my son, John Grigsby Davis; to my eldest son, James Kincheloe Davis; to my second eldest son, William Gibson Davis; to my son, Isaac...
    To my eldest daughter, Melinda Wilson; to my second eldest daughter, Mary Posman; and to my third eldest daughter, Maria Fort...
    Judgment against Culbert Harrison of Nelson Co. Kentucky I leave to Robert Wycliffe, of Lexington, Ky. and Charles A Wycliffe, of Nelson Co., Ky.
    To my fourth daughter, Lorian Davis
Written: 28 April 1824   John C. Rochester, Exe.
Witnesses: John C. Rochester and Jesse K. Davis
Recorded: 22 May 1824
Andrew Davis to Caroline McClanahan 29 Aug. 1833 8
Betsey Jane Davis to Trussey O'Rear 14 May 1835 29
Charles Davis to Jane Cole 14 April 1822 35
Elizabeth Davis to William Davis 19 April 1832 150
Elizabeth Davis to Thomas McClanahan 26 May 1833 5
Elvira Davis to James Parker 24 Sept. 1837 75
Emily Davis, daughter of Phillip E. Davis, dec. to John
    Robertson 14 April 1842 149
Jain Davis to Francis S. Wadley 14 Jan. 1844 67
James Davis to Susan Hunt 21 Oct. 1827 86
James Davis to Fanny Carpenter 25 Nov. 1828 88
Jeremiah Davis to Dorenda Gilbreath 4 Sept. 1839 102
Jane Davis to Gersham Compton 27 Feb. 1820 11
Jane Davis to Joseph M. Laune 7 Nov. 1835 42
John Davis to Mary Stephens 11 June 1835 45
Joseph L. Davis to Susan T. Richardson 14 Jan. 1836 43
Justian Davis to James Burrus 1 June 1848 263
Leonard Davis to Sarah Davis 4 May 1848 263
Mary A. Davis to Robert A. Wilson 8 Dec. 1839 108
Mary Jane Davis to Daniel Milton White 1 Jan. 1841 124
Nancy Davis to William Harris 31 Dec. 1834 27
O. P. Davis, Macon Co., Mo. to Sarah L. Robinson 12 Sept. 1843
    160

Sally Davis to George Tennille 21 Nov. 1819 6
Sarah Davis to Leonard Davis 4 May 1848 263
Susan Davis to Hustand McFarland 29 Aug. 1839 99
Susan Davis to Ira Page 14 Aug. 1844 179
Thomas W. Davis to Emiline Doyle 19 Sept. 1833 5
Warren Davis to Hannah Kenchloe 5 July 1829 105
William Davis to Mahala McFarland 20 Jan. 1823 40
William Davis to Elizabeth Davis 19 April 1832 150

Daniel Day to Permelia May 22 Feb. 1838 77

Polly Deakin to James Moore 24 Dec. 1832 1
Sinthy Deakin to James Robsinson 15 Jan. 1829 101

George W. Dean to Rachel D. Johnston 17 March 1838 85

John Deckard to Polly Crawford 6 Sept. 1832 153
Margaret A. Decker to Nicholas B. Soleman 23 July 1846 216
Nancy G. Deckard to John L. Drinkwater 25 July 1844 173
Sally A. Deckard to Archibald A. Drinkwater 29 Feb. 1848 253

John Dehart, Howard Co., Mo. to Lydia Margaret Lace 24 Feb. 1842 141

Joshua Dell to Polly Woods 10 May 1821 21

George Dempsey to Sarah Barnett 13 Aug. 1840 128

Reuben Dennington to Tititha C. Davidson 19 July 1838 84

Anthony W. Dennis to Emily Houx 3 Dec. 1836 44
Elizabeth Dennis to James L. Forsythe 26 March 1840 108
Samuel Dennis to Elizabeth Arhart 28 Feb. 1831 129
Sarah Dennis to Elias Barker 20 July 1829 105

Thomas Densman to Nancy Yarnal 7 Sept. 1826 65
Thomas Densman to Sally Robinson 18 Feb. 1827 69

Sarah Ann Dermsey to Obadiah F. Ballard 12 June 1843 156

Lucinda Derrill to Thomas Moore 3 July 1829 106

Jacob Devaul to Caroline F. O'Bryan 10 Oct. 1847 241

Mary M. Dewey to Nathaniel Parrett 7 Oct. 1847 241

Hannah Dewitt to William Potter 14 May 1843 157
Larkin Dewitt to Hannah Ewing 20 July 1820 114
Polly Dewitt to Elijah Farley 13 Oct. 1842 150
Thomas Dewitt to Rebecca Gibson 9 March 1845 185

Hiram Dial to Elizabeth Biggs 13 Sept. 1830 125
Stephen Dial to Deborah Stone 27 Aug. 1820 16

James Dickard to Christina Crawford 12 Sept. 1819 4

Frances A. Dickerson to Isiah F. Houx 6 Jan. 1846 198

Carter Dicks to Nancy Bridgewater 17 Oct. 1839 102
Martha Dicks to William Bridgewater 17 Oct. 1839 104

Page 88 A2
Will of Ann H. Dickson
    To my daughter, Mary Jane Williams...
    To Marcus Williams...
Written: 15 April 1851
Witnesses: James Quarles, Isaac Lionberger, and David Lilly
Recorded: 25 January 1853
Miss C. A. Dickson to A. P. McCarty 22 Feb. 1849 10
Eliza Ann Dickson to James H. Renfro 27 Oct. 1841 135
George Dickson to Nancy Calvert 18 Nov. 1828 117
James Dickson to Mrs. Nancy Littlepage 4 Oct. 1846 98
Mary Isabel Dickson to Fenton G. Reavis 18 April 1839 98
Nancy Dickson to James Cole 25 Jan. 1836 43

Joan Diel to Mary Dietrich 20 Nov. 1850 37

Mary Dietrich to Joan Diel 20 Nov. 1850 37

Major Dillard to William Stephens 22 May 1845 192
Nancy Dillard to William Potter 18 Nov. 1819 7
Phoebe Dillard to William P. Rutherford 29 Dec. 1835 37
Phebe Dillard to Thomas Adams 22 Dec. 1842 152

William E. Dingle to Ann E. Cockrell 20 Aug. 1833 7

Elizabeth Dinwiddie to Stubblefield Morrison 2 Dec. 1830 129

John P. Dix to Rebecca Burchel 23 July 1846 216
Mary Dix to Nathaniel Sutherland 21 Dec. 1847 251

Martha Dixon to William Reynolds 9 Sept. 1843 175

Benjamin Doalson to Jeanneat L. McClanahan 7 Aug. 1836 54

Louisa Dodds to ___ Sidebottom 7 Jan. 1846 199
Sarah Dodds to William Miller 12 April 1846 212
Sophia Dodds to Benjamin Doolin 20 Jan. 1831 135

Elizabeth M. Dollis to Peter Stephens 14 March 1839 96

Mildred Dooly to James Hofferfinger 13 Feb. 1832 145

Martha Donagair to John Kennedy _ _ _ 1832 152

Eliza Donaghe to James Blankenship 21 Dec. 1831 1842

Catharine Donhouser to George Speebu 17 Nov. 1848 3

Nancy Donneldson to John Cranston 26 March 1835 27

Lewis Doran to Jane Martin 19 Jan. 1843 155
Thomas Dorn to Mary Ann Odinele 22 Dec. 1843 155

Mary Dorman to John Hastedt 11 March 1850 28

Page 224 A2
Will of James R. Douglas
    To Hardenay H. Taylor...
    To Elizabeth Douglas...
Written: 4 May 1853
Witnesses: S. Puckett and Daniel C. Steele
Recorded: 25 September 1858
Page 121 A2
Will of Ruth Douglas
    To my sons: Ralph Douglas, William Douglas, Charles Mason Douglas, and Joshiah Morgan Douglas...
    To my daughters: Emma Douglas and Mar D. Tutt...
    My son, Henry C. Douglas, Exe.
Written 20 June 1853
Recorded: 24 February 1854
Harding Douglas to James H. Taylor 15 Aug. 1843 161
Mary Ann Douglas to William J. George 7 Sept. 1848 1
J. T. Douglas, St. Louis Co., Mo. to Cornelia McPherson
    8 April 1847 238

George Douthet to Elizabeth Guyer 26 March 1846 215

Page 56 A2
Will of James Dow
    To the children of my first wife Charity, the daughter of Samuel Teeters: Ann Eliza and Henry...
    To the children of my present wife Elizabeth, the daughter of James Mahan: James Pennington, John A., Milton G., and Mary Ophelia...
Written: 14 Oct. 1843
Witnesses: J. Williams and John C. Ostrander
Eliza Ann Dow to S. L. Townsley 12 May 1844 171
James Dow to Elisebeth Mahan 13 May 1830 118

Emiline Doyle to Thomas W. Davis 19 Sept. 1833 5
Frances Doyle to Nathaniel Gibson 25 Sept. 1842 174
Matilda Doyle to John J. Morley 23 Oct. 1837 74

William Drafflin to Atalanta McCullough 8 Oct. 1840 116

Susan Dreshel to Drary Goodman 29 Aug. 1844 178

Page 93 A
Will of Hannah Drinkwater
    To my son, William...
    To my daughters: Polly Drinkwater, Eliza Drinkwater, Margaret Drinkwater, and my sons: John Drinkwater and James Drinkwater...
Written: 15 May 1835   Elijah Randolph, Exe.
Witnesses: Lawrence Hall and Alexander Johnston
Recorded: 22 June 1835
Archibald A. Drinkwater to Sally A. Deckard 29 Feb. 1848 253
Emanuel Drinkwater to Euphemia Scott 4 Feb. 1821 19
James I. Drinkwater to Margaret Dunkin 31 March 1847 228
Jane Drinkwater to Hogan Soloman 26 March 1845 189
John L. Drinkwater to Nancy G. Deckard 25 July 1844 173
Martha Drinkwater to Thomas T. Toler 3 June 1846 214
Mary Drinkwater to William Aton 14 Aug. 1836 59
Nancy Drinkwater to Elijah Towler 8 Nov. 1846 225
Polly Drinkwater to William Travis 27 Dec. 1821 24
Samuel Drinkwater to Sarah Goodman 8 Dec. 1844 181
Thomas Drinkwater to Mrs. Catherine Williams 21 May 1846 232
William Drinkwater to Nancy White 24 May 1836 60

Jesse Driskill to Sarah Good 26 Nov. 1847 250
Louisa J. Driskill to Alexander Wood 31 Jan. 1850 29
Moses Driskill to Sophia Turner 20 Nov. 1848 2
Nancy Driskill to William Johnson 17 June 1840 113
Thomas Driskill to Mrs. Mary Turner 28 Aug. 1839 101
William Driskill to Susan Williams 27 Jan. 1839 95

George C. Dugan to Harriett J. Walls 7 Jan. 1849 5

Page 47 A2
Will of Delatha Duncan, widow of Isaac Duncan, dec.
    I wish a tombstone like the one that is over my deceased husband to be placed over my grave and it is my wish that all the remainder of my estate go to my beloved niece, Jane Williams.
Written: 21 Aug. 1849
Witnesses: James Parsons and John Logan
29 March 1851
Page 37 B
Will of Isaac Duncan
    To my wife Delithy...
    To my sons: William Duncan, Browning Duncan, Phillemon Duncan...
    Continued

To my daughter, Sarah Chism, late Sarah Embree...
Meriah Ross gets as much as her mothers part.
To my daughter, Susan Ann Ross who is ded who left two girls and the oldest was named Susan Jane and Susan Jane is ded. It is my wish for Ann Meriah to have her mothers part.
To my daughter, Ruth Briscoe...
My son in law, William Briscoe, Exe.
Written: 29 August 1840
Witnesses: Hugh Baxter and Shadrack Morris
Recorded: 25 November 1842

Frederick Duncan to Martha E. Parks 10 Oct. 1839 103
Henry G. Duncan to Elizabeth G. Koontz 2 May 1844 171
Isaac Duncan to Delitha Wiley 5 May 1834 21
Jeptha Duncan to Mary Read 31 Dec. 1834 24
Martha C. Duncan to John H. Kelly 14 Nov. 1849 23
Margaret Duncan to James I. Drinkwater 3 March 1847 228
Mary C. Duncan to Richard M. Sparks 8 Jan. 1850 29

Berry Dunham to Margaret Fisher 5 Aug. 1832 155
John Dunham to Saritha Seat 21 June 1832 153

Amanda Dunn to Jacob B. Hovey 20 Oct. 1850 35
Joseph W. Dunn to Nancy Melott 21 Jan. 1845 185
Mariah Dunn to Henry E. Moore 9 July 1836 63
Mary Dunn to Levi Talbot 19 Feb. 1843 152

Page 150 A2
Will of John Durbin
    To my sister, Agnes
    To the sisters of my deceased wife, $1000.
Written: 28 May 1854
Witnesses: John W. Tunnell, D. H. Hamilton, and W. P. James
Recorded: 24 June 1855

John Durnell to Mary Howles 16 May 1847 230

Harriett Dush to Fielden White 29 Feb. 1848 257

Elizabeth Eckhard to Henry L. Norfu 23 Dec. 1849 23

Ann Edgar to Soloman Brown 21 March 1821 19
Henrietta Jane Edgar to William S. Fawkersley 26 Jan. 1848 252
James M. Edgar to Eliza Collins 5 Nov. 1837 77
William Edgar to Mary J. Caldwell 4 Nov. 1847 250

William Edmons to Mary Catherine Reavis 4 Nov. 1845 197

Anderson Edwards to Elizabeth Larew 24 Jan. 1836 44
Cornelius Edwards to Mary A. Scott 21 April 1849 11
Elizabeth Edwards to Joshua Martin 4 Oct. 1832 156
Susanna Edwards to William Powers 4 May 1823 42
William G. Edwards to Catherine McClanahan 20 Nov. 1845 200

Page 2 A2
Will of Jacob Eller
    To my wife, Susannah Eller...
    To my sons: David George, Robert, James, and Christopher Columbus...
    To my daughters: Mary Hungerford, Martitia Jamison, and Harriet Eller...
    My friend, Lawrence O. Stephens, Exe.
Witnesses: G. W. G. Thomas and John C. Richardson
Written: 15 July 1847
Recorded: 8 November 1847
David Eller to Martha Jane Oglesby 9 Dec. 1847 245
Harriett E. Eller to Rev. Hugh W. Wear 15 April 1847 230
James M. C. Eller to Eleanor Cole 6 April 1832 145
Martitia Eller to James W. Jamison 7 April 1836 49
Rebecca Eller to Turner Adams 26 Jan. 1834 14

Elizabeth Ellice to George Shipley 25 March 1830 113

Amenicus Elliott to Elizabeth Ashcraft 28 April 1848 258
Ann Eliza Elliott to Richard Yartin 20 Aug. 1832 159
Edmond P. Elliott to Mariah H. Conner 14 Aug. 1843 158
Elizabeth Elliott to Robert C. Bell 27 July 1845 194
Henry Elliott to Eliza A. Conner 11 July 1844 176
Henry Elliott to Sama O'Bryan 20 Oct. 1847 242
Jackson Elliott to Patsy Briscoe 10 Sept. 1840 114
John M. Elliott to Eliza Scott 16 Dec. 1841 137
Mary Ann Elliott to George Conrad 23 May 1850 31
Martha Jane Elliott to Col. Thomas M. Cordry 23 Sept. 1841 132
Rose A. Elliott to Thomas B. Wallace 3 April 1838 80

Page 37 A2
Will of William Ellis
    My late son in law, David I. Patteson...
    To my daughters: Elizabeth H. Patteson and Mary Louise Ellis...
    To my daughter, Martha Gray, land in Spotsylvania Co., Va.
    To my sons: Thomas Joseph, William Henry...
    To my wife, Ann W.
    My sons, Thomas Joseph and William Henry, Exe.
Written: 10 January 1845
Witnesses: Levy Chandler, Jesse George, and Hillary Harris
Recorded: 26 August 1850
Elizabeth K. Ellis to John W. Leftwich 28 Aug. 1845 193
Isaac M. Ellis to Millie Bailey 1 Nov. 1849 27
Mary L. Ellis to Peter Miller 10 March 1845 185
Thomas J. Ellis to Martha M. Fore 26 April 1848 256
William Ellis to Ellender Hughes 14 Sept. 1829 107
William U. Ellis to Ann Maria Johnson 3 Nov. 1846 220

Elizabeth Ellison to Daniel Cline 15 May 1834 21
Mary Ellison to Samuel Awford 13 Oct. 1840 118
William Ellson to Martha Williams 31 Dec. 1823 44

George W. Embree to Elizabeth Titsworth 19 Jan. 1848 251
Polly Embree to Henry Bowsfield 28 April 1823 43

Peyton Embrow to Cynthy Ann McFarland 22 May 1849 17

John G. Encke to Louisa H. Stahr 9 May 1850 31

Howard D. English, Boon Co., Mo. to Martha H. Mucker
    25 Dec. 1849 25
Martha Ann English to Charles Moore 27 July 1848 265

Gabriel R. Eoford to Nancy Epperson 8 April 1849 16

Jessie Epperson to Mrs. Susan Branson 2 Oct. 1850 33
Nancy Epperson to Gabriel R. Eoford 8 April 1849 16
Susannah J. Epperson to Abner Brisendien 30 July 1849 16

R. Epison to Sarah B. Gabriel 8 Aug. 1844 176

Granville Erwin to Florinda Steel 10 Jan. 1843 153
    The former of Pettis Co., Mo.
Larkin Erwin to Elizabeth Jane Barnett 21 Oct. 1841 138
Rebecca Erwin to James Daniel 5 Oct. 1848 2

Andrew Estes to Susanna Estes 16 Feb. 1829 99
Mary Estes to Green Woods 30 Nov. 1821 26
Nancy Estes to Elija Spence 29 Nov. 1830 126
Nancy Estes to Hartley White 31 March 1833 1
Sally Estes to William Hall 9 Dec. 1819 9
Susanna Estes to Andrew Estes 16 Feb. 1829 99

Page 102 A
Will of Achilles Eubank
    To my wife, Nancy...
    To my children: Achilles Jackson Eubank, William Thomas Eubank, Richard Eubank, Joseph James Eubank after they arrive at lawful age each have their share by commissioners appointed by the court governing the case.
    I have given to my children born to me by my first wife all I wish them to have of my estate. That is to say Ambrose B. Eubank, Milly Calloway, Stephen Eubank, Elizabeth Calloway, Polly Quesenbury, and Frances Rollins.
    My best friend, Lawrence C. Stephens, Exe.
Written: 26 August 1838
Written: Thomas Best, Joseph Stephens, John Bigham, and George W. Cathey
Recorded: 4 December 1844

Achilles Eubank, aged about 79 to Nancy Wear, aged about 27
    years 13 Aug. 1837 70
Mary Jane Eubank to William Caughman 31 Aug. 1850 32
Susan Eubank to James McCullucy 31 Nov. 1844 181

Page 430 A2
Will of Julia H. Evans
    To my son, Thomas Edwin Evans...
    To my mother, Sarah Graham...
    To my brothers: William Thomas Graham, Charles Buchanan
Graham, and Emmett Noah Graham...
    To my sisters: Amanda Victoria Bradley and Harriett
Graham...
    J. M. McCutchen, Exe.
Written 6 June 1867
Witnesses: J. M. McCutchen and W. T. Gentry
Recorded: 21 March 1870
Alexander Evans to Margaret Jolly 13 Dec. 1840 119
Dianna Evans to Silas P. Arbuckle 7 Sept. 1831 138
James Evans to Melinda Smith 4 June 1844 171
Jerrumah Evans to Thomas Alley 7 Feb. 1832 142
Louis F. Evans to Mary Ann Allison 8 July 1847 238
Sophia Evans to James Cole 21 Oct. 1847 243

Polly Everson to William Parvy 3 Jan. 1820 13

Betsey Ewing to Charles R. Berry 16 Dec. 1824 50
George M. Ewing to Lucinda Rubey 27 May 1824 50
Hannah Ewing to Larkin DeWitt 20 July 1820 5
Isaac Ewing to Mildred Howard 29 July 1841 132
June J. Ewing to William Rubey 6 Sept. 1821 23
Margaret D. Ewing to Robert Sloan 13 Dec. 1826 67
Mary A. Ewing to Archibald Kavanaugh 11 July 1821 21
Mary Jane Ewing to William Z. Fields 28 Jan. 1840 111
Sidney R. Ewing to Joshua Campbell 6 Feb. 1823 41
William C. Ewing to Lucretia P. Corum 3 Feb. 1845 188
Winifred W. Ewing to Henry Rubey 26 Feb. 1822 30

Page 370 A2
Will of William Fairfax
    To my wife, Elizabeth...
Written: 2 Jan. 1866
Witnesses: R. A. Page, John Rootcap, and James H. Walker
Recorded: 21 February 1866

Elijah Farley to Polly Dewitt 13 Oct. 1842 150
A. Farley to Ann Casteel ___ 1840 120
Mary D. Farley, daughter of Daniel and Frances Farley to
    Isaac Jones 27 June 1843 156

Page 52 A
Will of Micajah Farris
    To my wife, Nancy...
    To my youngest daughter, Louisa Farris...
    To my children, towit William Farris, Polly Turley, Ephraim Farris, Ruth Tool, Jane Fisher, and Louisa Farris...
    My son, Ephraim, Exc.
Written: 25 Feb. 1832
Witnesses: Ludwill Allen, John Cramar, S. W. Macmahan, and James Flack
Recorded: 21 September 1832

Ann Farris to John Moreland 10 Feb. 1825 72
Clareny Farris to William Stephens 6 Jan. 1827 69
E. Farris to Evalina O'Bryan 21 April 1849 11
Eli Farris to Sevina Ardilon Miller 3 Nov. 1837 55
James Farris to Sarah Bankston 15 Jan. 1826 57
James Farris to Jane Casady 26 April 1838 81
Jane Farris to John Fisher 6 Oct. 1831 141
John Farris to Mary Westbrook 17 Dec. 1826 67
Louisa Farris to James Taylor 22 May 1834 21
Thomas W. C. Farris to Lydia Morley 8 Oct. 1826 65
Hannah Fawbush to Clelum Ross 6 Dec. 1820 18

William S. Fawkersley to Henrietta Jane Edgar 26 Jan. 1848 252

Frances Feek to John McAllister 29 March 1837 71

Page 294 A2
Will of John Felton
    To my wife, Christina formerly Lessnich
        (Will written in German)
Written: 14 January 1861
Witnesses: J. I. Felton and Stephen Young
Recorded: 1 March 1861

George Fenwick to Julia Ann Herndon 31 Aug. 1837 75

Harris Horns Furgarson to Sarah Thomas 4 June 1850 32
Martha Ann Ferguson to Henry Moreland 26 Nov. 1841 138
Miss M. A. Ferguson to B. McCarty 19 Dec. 1843 165
Mary Ann Ferguson to John W. Field 12 May 1842 143

Martillus Ferrill to Mrs. Mary Jane Waller 7 March 1837 65
Peter Ferrill to Polly Ann Byler 5 April 1832 149
Peter H. Ferrill to Susan J. Meredith 9 March 1836 48
Sarah U. Ferriott to Charles R. Muggah 23 July 1846 215

Benjamin A. Ferrel to Lucy C. Standley 13 Feb. 1829 99

Page 78 A2
Will of James Fields
   Samuel Roe, Jr. shall sell all my property and I bequeath to Samuel Roe, Jr. and Martha Ann Roe, share and share alike.
Written: 3 July 1852
Witnesses: S. A. Summers, Samuel Roe, and Peter Wilson
Recorded: 31 August 1852
James Fields to Lucy Ross   22 Dec. 1831   139
Jesse Fields to Martha Ann Oglesby   14 Nov. 1833   12
John W. Fields to Mary Ann Gerguson   12 May 1842   143
John Walker Fields to Harriett S. McCutchen   11 July 1837   70
Lerry M. Fields to Elverton Caldwell Westbrook   11 Jan. 1849   6
Salina Fields to Ambrose C. Lampton   9 April 1847   229
William Z. Fields to Mary Jane Ewing   28 May 1840   111

Martha Finch to William I. Steel   26 Sept. 1838   86

John Fine to Agnes Mitchell   30 Sept. 1826   75
Stephen M. Fine to Mary Beaty   24 Sept. 1835   33

Page 249 A2
Will of Mary Finley
   To my sons: Brutus W. Finley and Philander Finley...
   To the children of my deceased daughters Margaret Campbell and Sally Finley for reasons which appear to me to be good, but which it is unnecessary to mention, I shall give nothing and I only mention them to show that I had not forgotten them.
   To my children: Thomas B. Finley and Virginia Hancock...
   To my son in laws: Robert Crockett, Hugh Rhodes, and Rhodes Marshall...
   To my daughter in law, Nancy Finley...
Written: 26 July 1862
Witnesses: John A. Trigg, John F. Clark, and W. M. Clark
Recorded: 8 June 1865
Milton Finley, Saline Co., Mo. to Mary Wear   15 Aug. 1833   6
Wilker H. Finley to Mary Wallace   26 Feb. 1840   109

Hamilton Finney to Katherine Bruffee   28 Nov. 1847   245

Harriet Firk to Christian Brownfield   1 Oct. 1846   220

Joseph Firy to Margaret Morris   4 Jan. 1849   7

Caty Fisher to William McDaniel   16 March 1820   11
Henry Fisher to Nelly Gabainal   13 Dec. 1827   85
John Fisher to Elizabeth Stinson   28 Dec. 1825   62
John Fisher to Jane Faris   6 Oct. 1831   141
Joseph Fisher to Margaret Woolridge   1 Aug. 1842   146
Malinda Fisher to Samuel A. Sitter   8 Dec. 1836   57
Margaret Fisher to Berry Dunham   5 Aug. 1832   155

Maria L. Fisher to John Fluke 31 May 1842 143
Peter Fisher to Caty Carter 23 Dec. 1821 28
Polly Fisher to Harmon Bailey 16 Jan. 1828 87
Reuben Fisher to Elizabeth Bass 18 June 1832 167
Sabria Fisher to James Flack 9 June 1822 34
Trustman Fisher to Margaret Gess 19 March 1829 105
William Fisher to Eliza Smith 25 Dec. 1827 88

Catherine A. Fitten to Benjamin Weeden 27 March 1837 68
Mary J. Fitter to Daniel Weeden 19 Oct. 1842 148

James Flack to Silvey Fisher 9 June 1822 34

William Flint, Pettis Co., Mo. to Ann Porter 7 Nov. 1833 6

Page 132
Will of Jones H. Flournoy
    To my wife, Clara...
    To my children: Sarah Ann Flournoy, Eliza Margaret Flournoy, Mary Cornelia Flournoy, and Martha Flournoy...
Written: 7 April 1840
Witnesses: John Garrett and R. S. Wilson
Recorded: 30 May 1840
Clara Flournoy to Gideon E. M. Strange, Howard Co., Mo.
Sarah Flournoy to Andrew Adams 16 Dec. 1847 249

John Fluke to Mariah L. Fisher 31 May 1842 143

Page 43 A?
Will of Samuel Forbes
    To my wife, Caroline C. ...
    To my son, Watson P. ...
    To my daughter, Dela Fletcher...
    To my children: John M., Andrew M., Wesley G., Hannah Ross, dec. and her son, Samuel Ross and my deceased daughter, Emily Segraves whose three sons are now living viz John Segraves, Samuel Segraves, and William Jeptha Segraves...
    Also the children of my deceased son, Wesley G. towit James S. Forbes, Margaret Jane Forbes, William Forbes, Mary Forbes, and Zachary Taylor Forbes...
    A. S. Walker, Exe.
Written: 22 October 1850
Witnesses: Henry R. Walker and Daniel Wright
Andrew M. Forbes to Nancy M. Steel 23 Feb. 1831 132
Emily Forbes to Custis Segraves 6 Sept. 1837 72

Deale F. Forbus to Sary Ann Ross 17 Aug. 1848 1

Charles Force to Betsey Conner 7 Sept. 1819 4
Charles Force to Eliza W. Sombart 7 April 1845 168

NOTES

Elizabeth Ford to William Allison 14 Oct. 1841 134
Elizabeth A. Ford to Andrew T. Dashner 15 Oct. 1846 221
Nathaniel L. Ford to Narsissa Summers 1 Sept. 1844 178

Page 231 A2
Will of Thomas A. Fore, of the county of Christopher, Virginia
    To my father, Anderson Fore...
    I have slaves in the state of Texas in the care of my brother in law, Thomas I. Ellis of Gandalupe County.
    To my children...
    Dr. William H. Ellis and from Cooper County, Exe
Written: 22 July 1857
Witnesses: Samuel A. Pattison, Richard Plekinton, R. W. Flournoy, and Leonidas H. Fore
Recorded 24 December 1858
Martha M. Fore to Thomas J. Ellis 26 April 1848 256

Robert Forest to Eliza Ellen Dorron 2 Oct. 1837 72

Page 316 A2
Will of Nancy Forsythe
    To my daughters: Nancy Woolery, Polly Burger, and Lucy Phillips...
    To my children: Elizabeth Embry, Jailey Bradley, James Titsworth, and the two children viz Louisa Calvert and Newton Calvert of my deceased daughter, Priscilla Calvert...
    John Taylor, Exe.
Written: 12 June 1856
Witnesses: William B. Wallace and John S. Stephens
Recorded: 14 August 1862
Page 1 A2
Will of William Forsythe
    Mr. Samuel Chambers shall take charge of my beloved wife. After her death my estate shall be equally divided among Mr. Samuel Chambers three daughters viz Mary Elizabeth Chambers, Louisa Jane Chambers, and Martha Inzer Chambers.
    To my wife, Polly...
Written: 2 August 1847
Witnesses: James Parsons and John W. Logan
Recorded: 8 October 1847
James Forsythe to Nancy Tittsworth 5 Oct. 1841 135
James L. Forsythe to Elizabeth Dennis 26 March 1840 104
Joseph Forsythe to Thelida Saw 16 Feb. 1841 122
Linda Forsythe to John Glazier 9 April 1839 94
Margaret Forsythe to James H. Burns 22 May 1834 20

Page 43 A
Will of Spear Fort
    To Nancy Caulk, one English shilling
Continued--

To my children: Mary Wallace, David Fort, and Lewsinday Roberson...
Written: 11 February 1828
Witnesses: David Lilly and Jacob Chism
Recorded: 22 March 1828
John Fort to Dorinda Bell 19 Oct. 1828 97
Lucinda Fort to Charles Robertson 7 Nov. 1822 39

Andrew A. Foster to Mary Katherine Wear 16 Nov. 1841 135
Elizabeth M. Foster to Thomas Neal 27 Nov. 1850 34
Julia Foster to Jacob Harmon 12 Jan. 1834 16
Sarah M. Foster to Charles N. Wysong 1 June 1847 235
Thomas Foster to Elizabeth 4 Nov. 1835 35
William D. Foster to Mary Jane Baker 27 July 1848 264
Wilson C. Foster to Malinda Wear 16 Feb. 1841 122

Rosanna Fouch to George Volrath 18 April 1844 169

Elizabeth Frazier to William Baker 20 March 1831 132

James M. Freeman, Coon Co., Mo. to Rebecca A. Normbeck 31 March 1846 207

John R. French to Martha Reavis 25 April 1843 159

Catherine Fry to Jefferson Lord 15 Feb. 1849 8
Charles Frey to C. Bronhuisen 14 August 1849 17
Shaney Fry to Drury Venable 2 July 1837 69

Page 41 42
Will of James M. Fryer
    To my wife, Margaret...
    To my children towit Christney Fryer, Robert T. Fryer, Angeline Fryer, Maryan Fryer, Zeroldy Fryer, and Marthy Jane Fryer...
    Tandy E. Douglas and Thomas T. McCulloch, Exe.
Written: 7 April 1849
Witnesses: Spotswood M. McCulloch, Samuel Drinkwater, and Robert McCulloch
Recorded: 10 October 1850

Page 76 B
Will of Antony Fuchs
    To my wife, Rosina...
    To my daughters: Emelia Hedrick, Rosina, Stephena, and Sophia...
    To my sons: Charles and Francis...
    My son in law, Rinehard Hedrick and my wife, Exe.
Written: 26 July 1842
David Andrews and Casper Thro
Recorded: 15 August 1843
Amelia Fuchs to Reinhart Kissnich 8 Dec. 1840 118

Page 293 A2
Will of Frederick M. Fulkerson
    To my wife and after her death to her son, William Gray...
    To my daughters: Mary Ann Hayton and Lucinda V. Miller...
Written: 23 January 1861
Witnesses: William H. Ellis and H. I. Reavis
Recorded: 13 February 1861
Mary Ann Fulkerson to Andrew I. Hayton 27 July 1847 240

Elizabeth Fuller to Soloman Reed 12 March 1826 62

Bernet Furnish to Belsam Shepherd 23 May 1842 142

Joseph Furs to Mary Jane Barnes 18 Jan. 1846 204

Page 12 A2
Will of Jacob Gabriel
    To my three daughters: Sarah Epperson, Bashaba Gabriel, and Catherine Gabriel...
    To my son, Allen I. Gabriel, $100.
    to James P. Gabriel, $100.; to William I. Gabriel, $100.
    To my son, Jeremiah W. Gabriel, land
    To my son, Daniel I. Gabriel, land
    To my wife, Delila...
    To my two little sons, Benjamin F. Gabriel and Thomas B. Gabriel...
    To my two little grandsons, Jacob E. Gabriel and William I Gabriel, $1.00
    Delila Gabriel, Allen I. Gabriel, James P. Gabriel, and John R. Epperson, Exe.
Written: 21 March 1848
Witnesses: Michael Hornbeck, Robert Hornbeck, and James McClain
Recorded: 15 April 1848
Allen J. Gabriel to Nancy McClanahan 30 July 1840 113
James Gabriel to Polly Ann Goodman 1 Nov. 1838 89
John Gabriel, Jr. to Mary Vaught 14 Feb. 1827 73
Nancy Gabriel to Adam Weaver 1 Nov. 1827 85
Sarah Gabriel to John H. M. Miller 23 Nov. 1828 96
Sarah B. Gabriel to R. Epison 8 Aug. 1844 176
William J. Gabriel to Rebecca Goodman 19 Sept. 1850 39

Page 60 A2
Will of Hugh Gilbreath
    To my daughters: Catherine Stone, $250.; Nancy Woodward, $10., Jane Ryler, $50; Dicey Odenal, $50.
    To my son, John, $250.
    To my grand daughter; Eliza Ryler, $10.
    To my grand children, Hanna Plemmons, John Plemmons, and Nancy Plemmons, $50. each.
Continued--

Will of Hugh Gilbreath, Cont.

    To my children, James C., Durinday M. Davis, Hugh T., Nancy E. Carpenter, and Mary Ann Carpenter, $150. each.

    To my children Louisa Gilbreath, William M., Newlan A., Alfred W., Thomas J., Lucinda F. Gilbreath, and Manerva Ellen Gilbreath, $400. each.

    To my wife, Flora...

    George Crawford, Exe.

Written: 19 June 1850
Witnesses: David Jones, William Hunt, and Robert Denney
Recorded: 10 Feb. 1852

Dorenda Gilbreath to Jeremiah Davis 4 Sept. 1839 102
Eliza Gilbreath to Joab Dyler 17 Jan. 1829 103
Emily Galbreath to Henry Carpenter 27 Aug. 1846 217
Hugh Gilbreath to Geruna Smiley 30 April 1833 20
Hugh F. Galbreath to Catherine Carpenter 1 Oct. 1846 223
James Gilbreath to Frances Burns 5 March 1846 203
Jane Gilbreath to Thomas Dyler 9 April 1829 107
John Gilbreath to Martha Clayton 18 Feb. 1840 106
Peggy Galbreath to Andrew B. Harley 25 June 1820 15
Ronea Gilbreath to James G. Plemmons 10 March 1836 52

Page 138 A2
Will of Joshua Gale

    To my wife, Mahala...

    To the heirs of my brother, Jesse Gale, deceased, $4000.

    To my sister, Abagail Wallace, $4000.

    To my sister, Dolly Merryman, $4000.

    To my sister, Julia Bagby, $2000.

    To the heirs of my brother, William Gale, deceased, as follows: To his youngest daughter, Chloe Gale, $5.00. To Emily Carol and her sister, Mahala $1000., said children of the former William Gale, deceased.

    to my wife's sister, Hannah McGaffey of Texas, $4000.

    To my nephew, George S. Gale, $2000.

    $2000. in trust to my brother, Richard Gale, to be paid to the children of John Ray, deceased.

    To my brother, Thomas Gale, $1000.

    Mahala Gale, my wife and Richard Gale, my brother, Exe. In case of the death of Richard Gale, I appoint my nephew, Riley Gale, Exe.

Written: 10 May 1854
Witnesses: H. F. Mills and O. F. Potter
Recorded: 27 November 1854

Page 337 A2
Will of Robert W. Gale

    To my wife, Dorothy...

    To my children: William Temper Gale, Julia Lacy, wife of A. I. Lacy; Susan Campbell, wife of James M. Campbell; Josiah Gale; Robert Gale; and Margaret Gale

Written: 25 Oct. 1862 Recorded: 27 July 1863
Witnesses: Just. Williams and Henry C. Lewis

Emilee Gale to Robert Carroll 7 April 1845 234

Charles M. Gallagh to Sally Peters 16 June 1840 111

Anthony Ganter to Otela Schmultz, at the residence of Anthony
    Fox 4 Oct. 1842 145

James A. Gardner to Cynthia Jane Shirley 19 Nov. 1835 40
James A. Gardner to Mrs. Harthay Ann Smith 10 Nov. 1847 243

Elizabeth J. Garrett to Samuel B. Swearingen 28 Nov. 1844 183

Nathaniel Garten to Clementina Steel 15 Feb. 1831 131

Enoch H. Gatwood to Elenora Rose 28 Nov. 1850 35

Elizabeth Gatys to John Hunter 23 Dec. 1841 141

Gabriel W. Gaugh to Lucinda A. White 20 Jan. 1839 92

Page 181 A2
Will of Alexander Gay
    To my two grand children, Alexander Dwight Root and Lucy
Ann Root...
        To my sons: Joshua Gay and Thomas C. ...
        To my grand daughter, Lucinda Vandiver...
        To my grand daughter, Mary Eliza Wall...
        To my youngest son, George A. Gay...
Written: 3 December 1852
Witnesses: Saban Phillips, John Carroll, and Joshua O. Wilson
Recorded: 14 March 1856
Joshua Gay to Eliza Vandaver 24 Jan. 1850 27

Adaline George to Isaac Barton McFarland 8 July 1845 191
Alvin George to Jane Scott 11 April 1839 94
Alvirah George to Reuben McFarland 13 Sept. 1827 84
Elenor George to Thomas Allen 30 June 1831 135
Mr. H. George to Nancy A. Burnitt 8 Aug. 1850 33
Houston George to Ann Burris 7 Sept. 1835 45
Margaret George to James Martain 23 March 1830 116
Mary George to John Jones 7 April 1840 112
Nancy George to John A. Seltyne 19 Feb. 1846 256
Reubin George to Sally McFarland 1 April 1821 27
Thomas George to Emaline K. O'Dell 16 Dec. 1847 249
William J. George to Mary Ann Douglas 7 Sept. 1848 1

Page 388 A2
Will of Louis Gesel
    To my wife, Mary Anna...
    To my sister, Catharine Kemp; to John Kemp, in Iowa;
to Vincens Bleir...
Continued--

Will of Louis Gesel, Continued
    I also want my deceased wife, Catherine Gesel be dug up and buried on the new grave yard next to my grave, each of us furnished with a tomb stone.
Written: 15 July 1867
Witnesses: Jacob Cramer and Blasius Efinger
Recorded: 6 August 1867

Margaret Gess to Trustman Fisher   19 March 1829   105

Margaret Geyer, daughter of John Geyer, to Gabriel Cotton, 14 Oct. 1835   34

Thomas Gibs to Elizabeth Gibson   11 Nov. 1831   127

Elizabeth Gibson to Thomas Gibbs   11 Nov. 1831   127
John H. Gibson, Boon Co., Mo. to Susan B. Houx   14 Oct. 1843   163
Nathaniel Gibson to Frances Dogle   25 Sept. 1842   174
John H. Gibson to Martha Hill   11 May 1847   232
Rebecca Gibson to Thomas Dewitt   9 March 1845   185
Rhoda Ann Gibson to William Burgan   9 Sept. 1827   81
William U. Gibson to Lonurbille Branium   1 Oct. 1849   20
William Gibson to Mrs. Emily Masqrurier   4 June 1845   189

Benjamin Gilbert to Mary Neal   19 Dec. 1838   91
Benjamin Gilbert to Malinda Neal   27 June 1843   160
Mary Ann Gilbert to Andrew M. Carpenter   26 Oct. 1847   248

William Giles to Nancy Rymel   14 Oct. 1840   115

Delia Gillespie to Alfred Chadwick   24 June 1845   190

Mary Gillum to Jesse Moon   2 March 1828   90
Smith Gillum to Julia Ann Rice   18 Aug. 1842   147

John Gilmore to Frances Burch   22 July 1828   91
James Scott Gilmore to Nancy Burch   28 April 1826   62
Samuel Gilmore to Matilda Shirley   16 May 1830   120

Howard Gist to Elizabeth White   10 Oct. 1839   101
Thomas Gist to Peggy Robison   4 April 1830   121

Page 62 A
Will of Alexander Givens
    To my wife, Mary...
    To my son, Robert...
    To my daughter, Margaret Givens...
    To my grandsons: Rawleigh and Isiah, sons of Isiah Givens...
    To my children: John, Samuel, Alexander, William, Jane Tucker, and Elizabeth Carr...
Written: 16 August 1832   Recorded: 16 April 1833

Page 351 A2
Will of John S. Givens
    To my wife, Margaret S. ...
    To my daughters: Ann, Cynthia, Rhoda, and Margaret, and Mary Susan...
    To my sons: William M. and Nathaniel D.
    William D. Adams, Exe.
Written: 16 May 1865
Witnesses: E. C. Evans and Just. Williams
Recorded: 16 June 1865

Page 234 A2
Will of Robert Givens
    To my wife, Susan...
    To my sons: Newton, Wesley, Robert, Alexander, and James M. ...
    To my daughters: Susan, and Margaret Calvert...
    Alexander and James M. Givens, Exe.
Written: 7 November 1858
Witnesses: Jesse Ogden and Justinian Williams
Recorded: 28 February 1859

David Givens to Louisa Skidmore 4 Feb. 1847 228
Mary Givens to Joseph Westbrook 12 Aug. 1841 133

M. Givney to Mary Stocknill 4 Jan. 1831 140

James H. Glasgow to Harriet Amanda Cramer 12 Oct. 1836 64

Samuel Glass to Lucinda McFarland 26 Nov. 1827 70

John L. Glazebrook to Mary Jane Holand 23 Oct. 1828 101

Charles Glazier to Frances A. Parsons 25 March 1841 156
John Glazier to Linda Forsythe 9 April 1839 94

Virginia W. Gooch to Charles T. Lewis 23 Oct. 1845 194

Sarah Good to Jesse Driskill 26 Nov. 1847 250

Lucinda Margaret Goodard to Joshua L. Boyd 27 April 1844 174

Lucy Jane Goode to Robert Carpenter 21 Sept. 1847 250

A. C. Goodin to Eliza D. Miller 29 Dec. 1840 123
Joseph H. Gooden to Jaine Allen 14 March 1820 12

Drury Goodman to Susan Dreshel 29 Aug. 1844 178
Frances Goodman to William C. Shields 17 Sept. 1848 266
Rebecca Goodman to William J. Gabriel 19 Sept. 1850 39
Sarah Goodman to Samuel Drinkwater 8 Dec. 1844 181
William Goodman to Sarah Conner 21 March 1830 121
William Goodman to Dolly Robertson 19 Feb. 1826 56

Harriet Goodno to Isaac Thomas 9 April 1829 102
Martha Goodno to William Gartner, Jr. 1 March 1848 253
Vina Goodno to John Boyd 21 Aug. 1833 12

Margaret Gott to Finis E. Kirkpatrick 20 Feb. 1827 77

Mary Ann Graham to W. B. Murdock 13 Nov. 1844 185
Mary Susan Graham to Thomas Baskerville 11 Jan. 1849 257
Noah Graham to Sally Meredith 11 March 1830 117

John Graves to Deany Rees 4 Feb. 1834 15
William Graves to Ellen Thompson 16 Feb. 1843 152

Page 434 A2
Will of Mary Gray
    To my friends, Jesse and Elizabeth E. Homan
    C. N. Smith, Exe.
Written: 6 May 1870
Witnesses: B. K. Thompson and R. G. Stockton
Recorded: 6 June 1870
Francis M. Gray, Moniteau CO., Mo. to C. Hammons 15 July 1847 237
John T. Gray to Louticia McClanahan 27 Dec. 1846 225

Jane Green to Micajah Murphy 20 June 1841 129
John Green to Nancy Doyd 6 May 1819 3
Lindsey Green to Lucinda Claypole 23 Dec. 1843 174
Lucinda Green to Joseph Roberson 11 June 1846 214
Polly Green to William Sphonhimore 22 April 1824 47

Page 322 A2
Will of James Greenhalgh
    To my wife, Nancy A. ...
    To my daughter, Eliza Jane Crawford...
    To my sons: Alexander H. and John...
    Alexander H. Greenhalgh, Exe.
Written: 30 June 1855
Witnesses: P. R. Hayden and E. R. Hayden
Recorded: 30 December 1862

Eliza J. Greenhalt to John Crawford 28 April 1849 11

Jesse Greer to Nancy Durch 5 July 1832 162
Thomas Greer to Nancy Shields 23 Jan. 1834 15

Page 331 A2
Will of Elizabeth Gregory, County of Woolford, State of Kentucky
    To my sisters: Mary Gregory and Emilene Loyd...
    To my niece, Sally Ann Nicholson...
    To John Juned and Amanda Nicholson...
Written: 30 Sept. 1853   Recorded: 10 June 1863
James E. Ball and Swift Darnall, Woolford Co., Ky.

John A. L. Grice to Rebecca McClanahan   12 March 1837   66

Page 116 A2
Will of David Griffith
    To my nephews: Griffith Williams, David Williams, Walter Williams, Jonathan Williams, and my niece Hannah Davis...
    To my friends: Mrs. Jesse Main, Dr. Main, William Paine, James E. Paine, Daniel Laurie, and Rev. William Terry...
    William H. Trigg, Exe.
Written: 6 January 1854
Witnesses: F. M. Caldwell and John Hopewood
Recorded: 16 January 1854

Lavina Grove to Burton Lawless   10 March 1847   235

Albay Guyn to Elisha Spivey   26 Aug. 1822   37
Joseph Gwinn to Luvancy Mullins   29 March 1840   113

Elizabeth Guyer to Joseph A. Potter   1 Sept. 1825   55
Elizabeth Guyer to George Douthet   26 March 1846   215

Page 320 A2
Will of William Haas, a native of the Village of Hobitzheim near Damstadt in Germany
    To my wife, Maria...
    My son, William O. is a brutal son and a headless spendthrift, I exclude him hereby from all inheritance and partition of my personal and real estate.
    His son, William, my grandson, a child about four months of age we have in our family to nurse and which we will try to raise and educate to a fit and useful member of the human family.
    My daughter, Fredericka married against my most paternal remonstrances, a brutal and a worthless subject and giving thereby a most pernicious example to demoralize perhaps some of my other children. This fellow, in my absence from home, insulted my wife, my daughter, Rosine and Wilhemmina with the most brutal, vulgar, and disrespectful language, closing with "I take my revenge on you". Never have we given this branded individual any cause for such insulting behavior and I pray my children to beware of him forever--he is an unclean spirit I exclude her also as above from all inheritance and partition of my personal and real estate property.
    To my grand daughter, Marie Roeschel, or to her father, Ernest Roeschel...
    To my daughters: Rosine E. Roeschel and Elice, wife of H. Helfrich and Wilhelmine and to the children of my daughter, fredericka...
    To my sons, Archibald and Andrew...
Written: 23 April 1862   Recorded: 12 Nov. 1862
Witnesses: Elisha Stanley, Chr. Keill, and William Harley

Andrew Haas to Emilee Sombart 1 Feb. 1849 6
John Haas to Elizabeth B. Crawford 26 Nov. 1840 118

William Haggans to Elizabeth Speery 28 Sept. 1839 100

George Hain to Sophia Aull 27 April 1845 197

Polly Haines to William King 6 Sept. 1832 155

William C. Halford, Morgan Co., Mo. to Martha M. Martin
    31 March 1839 97

Ann Hall to John Chaney 16 Jan. 1833 162
Giddida Hall to Reuben Smith 4 Jan. 1829 97
Martha Elizabeth Hall to Francis Manion Lamm 26 April 1849 13
Meekey Hall to Bradley Campbell 21 July 1829 108
Sally W. Hall to Robert L. Todd 31 Oct. 1850 33
William Hall to Sally Estes 9 Dec. 1819 33

Samuel Hammond to Catherine Story 19 March 1822 30

Page 5 A
Will of George Hammons
    To my wife, Sarah...
    To my heirs, Nancy Vaunn...
    To my sons: Samuel and Harbert...
    Sarah, my wife and John Hammons, Exe.
Witnesses: Elijah Randolph and Richard Stanford
Recorded: 17 September 1821
Harland Hammons to Elizabeth Plemons 11 Nov. 1829 98
John Hammons to Sally Shockley 5 July 1829 106
C. Hammens to Francis M. Gray 15 July 1847 237
Catherine Hammons to Nevil Johnson 17 July 1833 5
Nancy Hammons to Caleb W. Houx 15 Jan. 1848 250
Sarah Hammons to Thomas Vaughn 14 Oct. 1829 110

Abel G. Hampton to Sarah Rennison 27 Jan. 1832 143
Albert Hampton to Ann Moon 23 Feb. 1840 109
James Hampton to Mary or Polly Strain 17 Aug. 1828 93
James Hampton to Cintha Williamson 2 April 1846 206
Willaim D. Hampton to Frances Mullins 9 Nov. 1823 44

Willie P. Hamrick to Jane Potter 8 Feb. 1844 168

Stephen K. Hancock to Joy Roberts Given 3 Feb. 1830 112

James Handlin to Mrs. Nancy Adams 28 May 1840 110

Elizabeth Haney to Absalom Stephens 28 Feb. 1833 166

Isiah Hannah to Mary Rector 22 Nov. 1827 87
John Hannah to Almira A. Hutchinson 2 Dec. 1841 136

Amanda Hannon to Thomas I. Stark 3 March 1847 236

Eli W. Hardcastle to Mary B. Page 1 Aug. 1844 176

Mark G. Hardin to Sarah Barnahart 4 July 1847 232

Robert Harlan to Columbia L. Bidstross 18 March 1847 229

Andrew B. Harley to Peggy Galbreath 25 June 1820 15

Martha J. Harlow to Andrew Couts 28 April 1847 231

Caroline Harmon to Wilson Cook 31 Oct. 1844 179
Henry Harmon to Mary Ann Cook 27 Oct. 1842 150
Jacob Harmon to Julia Foster 12 Jan. 1834 16
Jroen Harmon to Calvin Cook 13 Nov. 1849 26
Peter Harmon to Maria Smith Rec. 7 April 1828 90
Samuel Harmon to Polly Bennett 21 Aug. 1838 86

Abigail Harper to William Burnard 4 Aug. 1825 52
Elizabeth Harper to Rolley Hughes 20 Aug. 1826
Harvey Harper to Priscilla Peters   March 1827 77
Martha W. Harper to George W. Bruffee 17 March 1842 141

William Harriman to Caroline E. Mayo 28 March 1848 260

Alfred Harris to Elizabeth A. Colhoun 6 Dec. 1847 253
Anderson W. Harris to Gaberelah Nelson 25 Jan. 1844 168
Eliza Ann Harris to John Martin 4 Sept. 1850 36
Elizabeth Harris to Samuel Reed 26 April 1840 109
Mrs. Emily Harris to Richard Williams 26 June 1841 130
George W. Harris to Mary F. Tyler 9 Nov. 1841 136
Hannah Harris to John M. Price 14 May 1848 259
Henry Harris to Sarah Burris 1 Aug. 1847 239
James Harris to Martha Hoozer 4 Sept. 1839 103
John Harris to Martha Elizabeth Jones 12 Sept. 1850 34
Lucinda Harris to John McDuffee 29 June 1845 191
Lucy Harris to Edward Snodgrass 21 Feb. 1836 50
Margaret Harris to Benoni Johnson 1 June 1846 212
Martha Harris to Jabez Jones 20 Oct. 1831 141
Martha Harris to Shelton Huster 24 Jan. 1833 156
Mary Harris to Christopher Combs 10 March 1847 233
Nancy Lovina Harris to Henry McCurly Rec. 26 July 1826 63
Nancy Harris to Edward Snodgrass 19 Dec. 1830 128
Mrs. Nancy Harris to Thomas A. Johnson 15 Jan. 1850 28
Reuben B. Harris to Ann Brown 22 June 1820 6
Robert Harris to Nancy Berger 19 Sept. 1838 94

Sampson Harris to Midist Westbrook 24 Dec. 1829 116
Samuel Harris to Nancy Cole 22 Sept. 1839 101
Thurman Harris to Rebecca Wells 12 Feb. 1849 10
William Harris to Nancy Davis 31 Dec. 1834 27
William Harris to Adelia H. Turley 4 May 1843 158

Page 405 A2
Will of R. C. Harrison
    To my wife, Theodocia...
    To my only child, Sallie Ann Castleman...
    Judge Benjamin Tompkins, Exe.
Written: 8 October 1857
Witnesses: J. W. Draffen and Washington Adams
Recorded: 30 May 1868
Page 410 A2
Will of Theodosia Harrison
    To my daughter, Sally Ann Castleman...
Written: 22 June 1868
Witnesses: John L. O'Bryan and R. F. O'Bryan
Recorded: 3 November 1868
James Harrison to Nicy Hatfield 17 Sept. 1832 157
Sidney Ann Harrison to Willis H. Tackett 23 Dec. 1847 249
Page 62 A2
Will of George C. Hartt
    To my wife, Maria
    To my daughters: Lucretia Hartt, now Lucretia C. Peyton;
and Sarah Louise Parks, wife of Thomas Parks...
    To my sons: Albert G. and George Culver...
    To my grandchildren: Amanda and Lavina Hartt...
    George C. Hart and Thomas Parks and Wm. H. Trigg, Exe.
Written: 28 Sept. 1852
Witnesses: C. Terry, A. Kuchelon, and James Quarles
Recorded: 10 October 1852
Barnett Hart to Ann E. Kilger 27 July 1842 146
Lucretia Hart to Dr. H. Pace 11 July 1833 4
Sally Hart to Thomas Parks Given 2 July 1830 121

Greenville J. Harvey to Margaret Wisdom 13 Jan. 1850 30
Henry Harvey to Salinda Turley 4 Dec. 1832 166
Henry B. Harvey to Martha E. Caton 8 Nov. 1840 116
James Harvey to Mary Allison 11 Jan. 1835 24
Noah Harvey to Martha Jane Longan 28 May 1846 220
Reuben V. Harvey to Mrs. Barbary Ann Allen 7 May 1836 51
Sarah Ann Harvey to William Durrus 20 Dec. 1843 169
Susan Harvey to Andrew Whitlow 3 Feb. 1842 139

Page 3 A
Will of John Hassell, Senior, Hickman Co., Tennessee
    To my wife, Joanna Hassell...
Continued--

Will of John Hassell, Continued
    To my sons: Zebulon, Joshua, and John, Jr. ...
    To my daughters: Elizabeth Hassell, Joanna Warrington, and Mary Collins...
Written: 12 October 1812
Witnesses: Robert Mack, P. R. Booker, and Mathew Maye
Recorded: 6 March 1820

Edward Hazel to Sarah Yarnas 30 Jan. 1831 127

John Hastedt to Mary Dorman 11 March 1850 28

Betsey Ann Hasty to Joseph Boyd 6 Feb. 1836 47
John Hastey to Elizabeth Westbrook 18 Dec. 1838 91

Alexander Hatfield to Elizabeth Smith 20 Aug. 1826 76
Nicy Hatfield to James Harrison 17 Sept. 1832 157
William Hatfield to Polly Bass 14 Oct. 1832 160

Moses A. Hawkins to Cynthia Calvert 28 Aug. 1844 178

Page 172 A2
Will of Peyton R. Hayden
    To my wife, Maria...
    To my two youngest sons: Peyton R., Junior and Boyle...
    To the children of my deceased daughter, Amanda Bacon...
    To my sons: Alexander C., R. Ermit, Henry C., and Augustus W. ...
    To my son in law, husband of my deceased daughter, Amanda, Robert B. Bacon...
    To my son, Rush...
    My friend, Isaac Lionberger and my wife, Exs.
Written: 4 August 1855
Witnesses: Washington Adams, Dr. Samuel I. Tutt, and George H. C. Melody
Recorded: 26 January 1856

Amanda Hayden to Robert B. Bacon 1 Sept. 1840 114

Howard Hayes to Isabel Morris 29 Oct. 1829 110

Andrew I. Haytor, Howard Co., Mo. to Mary Ann Fulkerson
    27 July 1847 240

Benjamin Hearn to Mary Burns 22 May 1845 189

Eliza Heath to William S. Sherman _____ 1836 52
Moses Heath to Delila Moon ? Jan. 1826 56

Elisha B. Hedley to Wilmouth S. Jones 15 Sept. 1842 149

Jonathan Hedrick to Elizabeth Travilion 23 Dec. 1824 51
Sarah Hedrick to William W. B. Steel 18 Feb. 1836 49

James Hefferfinger to Mildred Dooly 13 Feb. 1832 145

J. D. Heironymous, Pettis Co., Mo. to Miss M. A. L. Boyles
    22 Oct. 1846 220

Page 386 A2
Will of Gottleib Hollenkoetter
    To my daughter: Anna Minna...
    To my sons: Friedrick, Johann Heinrick, and Johann Hermann...
Written: 19 February 1867
Witnesses: C. August Mieller and F. Adam Stegner
Recorded: 18 March 1867

George W. Helmreick to Sabela Weaver 12 Oct. 1843 163

Margaret Henchlew to Jesse Reed 13 Aug. 1833 7

Elizabeth Henderson to Peter T. Bowls 26 Sept. 1822 30
Isaac Henderson to Mary Woolery 6 July 1839 98
John T. A. Henderson to Malinda Rubey 25 March 1830 114

James Henry to Nancy Williams 23 Feb. 1840 109
John Marquis Henry, Pettis Co., Mo. to Eliza Oglesby
    26 Oct. 1842 150
Mary T. Henry to James McIntosh 28 Aug. 1846 219

William Henshaw to Sarah A. Caldwell 24 Aug. 1843 41

Charles Herndon to Rebecca Craner 12 Nov. 1835 41
Julia Ann Herndon to George Fenwick 31 Aug. 1837 75
Nancy Herndon to James A. Davenport 27 April 1840 112

William L. Heston, Cole Co., Mo. to Martha A. Martin
    27 Dec. 1838 93

Eliza Ann Hickman to James Orured 7 Jan. 1847 226
Samuel Hickman to Susan Shoemaker 1 June 1848 259
Sarah Ann Hickman to George H. Stephens 9 March 1848 254

Franklin W. Hickocks to Mary E. Simmons 28 Oct. 1841 138
Harriet Elizabeth Hickok to Henry Mark Myers 2 Nov. 1842 148
Martha Hickox to T. Abbott 15 Nov. 1847 256

Frances Nix to Elijah McFarland 8 March 1821 22
James Hicks to Harriet Houx 15 Nov. 1842 148
Sary Hix to Alexander McFarland 10 Aug. 1821 22

Alegilina M. Higguson to Samuel F. Higgerson 29 Oct. 1867 262
Samuel F. Higgerson to Alegilina M. Higguson 29 Oct. 1867 262

John Higginbotham to Louisa Springfield 21 Jan. 1841 121

Thomas Hightwoer to Mary Larrimore 4 Sept. 1845 202

Page 209 A2
Will of John A. Hill
    To my wife, Elizabeth...
    To my heirs: James Williams and Cammelia, his wife and Thomas Gay and Mary Ann his wife, John A. Hill, William M. Hill, and Washington Hill...
    To my sons: Thomas C. Hill, Andrew D. Hill, Jonathan Hill, and Gilbert Hill...
    Thomas C. Hill, Exo.
Written: 30 Sept. 1857
Witnesses: David Holeman and William Harrell
Recorded: 27 January 1858

Brackstrom Hill to Elizabeth McFarland 2 May 1849 15
Camilla Hill to James Williams 31 Aug. 1848 264
Charity Hill to James Vaughn 4 Nov. 1837 77
David S. Hill to Mary Meredith 27 Feb. 1840 107
Elizabeth Hill to Jesse Newman 25 Feb. 1846 202
James Hill to Polly McFarland 1 Oct. 1821 27
James M. Hill to Angeline Cole 5 Jan. 1848 250
John Hill to Luckey Jones 15 Oct. 1820 33
John Hill to Sophia Petty 22 Sept. 1844 174
Joseph Hill to Jane Martin 22 Feb. 1839 97
Margaret Hill to Jacob Cline 12 Sept. 1842 147
Martha Hill to John H. Gibson 11 May 1847 232
Martha Ann Hill to James Allen 13 March 1843 159
Milly Hill to John Vaughan 3 Jan. 1843 151
Winniford Hill to William Williams 19 Dec. 1850 38
Thomas N. Hill to Mary Briscoe 8 March 1848 254

Polly Hinley to William Swearingen 2 Sept. 1819 7

Anna Hines to John J. Gravesn 24 June 1849

William Hoberecht to Kareline Loekner 10 May 1850 30

Page 51 A2
Will of Samuel D. Hocker
    To my wife, Elizabeth ...
Written: 1 Nov. 1849
Witnesses: M. Bowers and William H. Trigg
Recorded: 23 April 1851

Martha Hoffman to Henry Nauman 1 Nov. 1849 24

Page 351 A2
Will of David Hogan
Continued---

Will of David Hogan
    To my wife, Elizabeth P. ...
    To my daughters: Sarah and Elizabeth G. Wilson...
    To my sons: John D., David, William, James, George W., Moses D., Wilkerson, and Robert H. ...
    To Hortensia G. Hogan wife of John D. ...
    To Cornelius V. Hogan, wife of William H.
    Anthony Smith Walker, Charles S. Bohannan, Wilkerson Hogan and William Hogan, Exe.
Written: 8 February 1867
Caralee Hogan to William D. Cline 14 Oct. 1847 249
Moses D. Hogan, Pettis Co., Mo. to Mary N. Wright 12 June 1849 18

Elizabeth Hog to Leonard Thompson 15 March 1832 147
Jane Hogg to Patrick Lemey 20 Dec. 1819 7
Hezekiah Hogue to Malissa Howard 25 Sept. 1832 157

Elizabeth Holt to Elijah Job 14 April 1840 113
George Holt to Lucinda Stevens 24 Nov. 1833 10
Levy Holt to Manerva Williams 10 Jan. 1839 95

Hiram M. Homan to Eliza J. Cline 13 Jan. 1842 140

James H. Hongerford to Margaret Ohowall 1 May 1843 157

Jane Hood to John Shaw 14 Feb. 1832 144

Ann Hoof to William Shirley 17 Dec. 1829 133

Elijah Hook to Hannah Shoemaker 20 Aug. 1839 99
E. Hook to Mary Shoemaker 15 July 1849 15
James Hook to Mary Proctor 12 Dec. 1833 13

Elizabeth Hooser to Abraham Baxter 25 Dec. 1843 169
Jane Hoozer to Thomas Stephens 11 Aug. 1839 103
Melinda Hoozer to William A. B. Smith 24 Sept. 1835 46
Martha Hoozer to James Harris 4 Sept. 1839 103
Sally Hooser to Joseph Snodgrass 1 Dec. 1825 62

Andrew Hornback to Sally Wood 12 Jan. 1837 61
Andrew Hornback to Elizabeth Wood 30 July 1846 222
James Hornbeck to Emaline Scritchfield 27 July 1831 136
Michael Hornbeck to Ann Elizabeth Westrook 18 June 1846 136
Rebecca A. Hornbeck to James M. Freeman, Boen Co., Mo., 31 March 1846 207
Samuel Hornback to Eleanor Bass 21 Nov. 1833 12
Robert Hornbeck to Angeline Anderson 212

Mary Catherine Hoss to Lewis Katz 3 March 1843 155
Katherine House to John Thornton 7 Dec. 1820 17
Priscilla House to Hiram Howard 16 July 1848 262

Page 33 A2
Will of Emanuel Hornsberger of the County of Rockingham,
   State of Virginia
   To my brother, John Hornsberger...
   To my sister, Pushnell...
   To William I. Hornsberger, all real estate in the state
of Missouri.
   To my niece, Mary Conrad, of Cooper County, Mo.
   William I. Hornsberger, Exe.
Written: 25 July 1844
Witnesses: Jacob E. Hornsberger and Adam Hornsberger
Recorded: 23 April 1850

Page 247 A2
Will of Placebo Houston, State of North Carolina, Iredell Co.
   To my daughter, Lucy H. Mutz...
   To the five sons of my deceased daughter, Sarah Louise...
   To John Augustus Houston, son of my deceased son, Augustus
C. Houston...
   Thomas F. Houston and John H. Dalton, Exe.
Written: 2 March 1852
Witnesses: A. S. Young, J. M. Love, and John M. Young
Codicil to the foregoing will
   To my daughter, Lucy M. Mutz...; to my daughter, Louisa
Reinhardt's children...; to my daughter, Mary Cecelia Dalton...
   To my son, Thomas F. ...
Written: 3 March 1852
Witnesses: A. S. Young, J. M. Love, and John M. Young
Recorded: 6 June 1859

Page 377 1A
Will of Frederick Houx
   To my wife, Margaret...
   To my son, Jacob, of Livingston Co., Mo. ...
   To my grandson, Theodore Gibson...
   To the children of my deceased daughter, Emily Edgar viz
Susan Spratten, Eliza Cowles, Margaret Dennis, Thomas Dennis,
Sarah Dennis, Wayne Ann Dennis, Nancy Edgar, and Emily Edgar...
   To the children of my deceased daughter, Ragena Waller...
   To my children: Elizabeth McFarland, wife of John S.
McFarland. J. E. Houx, Jacob Houx, Isaah Houx, Mahala Wallace,
wife of B. M. Wallace, Jane Ferrell, John W. Houx, and Malinda
Snider...
   To my daughter, Harriet Hix, wife of James Hix...
   Harvey Bruce and John M. McCutchen, Exe.
Written: 16 May 1859
Witnesses: Joe S. Stephens and George G. Vest
Recorded: 1 December 1866

Page 111 A2
Will of Jacob Houx
    To my wife, Margaret...
    To my son, Thomas C. ... and my sons, Phillip and Thomas...
    R. Smith, Exe.
Written: 20 October 1853
Witnesses: J. Kille McCabe, John Miller, and S. A. Summers
Recorded: 24 November 1853

Mrs. A. B. Houx to G. B. Miller 17 Dec. 1849 27
Caleb W. Houx to Nancy Hammon 18 Jan. 1848 250
Catharine Houx to William Cramer 1 Feb. 1827 75
Dolly Houx to Jesse Josserton 23 June 1834 75
Edward Houx to Margaret Riggs 3 Feb. 1847 228
Eliza Houx to William Martin 8 Feb. 1849 9
Emily Houx to Anthony W. Dennis 3 Dec. 1836 44
Frederick E. Houx to Elender B. Crawford 26 March 1835 31
George Houx, Lafayette Co., Mo. to Eliza Sloss 16 Jan. 1834 14
Harriett Houx to James Hicks 15 Nov. 1842 148
Isiah F. Houx to Frances A. Dickerson 6 Jan. 1846 198
Jacob Houx to Peggy Massy 27 May 1827 78
Louisa Houx to Peter W. Collins 14 Sept. 1841 136
Mahala Houx to Harvey B. Wallace 16 Nov. 1840 117
Margaret Houx to Valentine Bell 2 Dec. 1830 136
Mary Jane Houx to Thomas H. Miller 8 Jan. 1832 142
Phillip Houx to Margaret Morrow 14 Sept. 1824 48
Polly Houx to David Ross 1 Nov. 1832 157
Susan Houx to John Lewis 17 March 1831 130
Susan D. Houx to John H. Gibson 14 Oct. 1843 163

Jacob B. Hovey, Independence, Mo. to Amanda Dunn 20 Oct. 1850 35

Arrey B. Howard to Annjalenah Ray 6 Jan. 1831 129
Charles Howard to Elizabeth Mulkey 26 April 1820 14
Elizabeth Ann Howard to Stephen Howard 9 May 1849 12
Edmond Howard to Polly Robinson 10 June 1824 46
Hiram Howard to Lucinday McKenney 3 June 1830 119
Honor Howard to Henry Cowin 8 July 1819 3
Jane Howard to William Reynolds 10 Aug. 1848 263
Kesiah Howard to Charity Allee 1 April 1825 53
Leroy Howard to Penelopy Wood 27 Dec. 1833 16
Lusetta Howard to Richard Tolbert 29 Sept. 1846 223
Malissa Howard to Hezekiah Hogue 25 Sept. 1832 157
Martha Jane Howard to George W. Son 8 Aug. 1850 34
Mildred Howard to Isaac Ewing 29 July 1841 132
Mrs. Penelope Howard to Abram Byler 5 March 1844 168
Stephen Howard, Moniteau Co., Mo. to Elizabeth Ann Howard
    9 May 1849 12

Eliza C. Howe to George T. Rucker 20 Oct. 1849 20
Continued---

Harvy Howe to Rachel Steel   4 Dec. 1830   126
Martha Ann Howe to James K. Waysmen   13 April 1843   154
Mary Ann How to Warner Compton   13 April 1848   255
M. A. How to Joseph C. Roy   17 April 1845   188
Oliver R. Howe to Martha M. Seat at the residence of John B.
    Seat   21 Dec. 1840   5
William Howe to Charlotte Jones   6 Dec. 1820   18

Elizabeth L. Howerton to Anthony Coloby   21 April 1841   131
Jefferson Howerton to Jane Casteel   24 April 1838   79
Jeremiah Howerton to Elizabeth Casteel   24 April 1838   79

Edward H. Hubbard, Bates Co., Mo. to Emily Scott   26 Aug. 1847   244
James Hubbard to Betsy Rees   Given   17 Nov. 1831   137
Mary D. Hurbard to John L. Tucker   2 Jan. 1845   182

Absalom Huff to Newramy Mullin   20 Jan. 1820   10
Alfred Huff to Sarah Carpenter   15 May 1845   190
Calvin Huff to Safurny Witt   6 April 1847   235
Drocas Huff to William Snodgrass   29 Dec. 1836   58
Peter Huff to Frances Martin   19 Sept. 1824   48
Rebecca Huff to John Snodgrass   6 April 1845   187

Miss F. A. Huffman to Charles M. Brucking   20 May 1845   190

Rudolph A. Hufford, Barry Co. to Harriett Wattimiman
    1 Nov. 1840   116

Page 49 B
Will of Samuel Hughes
    To my daughters: Nancy Hughes and Mercy Hughes...
    To John Watson Hughes, son of Mercy Hughes...
    To my son, Rice...
    Harmon H. Bailey and John G. Miller, Exo.
Written: 1 March 1841
Witnesses: T. G. Thompson, Robert Stuart, and Rebecca Briles
Recorded: 25 November 1842
Daniel G. Hughes to Elizabeth Woods   13 Jan. 1825   89
James Hughes to Polly A. McFarland   16 Sept. 1848   4
Ellender Hughes to William Ellis   14 Sept. 1829   107
George K. Hughes to Rhody Boyle   30 Nov. 1838   69
Jane Hughes to John Rew   9 Jan. 1831   128
Kesiah Hughes to Elias Calvert   25 April 1839   96
Mary Hughes to Charles D. Mitchell   18 Oct. 1843   162
Roland Hughes to Josephine Bradley   27 Nov. 1841   137
Rolley Hughes to Elizabeth Harper   20 Aug. 1826   76
Sarah Hughes to Enoch Wethers   15 March 1838   82
Susannah Hughes to John Carrall   3 August 1837   70

Martha Huklin to William Ish   7 June 1819   14

Mariot Humphreys to Charles Shoemaker 1 Feb. 1827 73

Eliza Ann Hungerford to Rufus Shoemaker 28 Aug. 1823 43

Elizabeth A. Hunt to William M. Taylor 12 Jan. 1845 182
Gilpha Hunt to William Apperson 8 Nov. 1849 21
James Hunt to Margaret Hunt 10 Nov. 1825 57
Jonathan Hunt to Martha Lee 12 Dec. 1844 181
Margaret Hunt to James Hunt 10 Nov. 1825 57
Martha E. Hunt to Robert C. Combs 25 Feb. 1834 172
Mary Hunt to Lewis D. Reavis 23 June 1836 52
Meranda A. Hunt to John H. Taylor 10 Aug. 1845 193
Susan Hunt to James Davis 21 Oct. 1827 86

Elizabeth Hunter to James Lamb 25 Feb. 1841 126
John Hunter to Elizabeth Gatys 23 Dec. 1841 142
Marthy Hunter to James Snodgrass 15 Jan. 1846 199

Nathaniel Hurdeson to Sarah Cahanbergar 2 March 1843 253

Nancy Hurley to Joseph Castello 24 May 1826 64

Page 334 A2
Will of Clayton Hurt
    To my wife, Mary Ann...
    To my three daughters: Nancy A. Bales, Rebecca Brown, and Julia A. Shannon...
    To my sons: William Benijah and Clayton...
    James H. Baker, Exe.
Written: 21 January 1862   Recorded: 3 July 1863
Witnesses: D. C. Lionberger and David Lincoln
Page 345 A2
Will of Mourning Hurt
    To my wife, Clara...
    To my son, William Albert...
Written: 18 January 1864   Recorded: 3 June 1864
Witnesses: James H. Baker and Joel Hurt
Nancy Hurt to Elija Bales 26 Oct. 1843 161
Renezah Hurt to Emaline Robertson 23 Aug. 1844 173
William Hurt to Catherine Robertson 12 Sept. 1837 71

John W. Huse to Susan Miller 8 Feb. 1848 252

Adeline Huston to John Piper 16 April 1829 103
Eliza Huston to John B. Stean 11 Aug. 1836 64
Sarah Huston to William McMahan 5 Jan. 1826 56
Shelton Huston to Martha Harris 24 Jan. 1833 165

Page 182 A2
Will of Nathaniel Hutchinson
    To my wife, Mary...
    To my deceased daughter, Elizabeth Bingham's two children
    To my daughter, Mary Ann Smith...
    To my sons: Joseph C. and Horatio H. ...
Written: 30 January 1856   Recorded: 23 April 1856
Witnesses: Washington Adams and R. S. Wilson

Almira A. Hutchinson to John Hannah 2 Dec. 1841 136
Elizabeth Hutchinson to Samuel J. Tutt 2 Feb. 1843 153
George Hutchinson to Frances Cordrey 4 July 1843 160
James Hutchinson to Martha V. Tutt 18 Dec. 1845 198
John H. Hutchinson to Sally Moore 13 Aug. 1822 39
Margaret H. Hutchinson to Bennett C. Clark 9 Sept. 1841 133
Mary Ann Hutchinson to Thomas R. Smith 25 July 1839 99
Nancy J. Hutchinson to William H. Cropper 17 Jan. 1850 28
Sarah Ardell Hutchinson to William S. Speed 15 June 1846 215

Jacob Ingram to Jane H. Martin 22 Nov. 1842 153
John Ingram to Elviry Smiley 23 Aug. 1827 30

Hypasia Ann Isball to A. N. Wright 7 Sept. 1841 133
William E. Isbell to Katherine Litney 25 Sept. 1849 19

William Isba to Martha Huklin 7 June 1819 14

John Jackson to Abaline Anderson 23 March 1834 18

Mary Ann James, Pettis CO., Mo. to Jesse Thomas 28 Oct. 1841 135
James James to Elizabeth Morris 2 May 1841 127
Nancy C. James to James L. Moody 6 Sept. 1849 178
Virginia M. James to James Monroe Nugent 26 Nov. 1850 35

James N. Jamison to Lucy Ann Townsend 10 March 1846 131
Elizabeth Jamison to Silas Yarnel 21 July 1841 131
Ephraim Jamison to Margaret Wallace 21 July 1841 131
James W. Jamison to Martitia Eller 7 April 1836 49
Lucinda Jamison to George W. Wallce 1 May 1838 80

Delaney Jarvis to Cummiurs Meilum 12 Aug. 1845 195

Elizabeth Jeffries to Cecero Brown 28 Sept. 1819 14
James Jeffreys to Emilee Bruce 11 Oct. 1849 21
Miss Jeffries to Darius E. Putnam 7 May 1849 24

Page 130 A
Will of Martin Jennings
    To my wife, Elizabeth and my children...
Written: 27 May 1833   Recorded: 7 May 1841
Witnesses: G. W. Wright, Arch. Kavanaugh, and G. Tutt

Diana Jennings to Elisha Jennings 8 Jan. 1846 199
Eli Jennings to Mary Ann Jennings 15 Nov. 1846 223
Elisha Jennings to Diana Jennings 8 Jan. 1846 199
Elizabeth Jennings to Mathew M. Ralston 18 Oct. 1849 21
Elizane Ann Jennings to James Campbell 4 April 1820 19
James M. Jennings to Nancy Jennings 28 Dec. 1843 165
Mary Ann Jennings to Eli Jennings 15 Nov. 1846 223
Nancy Jennings to James M. Jennings 28 Dec. 1843 165

Karen Jeringen to William Simons 1 July 1830 86

Abraham Job to Margaret Reeves 13 Oct. 1822 36
Bartholmew Job to Morgan Williams 21 Nov. 1833 12
Elijah Job to Elizabeth Holt 14 April 1840 113
Susan Job to Nicholas J. Scrumm 8 July 1849 17

Page 413 A2
Will of Miles Johnson
    To my wife, Jane K. ...
    To my step-daughter, Nancy E. White and to my step-son, George Henry Crop
Written: 24 August 186_   Recorded: 4 February 1869
Witnesses: L. C. Hawkins and John Woods
Alexander W. Johnson to Mary Logan 5 Nov. 1839 108
Amanda Johnson to Henry C. Woolery 3 Feb. 1858 28
Ann Johnson to Hezekiah Warden 3 Jan. 1823 71
Ann Maria Johnson to William U. Ellis 3 Nov. 1846 220
Artemisia Johnson to James Scott 20 June 1849 19
Barnet Johnson to M. Wear 7 Dec. 1848 3
Benoni Johnson to Margaret Harris 1 June 1846 212
Clark Johnson to Barbary Millsap 1 Jan. 1826 54
David Johnson to Mournin Kelly 15 Jan. 1827 73
Ettel Johnson to Elizabeth Travis 23 Dec. 1821 24
James Johnson to Nancy Socket 1 July 1827 81
James Johnson to Maryan Taylor 9 Feb. 1830 114
Jesse Johnson to Becky Von 18 Nov. 1827 84
John Johnson to Sarah Moore 24 Dec. 1820 22
John L. T. Johnson to Elizabeth Ann Robertson 17 Dec. 1835 42
Lucinda Johnson to Mathew Adams 23 Oct. 1827 86
Mahala Johnson to John Von 24 July 1828 93
Margaret Johnson to Phillip M. Lockwood 17 Oct. 1850 35
Mary Jane Johnson to John Wilson 30 Oct. 1843 163
Nevil Johnson to Catherine Harmons 17 July 1833 5
Rachel Johnson to Thomas Quick 8 Nov. 1827 86
Rebecca Johnson to William Swearingen 29 March 1832 146
Susannah R. Johnson to Samuel McDaniel 12 Sept. 1830 123
Tabin Johnson to Rebecca O. Cannion 28 Aug. 1833 4
Thomas Johnson to Liddy Keaney 9 June 1827 70
Thomas A. Johnson to Mrs. Nancy Harris 15 Jan. 1850 28
Vincent Johnson to Lucy Allison 2 Oct. 1823 46
William Johnson to Nancy Driskill 17 June 1840 113

Jacob Johnston to Prudence Story 23 Dec. 1825 55
K. A. D. Johnston to Eleanor I. Wear 19 March 1845 185
Margaret E. Johnston to John W. McClain 27 Sept. 1842 146
Nancy June Johnston to David McClain 18 Nov. 1847 247
Rachel D. Johnston to George W. Dean 17 March 1838 85
Susan E. Johnston to Phillip W. Shoemaker 24 Feb. 1850 29
Wesley Johnston to Mary Druffee 17 March 1831 130

Page 92 A
Will of Joseph Jolly
    To my sons: John and William...
    To Mary Ann Guyn
Written: 11 May 1835   Recorded: 6 June 1835
Witnesses: William E. Huff and J. J. Huff
Page 176 A2
Will of William Jolly
    To my daughter, Margaret Evans, wife of Alexander C. Evens
    To my grandson, Andrew I. Cole...
    To my daughter, Nancy Ann Hazell, wife of Zeburn Hazell
    To my daughter, Mary Ann... and to my daughter, Tabitha J.
    To my sons: Urah H., Berryman F., and Joseph W. ...
    The daughter's uncle, David Jones is to take charge of the two girls, Mary Ann and Tabitha J.
    David Jones, Exe.
Written: 5 August 1852   Recorded: 10 March 1856
Witnesses: William C. Lowry, G. L. Bell, and A. Koontz
Elizabeth Jolly to William J. Cole 7 June 1838 83
Joseph Jolly to Rebecca Cathey 8 Dec. 1836 59
Julia Ann Jolly to Thomas Conner 27 Dec. 1849 6
Margaret Jolly to Alexander Evans 13 Dec. 1840 119
Uriah Jolly to Mary M. Ulesse 9 Sept. 1847 241
Nancy A. Jolly to Mr. Seaburn C. Hazel 4 Dec. 1845 198
William Jolly to Sally Nanney 12 March 1826

Christopher Johns to _____ 6 Dec. 1832 160

Page 347 A2
Will of Henry Jones
    To my three children: Jonathan R., Sandy E., and Sue E. ...
    To my other children: William, James, Samuel, Wilmoth...
    The estate of my wife belonging to her father's estate, Jonathan Huff, dec. ...
    To my wife, Susan...
    Jonathan R., Sandy E., Sue E., and Mary U. Suggs, the children of my present wife.
Written: 18 May 1864   Recorded: 13 December 1864
Witnesses: Henry Jones, M. J. Huff, and Mary U. Suggs

Page 253 A2
Will of James Jones, born in North Carolina
    To my wife, Mrs. Elizabeth Jane Jones...
    To my daughter, Mary Jane Jones
Written: 8 August 1859   Recorded: 29 September 1859
Witnesses: E. H. Harris, Newton Woolfolk, and John W. Young
Page 175 B
Will of Joshua Jones, County of Greene and State of Missouri
    To my brother, Caleb Jones...
Written: 20 February 1841   Recorded: 16 Dec. 1846
Witnesses: L. D. McKenney and W. B. Farmer

Benjamin Jones to Jane Jones 28 March 1827 76
Catherine Jones to Charles McCray 17 March 1836 48
Charlotte Jones to William Howe 6 Dec. 1820 18
Cynthia Jones to William Westbrook 28 March 1822 31
David H. Jones to Martha Ann L. Townson 30 March 1837 66
Elizabeth Jones to Francis McKenny 25 July 1832 156
Emiline Jones to William Blanchard 25 May 1839 96
Emily H. Jones to Alexander Parks 13 July 1843 159
Frances Jones to Enoch Francis Woolery 12 March 1846 204
Hannah Jones to Nathan Cooper 30 Jan. 1834 14
Isaac Jones to Mary B. Farley, daughter of Daniel and Frances
    Farley 27 June 1843 156
Jabez Jones to Martha Harris 20 Oct. 1831 141
James Jones to Margaret Randle 1 June 1840 263
Jane Jones to Benjamin Jones 28 March 1827 76
Jesse Jones of the state of Kentucky to Agnes Jane Taylor
    20 March 1837 66
John Jones to Mary George 7 April 1840 112
Josephine D. Jones to John B. Perry 30 Dec. 1845 197
Lewis C. Jones to Mary McCrary 10 Aug. 1837 71
Luckey Jones to John Hill 15 Oct. 1820 33
Martha Elizabeth Jones to John Harris 12 Sept. 1850 34
Mary Frances Jones to John W. Nash 18 May 1841 128
Nancy Jones to Samuel Parks 16 Nov. 1826 68
Nancy Jones to Thomas Stockstill 11 June 1832 2
Nancy D. Jones to James W. Bosell 4 March 1846 214
Parthena Jones to Enoch J. Rector 14 Feb. 1839 96
Polly Jones to James McFarland 16 Oct. 1832 156
Sally Jones to Benjamin A. P. Longan 24 Oct. 1824 48
Samuel F. Jones to Susan Coffman 9 Dec. 1847 245
Sarah Ann Jones to John H. Chinn 8 April 1840 112
Sarah M. Jones to James Reed 11 Aug. 1850 33
Thomas Jones to Rebecca Allison 1 Sept. 1844 100
Wiatt Jones, Moniteau Co., Mo. to Frances Runal ____ 1849 11
Wiley Jones to Pheby Talytell 10 Oct. 1847 246
William B. Jones to Dinretta Ogle 11 Feb. 1841 122
Wilmouth S. Jones to Elisha B. Redley 15 Sept. 1842 149

Mrs. Sarah Jorden to George Hett 11 Aug. 1845 191
James D. Jordan to Malissa Barnes 16 April 1839 95

Jesse Josserton to Dolly Houx 23 June 1834 20

Diedrick Karstens, Morgan Co., Mo. to Christine Schlotzhauer 20 Nov. 1850 34

Lewis Katz to Mary Catharine Hoss 3 March 1843 155

Archibald Kavanaugh to Mary A. Ewing 11 July 1821 21
Charles C. C. Kavenaugh to Tabitha C. McLean 15 Dec. 1830 130

Mary Ann Kealen to Jefferson Smith 10 March 1841 123

John Keegar to Susan Callaway 3 Oct. 1842 145

James Keeny to Modest Keeny 19 March 1832 161
Modest Keeny to James Keeny 19 March 1832 161
Liddy Keeny to Thomas Jefferson 9 June 1827 70
Martha C. Keeny to James Walters 28 Nov. 1842 153

Charity Kell to John Luster 9 Nov. 1825 54
John Kell to Nancy Martin 7 Feb. 1826 58
Mrs. Nancy Kell to Robert Rollins 24 Sept. 1846 217

Nancy Kelley to John C. Rochester 28 Feb. 1821 19

Silvester Kellogg to Elizabeth Ann Calvert 5 April 1832 145

Mrs. Deborah Kelly to James Ross 20 June 1847 236
Elizabeth Kelly to Archibald Woods 12 Sept. 1822 36
Edward Kelly to Mary Beatwright 3 March 1844 172
Esther Kelly to Joshua Cox 7 April 1823 42
James Kelly to Elizabeth Mullins 17 Aug. 1839 101
John H. Kelly to Martha C. Duncan 14 Nov. 1849 23
Lucy Kelly to David Peters 25 July 1825 52
Martha Ellen Kelly to William L. C. Patterson 23 April 1846 207
Mary Ann Kelly to Charles Lewis Miller 10 Nov. 1845 195
Mary Elizabeth Kelly to Richard R. Thompson 11 Jan. 1848 255
Mournin Kelly to David Johnson 15 Jan. 1827 73
Parthena W. Kelly to Joseph H. Nep 27 Feb. 1840 107
Rhoda Kelly to Robert Salmons . Jan. 1850 30
Sarah Kelly to Rice Callas 1 Dec. 1822 40

James Kelsey to Margaret Kelsey 16 Dec. 1831 139
Margaret Kelsey to James Kelsey 16 Dec. 1831 139
Elenor Kemper to John Guthridge Spieler 25 March 1843 154

Page 230 A2
Will of Leonard Kempf
    To my wife Catherine
Written: 18 September 1856   Recorded: 9 March 1859
Witnesses: Emmett R. Hayden and C. F. Hehle

Hannah Kenchloe to Warren Davis 5 July 1829 105
Mary Kenchloe to Samuel Riddle 24 Dec. 1839 104

Ann Kennedy to Samuel H. Saunders 28 June 1844 176
John Kennedy to Martha Donagair ___ ___ 1832 152

Mary Jane Kenrick to Joseph A. Potter 20 June 1849 19
Sidney Elizabeth Kenrick to Henry G. Potter 21 March 1849 12

Will of Mark Kerns
Page 325 A2
    Mark Kerns of the Borough of Chambersburg, County of Franklin, state of Pennsylvania
    To my mother, Naomi Fisher...
    My mother and my friend, Jobe Mann, Exe.
Written: 20 July 1862   Recorded: 12 March 1863
Witnesses: C. H. Duncan and Samuel R. Fisher

Ellen Kerton to John W. Bull 12 July 1846 213
Frances Kerton to Thomas Bacon 5 Jan. 1845 184
Thomas M. Kerton to Elizabeth Jane Bull 21 Dec. 1845 201

James L. Ketton to Nancy Card 1 March 1833 167

John Keyton to Margaret Briscoe Given 10 Oct. 1828 96
William H. Keyton to Nancy D. Cole 29 June 1826 63

George Leonard Khochn to Mary Ann Smith 6 Nov. 1846 2

Martin Kidwell to Sally Woods 16 April 1848 259

Ann W. Kilgore to Barnett Hart 27 July 1842 146

Elijah Kinchloe to Elizabeth Reed 26 May 1840 110
Zechariah Kinchle to Victerona Barnes 18 Jan. 1846 204

Henry C. King to Elizabeth Moon 13 Jan. 1848 252
Isaac King, Saline Co., Mo. to Margaret Pharis 29 Aug. 1844 177
Nancy Ann King to James H. Burris, Morgan Co., Mo.
    1 Sept. 1842 149
Nancy J. King at the residence of William King to James W. Little
    7 Nov. 1850 34
William King to Polly Haines 6 Sept. 1832 155

Milan Kirk to Ruth Boyd 26 July 1835 30
Nancy Kirk to Joseph G. Shoberenell 17 Dec. 1840 119

Wiette Kirkindall to Jane Stone 24 April 1832 152
William Kirkendoll to Malvina Amick 20 Feb. 1833 2

Finis E. Kirkpatrick to Margaret Gott 20 Feb. 1827 77
Margaret Kirkpatrick to Mathew Wooden 15 Jan. 1837 62
Martha Kirkpatrick to James J. Berry 1 Jan. 1822 29
Martha Ann Kirkpatrick to Matthias Cline 7 March 1841 127
R. Kirkpatrick to Elizabeth Bruce 9 Sept. 1847 240
Sarah Kirkpatrick to John Reed 20 March 1823 41
Sarah Caroline Kirkpatrick to Richard Rice 5 Sept. 1844 174

Reinhart Kissnich to Amelia Fuchs 8 Dec. 1840 110

Margaret Kivette to Greene Steele 17 March 1845 186

Page 409 A2
Will of George Klein
    To my wife, Genevieve...
    To my children: Emily, Rosa, Charles, Catherine, and Polly Kline...
Written: 30 Sept. 1854   Recorded: 3 November 1868
Witnesses: A. S. Shortridge, J. N. McCutchen, and J. L. St

Karoline Lockner to William Hoberecht 10 May 1850 30

William Knaus to Malvina Oglesby 26 Oct. 1843 165

Elizabeth Know to Henry Jacob Neff 15 Jan. 1850 31

Page 393 A2
Will of Joseph C. Koontz
    To my wife, Mary...
    To my sons: Dewitt C., Samuel, Alfred, George, and A. Hiram C. ...
    To my daughter, Mary E.
Written: 29 June 1867   Recorded: 29 Nov. 1867
Witnesses: N. Williams and Just. Williams
Benjamin F. Koontz to Martha Ellen Steel 23 May 1846 210
Elizabeth G. Koontz to Henry G. Duncan 2 May 1844 177
Mary Koontz to John Wilkerson 2 March 1840 254

Page 127 A2
Will of James Lacy
    To my wife, Lydia...
    To my sons: George W. and John K. ...
    John K., Exe.
Written: 27 March 1854   Recorded: 24 April 1854
Witnesses: S. A. Summers and Samuel Roe
Page 442 A2 Will of Julia Lacy
    To my sons: George G. and Robert A. and my daughter, Agnes
    My husband, Archibald J., Exe.
Written: 31 May 1870   Recorded: 5 November 1870
Witnesses: William D. Muir, Dorothy Gale, and W. H. Ellis

Page 163 A2
Will of John K. Lacy
    To my wife, Susan A. ...
Written: 26 June 1855   Recorded: 6 August 1855
Witnesses: J. J. McCabe and John Seith
Gravenor Lacy to Mary Patrick 24 Aug. 1837 73
John Kay Lacy to Susan Ann Hassie 29 Sept. 1825 32
Sarah Lacy to John W. H. Wooldridge 12 Oct. 1848 4
Page 1 A
Will of Moses Langley
    I will all remainder of estate to my wife, Sally till by children are raised..
Written: 23 February 1818 Recorded 6 January 1820
In the presence of Robert Boyd, William Frazor, and David D. Trotter
Mrs. Sally Langly to Nathaniel Bullard 21 Oct. 1819 7
Joshua Lakey to Polly Brown 20 Aug. 1819 9

James Lamb to Lizabeth Hunter 25 February 1841 126
Elizabeth Lam to John F. Clayton 24 Dec. 1844 183
Francis Nannion Lamm to Martha Elizabeth Hall 26 April 1849 13
John Lamm to Caroline Pusely 26 May 1838 82

William Lamont to Amanda Vanplank 18 Dec. 1844 180

Ambrose C. Lampton to Salina Fields 9 April 1874 229
John H. Lampton to Marilda A. Bruce 20 Feb. 1838 79
Malissa H. Lampton to William M. Berry 29 Nov. 1836 62
Manippa Lampton to Jefferson Shanklin 6 April 1837 69

Page 8 A2
Will of Hugh Lanimore
    To my wife, Fanny...
    To my daughter, Nancy Henderson, wife of George Henderson
    To my sons: George and Rowland...
    Rowland, my son, Exe.
Written: 8 December 1840   Recorded: 7 February 1848
Witnesses: Benjamin A. B. Longan and Andrew F. Duncan
Mary Lanimore to Thomas Hightwoer 4 Sept. 1845 202

Elizabeth Larew to Anderson Edwards 24 Jan. 1836 44

Joseph N. Laune to Jane Davis 7 Nov. 1835 52

Timothy Lawler to Mary Brian 4 March 1827 74

Martha W. Lawlin to Jeremiah Mizo 3 Sept. 1840 7

Mrs. Elizabeth Lawrence to Thomas Thomas 4 April 1841 125
William F. Lawrence to Mary S. Mills 13 Feb. 1839 94

Page 180 B
Will of William Lawless
    To Burton Lawless and his wife, Nancy...
    To my sister, Maryan Wilhelm...
    To my uncle Burton Lawless and his wife, Nancy...
    To my mother, Elizabeth Huston...
    To my brother, Benjamin Lawless...
Written 18 Nov. 1843   Recorded 10 April 1847
Benjamin Lawless to Elizabeth Townsend 29 Feb. 1844 170
Burton Lawless to Lavina Grove 10 March 1847 235
Lydia Jane Lawless to Samuel Teeter 24 July 1844 178

Elizabeth Layman to John Light 27 Oct. 1844 176

Eveline Lawrey to Heli Corum 23 July 1824 47

Page 66 A2
Will of Joseph Lee
    To my father, John Lee, Sr. ...
    To my mother, Catherine...
    To my brother, John...
    To my sisters: Marcilla and Elizabeth...
    John M. McCuthen, Exe.
Written: 6 February 1852   Recorded: 14 February 1852
Witnesses: S. A. Summers, John McCuthen, Alfred Simmons, and H. McFarlin
DerIndia Lee to Bird Parks 19 March 1840 112
Martha Lee to Jonathan Hunt 12 Dec. 1844 181

John W. Leftwich, Pettis Co., Mo. to Elizabeth K. Ellis
    28 Aug. 1845 193

Patrick Lemey to Jane Hogg 20 Dec. 1819 7

Susan Letchworth to David P. Mahan 17 Sept. 1820 17
Thomas Letchworth to Polly Chisholm 5 April 1821 20

Rody Levens to Jacob Stephens 24 July 1848 262
Washington Franklin Levens to Maranda Boles 3 March 1842 140
Zerilda H. Levins to Jackson J. Reavis 24 May 1838 83

Charles T. Lewis to Virginia W. Gooch 23 Oct. 1845 83
James Lewis to Elizabeth Oherrel 16 Sept. 1848 1
James P. Lewis to Phebe Mann 18 Nov. 1847 245
John Lewis to Susan Houx 17 March 1831 130
Joshua Lewis to Dicy Stone 8 Feb. 1823 41
Robert C. Lewis to Mrs. Rachel Stafford 29 June 1848 266
Susan Lewis to Henry Mills 20 August 1840 114
William Lewis to Mrs. Mary Ann Moore 23 May 1850 32

NOTES

John Light to Elizabeth Layman 27 Oct. 1844 178

Polly Lillard to William M. Rogers 1 May 1820 12 A

John P. Lilly to Samenda Ann Allison 11 Sept. 1843 160
Malinda J. Lilly to Samuel Thomas 4 July 1849 15
Nancy Lilly to David Byler 13 March 1832 149

Page 308 A2
Will of Elizabeth Linn, formerly of the state of Missouri at present a resident of the county of Accomack, in the state of Virginia
    To my grandsons: Lewis F. Linn and James Robert Linn
    To my friend, Dr. William R. Trigg...
    To my daughter, Mary Linn Browne, wife of Peter F. Browne..
    My daughter, Mary, Exe.
Written: 29 August 1861   Recorded:
Witnesses: John Akinson, George D. Wise, and Bagley Browne

Page 310 A2
Will of Isaac Lionberger
    To my wife, Mary Ann...
    To my younger children: Francis, Edward William Mann, Sally
    To my three older children: Robert, Mary Elizabeth, and Dewitt Clinton...
    To my daughter, Isabella, wife of James Woolfolk...
Written: 21 November 1861   Recorded: 5 March 1862
Witnesses: Abraham R. Lincoln and David Lincoln
Mary E. Lionberger to John C. Richardson 15 Feb. 1847 226
Mahalia Linsey to Spotswood Lengan 2 July 1826 65
Mary Lindsay to John Pollock 21 July 1821 92

Katherine Litnay to William E. Isbell 25 Sept. 1849 19

James W. Little to Nancy J. King at the residence of William
    King 7 Nov. 1850 34

Mary Jane Littlepage to Marcus Williams, Jr. 14 March 1839 95
Mrs. Nancy Littlepage to James Dickson 4 Oct. 1846 219

Margaret Lockhart to Kimber Barton 7 Nov. 1821 37

Phillip N. Lockwood, St. Louis, Mo. to Margaret A. Johnson
    17 Oct. 1850 35

Page 332 A2
Will of George W. Logan
    To my sisters: Matilda Logan and Jane Williams...
    To my wife, Mary F. ...
    James H. Baker, Exe.
Written: 5 March 1863   Recorded: 16 June 1863
Witnesses: J. P. Embree and John D. Johnston

George Logan to Catharine Tompkins 19 Nov. 1846 224
Jane Logan to Sandy J. Williams 10 June 1846 211
John W. Logan to Martha C. Parsons 6 May 1847 237
Mary Logan to Alexander W. Johnson 5 Nov. 1839 108

Margretome Loller to John Adams 15 Jan. 1846 203

George Long to Mary Raiter 7 Sept. 1842 145

Page 147 A
Will of Jane Longan
    To my niece, Elizabeth Scruggs and her husband, John...
    To Martha Longan and Susan Mahan...
    David P. Mahan, Exe.
Written: 8 March 1839   Recorded: 8 May 1841
Witnesses: Samuel Parks and William Allison
Benjamin A. B. Longan to Sally Jones 24 Oct. 1824 48
Frederick Longan to Emilee Reavis 8 May 1849 13
John D. Longan to Elizabeth Reavis 2 Sept. 1827 84
Lewis Lundford Longan, Cole Co., Mo. to Polly Randolph
    20 Dec. 1835 42
Martha Jane Longan to Noah Harvey 28 May 1846 220
Spotswood Longan to Mahalia Linsey 2 July 1826 220

Jefferson Lord to Catherine Fry 15 Feb. 1849 8

Elvira M. Lovelace to Oliver J. McFarland 27 June 1848 261

Lucy Ann Leville to Lafayette Carlos 13 June 1850 36

Page 296 A2
Will of James M. Lowry
    To my wife, Mary Jane...
    Samuel Franklin Cole, Exe.
Written: 6 February 1861   Recorded: 12 March 1861
Witnesses: G. T. Pendleton and Henry Corum
Hiram C. Lowry to Jane Steel 30 Aug. 1838 84
James M. Lowry to Mary Jane Cole 21 March 1847 232
Joanna Lowry to James C. Ross 5 June 1839 98

Will of Benjamin Ludwig
Page 402 A2
    To my wife, Margaret...
    To my children: Louise Ludwig, Catherine Bischoff,
Cathrina Willemine, and Doorte Scharlotte Ludwig...
Written: 7 March 1868   Recorded: 28 May 1868
Witnesses: David Schibb and Asa Morton

John Luster to Charity Kell 9 Nov. 1825 54

Dewitt Clinton Mack to Sally Ann Betts 2 Dec. 1847   244
Eliza Jane Mack to Francis Achlie 14 June 1846   211

Albert Calloway Maddox to Elizabeth Cobbs 25 Nov. 1841   139
Willoughby Maddox to Elizabeth Shirley at the house of
    Frederick Shirley   11 Nov. 1847   243

Page 242 A2
Will of Owen Magruder
    To my wife, Mrs. Sarah O. Magruder...
    To my daughter, Florence Greenlease...
    To my son in law, Dr. George T. Pendleton...
    To my son, William A.
Written 11 January 1859   Recorded: 16 March 1859
John W. Young and Jerome Harris, witnesses

Cynthia S. Mahan to George W. Simmons 25 Oct. 1836   88
David P. Mahan to Susan Letchworth 17 Sept. 1820   17
Elizabeth Mahan to James Dew 13 May 1830   110
James Mahan to Nancy Miller 8 Feb. 1829   102
Kitty Ann Mahan to Peter Borner 5 Dec. 1827   85
Louisa Mahan to Hank Scragg 20 March 1834   18
Mary Jane Mahan to Rhodes Paschal 22 Dec. 1846   225

James E. Major, Howard Co., Mo. to Frances B. Bernard
    24 March 1840   117
John A. S. Major to Mary M. Bernard 15 Dec. 1841   139

James Manela to Dorcas L. McClanahan 21 Nov. 1844   162

Lewis Manes to Elizabeth Brown 1 Jan. 1839   90

Presley Hanion, Van Buren Co. to Sally Ann Collins 6 May 1845
    187

Dr. George Wylde Mann to Mrs. Jessie Buchanan 28 May 1848   26
Mary Angeline Han to George N. Robertson 29 Aug. 1845   193
Nancy Man to John Vault 15 May 1826   64
Phebe Mann to James P. Lewis 18 Nov. 1847   245
Susan E. Mann to Eli B. Amick 11 Jan. 1849   8

Hannah Mar to Thompson Whitson 26 March 1820   11

Robert March to Nancy C. Anderson 6 Nov. 1836   56

Page 367 A2 Will of Joseph Marchand
    To my wife, Elizabeth
Written: 18 May 1855   Recorded: 2 Feb. 1866
Witnesses: John Kempf and Silvester Harstetter

Amanda Harland to A. F. Patton   16 March 1847   237

Evi Harley to Sarah Boyles   5 March 1833   3

Page 441 A2
Will of Isham Martin
    To my wife, Elizabeth...
    To my children: Margaret A. Renshaw, Jane Hill, Sarah Ann Snodgrass, Polly M. Baxter, Charlotte Snodgrass, Daniel D., John H., William A., and Martha N. Halford...
    Joel and Job Snodgrass and D. B. Martin, Exe.
Written: 26 Oct. 1870   Recorded: 16 November 1870
Witnesses: Moses and William Martin
Barbara Martin to John Wemple   9 Dec. 1849   22
Caleb Martin to Louisa Crowder   20 Nov. 1833   17
Elizabeth Martin to James Atkins   9 Jan. 1840   104
Frances Martin to Peter Huff   19 Sept. 1824   48
Page 78 A
Will of William Martin
    To my wife, Martha...
    To my eldest son, Isham; to my third son, Moses; to my second son, Soloman; to my fourth son, Aaron; to my fifth son, Joshua;
    To my daughters: Elizabeth Martin, Sarah Gist, and my youngest daughter, Martha Martin
Written: 25 July 1829   Recorded: 4 February 1835
Witnesses: Thomas Gist, Soloman Martin, and Aaron Martin
Isaac Martin to Mary Smith   22 Feb. 1827   78
James Martin to Margaret George   23 March 1830   116
Jane Martin to Michael Brown   21 Oct. 1830   124
Jane Martin to Joseph Hill   22 Feb. 1839   97
John Martin to Eliza Ann Harris   4 Sept. 1850   36
Jane Martin to Lewis Doran   19 Jan. 1843   155
Jonathan P. Martin to Margaret Shipley   6 April 1828   90
Joshua Martin to Elizabeth Edwards   4 Oct. 1832   156
Lucinda Martin to Peter Scott   30 June 1846   218
Malissa Martin to Thomas Cole   19 Jan. 1849   9
Margaret A. Martin to John W. Renshaw   12 Oct. 1835   41
Martha Martin to James Slenslan   30 July 1837   72
Martha A. Martin to William L. Heston   27 Dec. 1838   93
Martha N. Martin to William C. Halford   31 March 1839   97
Mary M. Martin to Benjamin Baxter   20 Sept. 1848   3
James Martin to Emilene Waters   1 Sept. 1841   134
Morman Martin to Andrew Russell   8 Aug. 1819   10
Nancy Martin to John Kell   7 Feb. 1826   58
Nancy Martin to Reuben Snodgrass   5 Oct. 1826   67
Nancy Martin to Stephen Stinson   2 Feb. 1832   156
Sarah Ann Martin to Job Sorgrass   18 June 1846   216
Valentine Martin to Jane Seat   11 July 1840   266

William Martin to Charlotte Burrus 21 Dec. 1843 169
William Martin to Eliza Houx 8 Feb. 1849 9
William F. Martin to Roady Ann Moore 12 Aug. 1841 129

Page 54 B
Will of Alfred Masquerier
    To my wife, Emely...
    To my brother, Lewis...
    To my sister, Mary B. Corum...
    My friends, Jordon O'Bryan and Hiram Corum, Exe.
Written: 17 December 1843 Recorded: 24 November 1843
Witnesses: John A. S. Tutt, Henry Corum, and N. Leonard
Alfred Masquirier to Emilee O'Bryan 28 Feb. 1837 67
Mrs. Emily Masquirier to William Gibson 4 June 1845 169

J. N. Mason to Arabella C. Taylor 16 Sept. 1841 132
James Mason to Nancy Wood 12 Sept. 1830 123

Page 36 A
Will of Massie: Silvanus
    To my wife, Margaret...
    To my children...
    Thomas Collins and Andrew Briscoe, Trustees
Written: 18 Dec. 1826 Recorded: 2 July 1827
Witnesses: Andrew Briscoe, Thomas Collins, and Francis Collins
Elizabeth H. Massey to Thomas B. Smith 10 July 1842 144
Frances Massey to Marion Seat 4 June 1845 169
Peggy Massy to Jacob Houx 27 May 1827 78
Susan Ann Massie to John Kay Lacy 29 Sept. 1835 32

Margaret Masel to George Ulever 6 Oct. 1847 242
Mary Ann Massel to John Christian Shupp 31 Oct. 1848 2

Caroline Masters to William Robertson 22 March 1832 148

Page 39 A2
Will of Isaac Maston
    To Elizabeth Smith and to the heirs of her body I bequeath five Negroes and the tract of land on which Thomas B. Smith now lives.
    To my brothers: Hudelt and William H., $1000. each
    To the heirs of my brother, John F., $1000.
    To my sister, Mary Walker, $1000.
    To my wife, Mary the remainder of my estate.
    My wife and Anthony S. Walker, Exe.
Written: 14 September 1850 Recorded: 13 Sept. 1850
Witnesses: J. Hobbs and H. E. W. McDoamon

David L. Mathews to Margaret S. Wear 7 Dec. 1848 3

Amanda Mattingly to Lewallen Rector 16 Oct. 1838 90

Peter Hauttby to Tabitha Thomas   17 Nov. 1842   149

Mrs. Elcy Maxwell to John Clayton   11 July 1849   16
Jefferson Maxwell to Rhoda Campbell   8 Dec. 1836   60
Samuel Maxwell to Permelia Moon   27 Dec. 1829   60

Lavinia May to David Tittsworth   14 July 1831   135
Permelia May to Daniel Day   22 Feb. 1838   77

Sally Mayfield to James Rickman   21 Dec. 1844   183
Stephen Mayfield to Miram Thompson   29 April 1846   210

Caroline E. Mayo to William Harriman   28 March 1848   260

John McAllister to Frances Feek   29 March 1837   71

John C. McAtha to Martha Berry   24 Dec. 1849   25

Page 272 A2
Will of James McBride, of Hamilton in the County of Butler and State of Ohio
    To my wife, Hannah...
    To my daughter, Laura Stembel, wife of Roger N. Stembel...
    To my son, Horace McBride...
    To my daughter, Marietta Saunders, wife of William P. Saunders...
    To my son, James McBride, Jr. ...
    Isaac T. Saunders, John W. Ervine, James Clark, and James D. Thomas, Exs.
Written: 27 May 1859   Recorded: 12 June 1860
Witnesses: William Beckett, J. Curtis, and Jacob Shaffer

Andrew McBrown to Helen Shoemaker   5 April 1848   255

John McCaleb to Elizabeth Smith   15 August 1839   99

Page 146 A2
Will of Charles McCabe
    To my wife, Elizabeth...
    To Maria Collins...
    Elizabeth McCabe, Exe.
Written: _ August 1853   Recorded: 1 January 1855
Minor Gibson, Margaret Maddox, and John Suddeth, witnesses

Page 31 A2
Will of Nicholas McCarty
    To my wife, Katharine...
    To my three children: Nancy T. Crawford, Benjamin F, and Ann Elizabeth McCarty...
Continued--

81

Will of Nicholas McCarty Continued
    To Nancy T., wife of James S. Crawford...
    To my two children: Peny F. McCarty and Ann E. McCarty...
    My friend, L. C. Stephens, Exe.
Written: 11 April 1845   Recorded: 13 April 1850
Witnesses: David Eller and Thomas L. George
A. P. McCarty to Miss C. A. Dickson 22 Feb. 1849 10
Ann T. McCarty to James L. Crawford 17 March 1836 48
Eliza J. McCartey to Hugh O'Donnell 3 May 1847 231
James McCartey to Betsey Miller 31 Oct. 1822 38
James McCarty to Polly Cole 9 May 1832 147
James McCarty to Mary A. A. McFarland 2 Oct. 1838 87
Mary A. McCarty to Joseph H. Moore 24 Jan. 1850 28
Nancy McCarty to Samuel Ritchey 19 Dec. 1824 49
S. McCarty to Miss M. A. Ferguson 19 Dec. 1843 165

Asa McClain to Mary Campbell 7 Jan. 1847 227
David W. McClain to Jaily Ann Stephens 4 Dec. 1845 200
Dr. David O. McClean to Elizabeth McClain 10 Sept. 1848 265
David McClain to Nancy June Johnston 18 Nov. 1847 247
Elizabeth McClain to Dr. David O. McClean 10 Sept. 1848 265
John W. McClain to Margaret B. Johnston 27 Sept. 1842 146
Mary Jane McClean to Wimrod Oglesby 26 March 1839 93
William C. McClain to Amelia Sullivan 27 May 1842 143
Tabitha C. McLean to Charles C. C. Kavanaugh 15 Dec. 1830 130

Page 168 A2
Will of Jobe McClanahan
    To my daughter, Mary Manelys heirs, namely, James, Job, and William A.
    To my son James' heirs, Manoly, Liddy Ann McClanahan, Emiline McClanahan, and Manerva McClanahan...
    To my son, David's heirs, namely, Eliza, Crecy An, and Mary Frances...
    To my sons: Thomas, Jackson, and Job S. ...
    To my daughters: Caroline Davis, Elizabeth Rumfe, Crecy Ann McClanahan, and Liddy Rennel...
    William H. and Thomas, my sons, Exe.
Written: 19 October 1855   Recorded: 30 October 1855
William H. Thornton, Jesse Jones, U. P. Pursley, and James Hammons

Page 112 A
Will of Joshua McClanahan
    To my wife, Evalina...
    To my six children: Melvina McClanahan, Jane Lucrey, Mary Sharp, Darcus Lavinia, Thomas M., and Sarah Ann...
Written: 11 January 1836   Recorded: 8 May 1837
David Jones, William Snodgrass, and Robert C. Nelson, witnesses
Absalom McClanahan to Mary Bazzel 8 Feb. 1844 167
Andrew McClanahan to Mariah Nelson 26 Dec. 1839 105
Andrew J. McClanahan to Elizabeth Broiles 21 Jan. 1841 126

Caroline McClanahan to Andrew Davis 29 Aug. 1833   8
Catherine McClanahan to William G. Edwards 20 Nov. 1845 200
David McClanahan to Elenor Rymal 26 June 1837 68
Dorcas L. McClanahan to James Manila 21 Nov. 1844 182
Eleanor McClanahan to John Christopher Musin 6 Oct. 1849 21
Eliza McClanahan to Moses Turner 30 July 1828 91
Enoch McClanahan to America Mills 2 Aug. 1838 85
James McClanahan to Nancy Wingate 20 June 1847 236
James M. McClanahan to Kiciah Rymal 26 Dec. 1837 77
Jeanneat L. McClanahan to Benjamin Doalson 7 Aug. 1836 54
John McClanahan to Sarah A. McDaniel 26 Nov. 1844 182
Louticia McClanahan to John T. Gray 27 Dec. 1846 225
Lyda Ann McClanahan to Newton Rimel 11 Aug. 1850 33
Mary McClanahan to William Anderson 12 Dec. 1845 214
Mary M. McClanahan to William Neely 5 Sept. 1833   8
Mary Sharp McClanahan to John McDaniel 15 Feb. 1841 125
Nancy McClanahan to James Cathey 12 Jan. 1822 26
Nancy McClanahan to Allen J. Gabriel 30 July 1840 113
Rebecca McClanahan to John A. L. Grice 12 March 1837 66
Thomas McClanahan to Elizabeth Davis 26 May 1833 5

Page 14 A
Will of Joseph McClure
    To my wife, Elizabeth...
    To my son, Charles... to my son, Andrew, balance of the money in North Carolina
    To my daughters: Sary, Kesiah, Elizabeth, and Nancy...
Written: 26 September 1820
Witnesses: James D. Campbell, Green B. Ellison, and Margaret Ellison
Isabel McClure to John Son 20 July 1821 22
Mary McClure to John Robertson 22 July 1821 22
Nancy McClure to John Woods 6 Sept. 1821 26

Page 133 B
Will of Henry McClury
    To my wife, Mary, 160 Acres of land in the Territory of Arkansas
Written: 6 January 1845   Recorded: 4 January 1845
Witnesses: John S. Poisel and Joseph Stephens

Margaret McCorch to Perry Crews 22 March 1849 14

Frances K. McCorkle to Charles Brownlee 5 Oct. 1848 4
Robert McCorkle to Elizabeth Yarnell 21 March 1847 235

Charles McCrary to Catherine Jones 17 March 1836 48
Mary McCrary to Lewis C. Jones 10 Aug. 1837 71

Page 104 A2
Will of Robert McCulloch
    To my wife, Patsy...
    To my daughters: Sarah Rail, Martha Taylor, Sophia Williams, and Lucy Ann McCullough...
    To my sons: Robert, Joseph, and Thomas...
    To my deceased daughter, Mary E. Douglas heirs...
    To my deceased son's, George W. heirs...
    To my son Spotswood M. ...
Written: 30 April 1845   Recorded: 29 August 1853
James Curry, James H. Goodman, Tandy I. Douglas, William H. Ellis, and Samuel Drinkwater
Elizabeth McCulloch to Absolom H. Frier 26 April 1838 81
James McCulloch to Susan Eubanks 28 Nov. 1844 161
Martha McCulloch to Ravenscroft S. Taylor, 7 Sept. 1843 161
Robert McCulloch, Jr. to Katherine Robertson, daughter of
    Edward Robertson 27 July 1837 69
Sarah McCullouch to William Rayle 16 Dec. 1835 40
Sophia McCulloch to Robert M. Williams 30 Dec. 1840 120
Page 109 A2
Will of Thomas McCullough
    To my children: Thomas T., Martha Douglass, Margaret Fryer, Sarah Reavis, Mary Ann Reavis, and Elizabeth Fryer...
    To the heirs of my daughter, Atlanta Draffen, wife of William Draffen...
    To my sons: Robert and John...
    To my two youngest daughters: Elizabeth Fryer and Atlanta Draffen...
    Tandy Douglas and Henry I. Reavis, Exe.
Written: 6 September 1845   Recorded: 12 November 1853
Witnesses: John A. Justice, James C. Cox, and William I. Cox
Atlanta McCullough to William Drafflin 8 Oct. 1840 116
Elizabeth McCullugh to Absolom H. Frier 25 April 1838 81
Sally McCullough to Henry I. Reavis 6 Nov. 1831 142

Henry McCurly to Nancy Levina Harris Rec. 26 July 1826 63

Page 397 A2 Will of Hiram McCutchen
    To my three children: Nelly, Alice, and Freeman...
    To Laura Mayo, aunt of my children...
    John M. McCutchen, Exe.
Written: 26 December 1867   Recorded: 10 March 1868
Witnesses: William Harriman and B. W. Green
Page 390 A2 Will of John McCutchen
    To my daughters: Ann Eliza Houx, Mary Jane McGoowin, Marinda Ann Bell, and America M. Witherspoon...
    To my son, John M. ...
    To my four grandchildren, Alonzo W., Mary Ellen, Eliza Jane, and Luella W., minor heirs of my deceased son, James C. .
Continued--

Will of John McCutchen Continued

    To my tow grandchildren, Sarah E. Fields, now Sarah E. Caldwell and Harriett Fields...

    To my grandson, Henry C. Glass, son of my daughter, Ann Eliza Houx, provided he should return from California to Missouri within five years after my death...

    John H. McCutchen, Exe.

Written: 3 January 1861

Witnesses: Jonas Brownfield, Oliver Zeller, Samuel Roe, Sr., W. P. Harriman, and William Harriman

Codicil

    The said Henry, son of Ann Eliza Houx died in Calif.

    I have given to my grand-daughter, Harriett S. Fields, now McCartney...

    I have given to my grandson, Alonzo W. McCutchen...

Written: 4 October 1866   Recorded: 8 November 1867

Witnesses: Frank G. McCutchen and William Harriman

A. McCutchen to Miss A. A. Sloan 27 Nov. 1848 3
Alfred McCutchen to Mary B. Weir 26 Aug. 1832 159
America Missouri McCutchen to Finis Anderson Witherspoon 19 Sept. 1850 33
Dean McCutchen to Patsy Ewing Sloan Given 27 Oct. 1829 109
Harriett S. McCutchen to John Walker Fields 11 July 1837 70
James C. McCutchen to Sarah Morris 3 Oct. 1844 210
James B. McCutchen to Sarah Ann Williams 4 Oct. 1832 160
John S. McCutchen to Fannie W. Tutt 17 Aug. 1847 239
Robert McCutchen to Nancy Young 20 Dec. 1831 144

Alfred McDaniel to Permelia Beck 2 Jan. 1849 6
Amos McDaniel to Dinna Smith 2 March 1845 187
Harvey McDaniel to Egley Ann Boulton 19 Oct. 1835 43
John McDaniel to Mary Sharp McClanahan 15 Feb. 1841 125
Mary A. McDaniel to Sidney Smith 30 Aug. 1840 265
Samuel McDaniel to Susannah R. Johnson 12 Sept. 1830 123
Sarah Ann McDaniel to John McClanahan 28 Nov. 1844 102
William McDaniel to Caty Fisher 16 March 1820 11
William McDaniel to Mary Conner 8 Feb. 1835 46

Abraham McDonald to Sally Parker 16 Aug. 1825 53
Hiram McDonald to Susan Parker 16 Aug. 1825 53

Mary McDonel to Ambrose Canada 25 Jan. 1827 69

James McDowell to Rachel McGee 7 June 1827 79
Susan McDowell to James Miller 23 Nov. 1843 165

John McDuffee to Lucinda Harris 29 June 1845 191

Archibald McDuffin to Sarah Woods 17 Jan. 1850 30
    Mr. McDuffin is of Macon County, Mo.

Page 19 A2   Will of John McElroy
     To my wife, Elizabeth...
     To my daughters: Mary Ann and Elizabeth...
     To my sons: Samuel, George, and John...
Written: 25 October 1846   Recorded: 12 December 1846
Witnesses: S. A. Summers and Samuel Roe

Page 123 A   Will of William B. McFarland
     To my wife, Nancy...
     To my sons: Joseph, John Howard, William Riley, and
Andrew Jackson...
     To my daughters: Sarah Steele, Lucinda, Polly Ann,
Sofia Caroline, and Rebecaka Louisa...
Written: 7 January 1839   Recorded: 6 February 1840
Witnesses: William Steele and William D. Vance
Alexander McFarland to Sary Hix 10 Aug. 1821 22
Amanda McFarland to Henry Webster 20 April 1835 28
Benjamin F. McFarland to Sary Ritchardson Given 3 Dec. 1830 132
Cynthy Ann McFarland to Peyton Erbrow 22 May 1849 17
David McFarland to Susan Ross 28 Jan. 1826 67
Elijah McFarland to Frances Hix 8 March 1821 22
Elizabeth McFarland to Brackstrom Hill 2 May 1849 15
Elizabeth Ann McFarland to William Rankin 4 April 1844 175
Elly McFarland to William Tucker 31 August 1826 66
Houston McFarland to Zelah Crawford 25 Oct. 1841 134
Hustand McFarland to Susan Davis 29 Aug. 1839 99
Huston McFarland to Eliza Crawford 7 Jan. 1835 28
Isaac Barton McFarland to Adaline George 2 July 1845 191
James McFarland to Polly Jones 16 Oct. 1832 156
John McFarland to Nancy Morris 1 July 1824 40
Julia McFarland to Isiah P. Smithers 31 Dec. 1845 199
Lucinda McFarland to Samuel Glass 28 Nov. 1827 70
Lucinda McFarland to John J. Carpenter 12 April 1840 111
Mahala McFarland to William Davis 30 Jan. 1823 40
Margaret L. McFarland to Isiah P. Srithers 21 Oct. 1841 133
Mary A. A. McFarland to James McCarty 2 Oct. 1836 87
Nancy McFarland to Alexander Stone 1 Dec. 1829 111
Nancy Ellen McFarland to James M. Allcorn 5 Feb. 1846 203
Oliver J. McFarland to Elvira M. Lovelace 27 June 1848 261
Polly McFarland to James Hill 1 Oct. 1821 27
Polly A. McFarland to James Hughes 18 Sept. 1848 4
Reuben McFarland to Alvirah George 13 Sept. 1827 84
Sally McFarland to Reubin George 1 April 1821 27
Samuel McFarland to Jane Morrow 15 Sept. 1824 50
Samuel P. McFarland to Mary A. Stephens 19 Oct. 1841 134
William McFarland to Lucinda Riggs 3 Jan. 1830 112
William Kelly McFarland to Mary Ann Moan 7 Oct. 1846 221
Elizabeth McGauchlin to Fenepe B. Carthea 28 Oct. 1845 200

David McGee to Elizabeth Boolen 14 July 1825 54
James McGee to Sarah Couder 5 Feb. 1850 26
Rachel McGee to John Stean 4 May 1826 61
Rachel McGee to James McDowell 7 June 1827 79
Robert McGee to Sarah McPerson 4 Jan. 1829 104

Margaret McGuire to John Parker 23 Dec. 1836 47
Sarah McGuire to William Woods Given 10 Oct. 1828 96
Thos McGuire to Mira M. Pollard 3 Nov. 1835 44
Timothy McGuire to Lidia Shoemaker 20 March 1845 190

James McIntosh to Mary T. Henry 28 Aug. 1846 219

Andrew P. Mckee to Sarinda Boyd 15 Dec. 1836 55

Francis McKenny to Elizabeth Jones 25 July 1832 156
Lucinday McKenney to Hiram Howard 3 June 1830 119

Kenneth McKensey to Eliza Smith 13 Jan. 1828 68

Page 204 A2 Will of Jesse Melson McMahan
    To my brother, Robert Davis McMahan...
    To my sister, Araminta, wife of John H. Sutherland...
    To my sisters: Melissa A., Sophia T., Azenith, wife of Robert K. Taylor; Louisa L., wife of John C. Oldham, Saline County, Mo.
    Robert McMahan, Exe.
Written: 14 April 1857   Recorded: 11 June 1857
Witnesses: William W. Goodrich, 42 Willowbly St., Brooklyn, N. Y. Office 74 Wall Street, New York City
    E. H. Phillips, 15 Light Street N. Y. New York City
Page 7 A   Will of Thomas McMahan, Senior of the Arrow Rock Twnship
    To my wife, Diana...
    My daughter, Elizabeth McGee, dec.
    My daughters: Mary and Susannah...
    To my sons: Samuel, Thomas, and James
    Thomas and James, Exe.
Written: 21 Jan. 1821   Recorded: 9 April 1821
Witnesses: Peyton Nowlin, Bryan T. Nowlin, and Peyton W. Nowlin
Page 166 A2 Will of Thomas McMahan
    To my wife, Margaret...
    To my daughters: Amelia E. Lewis, Janetta Piper, Samenda Bingham, Susan Brown, Louiza Jenkins, and Margaret J. McMahan...
    To my sons: Samuel G., William H. C., James, George, and Jesse...
    Jesse McMahan, Exe.
Written: 27 Dec. 1854   Recorded: 20 August 1855
Witnesses: N. C. Miller and L. L. Cooper

Acenith McMahan to Robert Taylor 27 June 1839 98
Araminta McMahan to John H. Sutherland 22 March 1838 76
Henry C. McMahan to Mildred Turley 23 Nov. 1848 3
John McMahan to Polly Millsap 27 Oct. 1836 63
John M. McMahan to Elzira Turley 19 April 1832 151
Saminda A. McMahan to Henry V. Bigham 31 March 1850 30
Samuel McMahan and Martha Miller 3 Dec. 1833 16
Samuel W. McMahan to Harriett Riddle 17 March 1833 2
Thomas McMahan, Jr. to Lucy Riddle 25 March 1830 115
William McMahan to Sarah Huston 5 Jan. 1826 56

Peter McMicle to Sarah A. Potter 20 Feb. 1844 171

Ann McNee to Joseph Stephens 17 Feb. 1825 72

Elizabeth McNeel to James Dell 13 Jan. 1826 60

Page 428 A2 Will of Edward D. McPherson
　　To my wife, Mary J. ...
　　To my daughters: Sarah Ann Hopkins, Cornelia Douglass, wife of John T. Douglass, and Louisa Ross, wife of William A. Ross...
　　To my sons: Edward D. and Henry...
　　To my grandchildren: Cornelia Douglas Hopkins, Lula Hopkins, Mary Hopkins, and Maria Hopkins...
　　John T. Douglas and Henry, my son, Exe.
Written: 2 December 1869   Recorded: 20 January 1870
Witnesses: E. Stanley, Robert B. Bacon, and James M. Nelson
Benjamin McPherson, Morgan Co., Mo. to Sarah Ann Woods,
　　daughter of Green Woods 8 Dec. 1839 105
Cornelia McPherson to J. T. Douglass 8 April 1847 236
E. D. McPherson to Mrs. Mary Young 6 Dec. 1842 153
Sarah McPherson to Robert McGee 4 Jan. 1829 104

Jeremiah Meadows to Anne Music 26 June 1819 2

Page 299 A2 Will of Catherine Meier
　　To my daughters: Christina, wife of Christian Andri and Caroline, wife of D. H. Kalkman...
　　To my son, Joseph A. Manhard...
　　Joseph Eppstein, Exe.
Written: 7 June 1860   Recorded: 25 June 1861

Isaac Mellott to Luelda Merton 25 Dec. 1849 25
Nancy Mellott to Joseph W. Dunn 21 Jan. 1845 185

Catharine Johnson Menifee to Wesley John Munylan
　　17 Aug. 1847 248
Mary Susan Menifee to Thornton Padget Bell 25 March 1847 234

Page 88 A
Will of Absolem Meredith
    To my wife, Polly...
    To my children: Mary M. Meredith, Rachael McFarlin, Sarah Graham, Thomas Meredith, Susan J. Meredith, and Absolem Meredith, and Joseph R. K. Meredith...
Written: 16 March 1835   Recorded: 6 June 1835
Witnesses: Azariah Bone and Samuel Roe
Absolem Meredith to Nancy Moss 2 Nov. 1843 164
Andrew T. Meredith to Polly Thomas 16 June 1846 213
Joseph R. K. Meredith to Elizabeth T. Moss 26 June 1844 210
Martha Meredith to Thomas C. Berry 10 Dec. 1849 23
Mary Meredith to David S. Hill 27 Feb. 1840 107
Sally Meredith to Noah Graham 11 March 1830 117
Susan J. Meredith to Peter H. Ferrill 9 March 1836 48
Thomas Meredith to Susanna Wooldridge 23 Aug. 1832 155

Mary Hannah Merrill to Charles West, at the residence of
    Wilson Merrill 10 Aug. 1841 129
Sarah Barton Merrill to John Coleman Ronald at the residence
    of Willson Merrill 24 Jan. 1843 151

Luelda Merton to Isaac Mellott 25 Dec. 1849 25

George Mett to Mrs. Sarah Jorden 11 Aug. 1845 191

John I. Meyer to Edetha Robinson 24 Dec. 1846 227

Jonathan Mickel to Mary Bowlin 19 Aug. 1835 36

Henry Middleton to Nancy Roberts, both of Simeon Co., Ky.
    8 April 1848 255

Hardy Midlin to Winney Scott 27 Nov. 1833 17

Sarah S. Miles to John W. Winders 2 Sept. 1847 239

Page 190 A2
Will of George Miller
    To my wife, Margaret...
    To my daughters: Louisa and Sophia...
    To my father in law, Christian Kohler, administrator
Written:
Witnesses: W. Sohrock, Hermann Becker, and Jocob Maurhuffer
Recorded: 1 November 1856
Page 152 B
Will of John Miller
    To my nephew, James Miller, Saline Co., Mo. land Called "Douglass" being in St. Louis County.
Continued--

Will of John Miller Continued

To my nephew John Miller, of Cooper county, land called "The Hurricane" lying in Howard Co., Mo. near Glasgow.

To Nancy Miller Lowry, daughter of Dr. John J. Lowry, of Howard Co., Mo. property situated on the southwest corner of the public square in the town of Fayette; also another lot in Fayette purchased of Benjamin Holliday.

To Mrs. Holliday, wife of Benjamin Holliday and her heirs forever when Alfred Bassey, the father of the said Mrs. Holliday shall convey all his rights...

Unto my nephew, William Miller, son of James Miller, Sr. of Ohio, land in St. Louis Co., Mo.

To Richard Miller, my nephew and son of James Miller of Ohio, land in Cooper Co.

To my nephew, James Parks, of Ohio, land in the town of Steuberville, Jefferson Co., Ohio.

To my Negro man called "Commodore" his freedom.

To James Miller, land in Howard Co.

To my friend, Dr. George Penn of Saline Co., Mo. real estate in Arrow Rock.

Unto my friend, James W. Smith, of Saline Co., Mo. real estate in Arrow Rock.

Unto my brother, James Miller, of Ohio, promissory note..

To my nephew, Joseph Miller, of Philadelphia, son of James Miller, of Ohio, the sum of $3000.

To my friend, Alonzo W. Manning, of St. Louis, Mo. land near St. Louis, which I hold in common with Col. John O'Fallon and my diamond breast pin which I usually wear.

To my friend, Mrs. Martha Mitchell of St. Louis, $150 to purchase a suitable momento of me.

To my friend, Mrs. Catherine Graham, wife of Major Richard Graham of St. Louis Co. the sum of $150, to purchase a suitable Momento of me.

To my friend Major Richard Graham my gold watch, chain, and seal.

To my friend, Col. John O'Fallon $100. to purchase a suitable momento of me.

To my sister Elizabeth Parks of Pennsylvania ¼ of the money remaining.

To my sister Jane Parks ¼ of my money remaining.

To the surviving children of my sister, Mary Lowry, dec. ¼ of the money remaining.

To my brother, James Miller of Ohio ¼ of my money remaining.

To John Miller Wilds, of Howard Co., Mo., son of Robert Wilds, 100 acres of land in Pike Co., Mo. commonly called "Eastin Tract" from Miles to Clarksville.

John O'Fallon, Richard Graham, Dr. John J. Lowry, James Miller, and Alonzo W. Manning, Exe.

Written: 27 March 1846   Recorded: 5 June 1846
Witnesses: Peter Ferguson, St. Louis Co., William H. Grimolds, Michael Hefferman, and John Graham

Page 371 A2
Will of Theobald Miller
   To Alias Bolin and his wife, Mena; Elizabeth Warner; Catherine Hazel; Margaret Ganier; Susa Miller: and John Miller..
Written: 14 February 1863   Recorded: 6 June 1866
Witnesses: G. H. Meyer and L. Nantz

Alexander S. Miller to Polly Cathey 1 March 1829 100
Ann Miller to Joriah Wood 21 Oct. 1824 46
Barnett Miller to Joel K. Briscoe 30 Oct. 1837 73
Betsey Miller to James McCartey 31 Oct. 1822 38
Charles Lewis Miller to Mary Ann Kelly 10 Nov. 1845 195
Eliza B. Miller to A. C. Goodin 29 Dec. 1840 123
Elizabeth Miller to Cornelius Cowen 22 March 1827 75
Elizabeth Miller to Jesse Shirley 17 Dec. 1835 40
Emily Miller to Clinton Young 23 Oct. 1831 137
G. T. Miller to Mrs. A. B. Houx 17 Dec. 1849 27
James Miller, Cole Co., Mo. to Susan McDowell 23 Nov. 1843 165
Jerry W. Miller to Jenac Roberts 7 Jan. 1832 140
John Miller to Elizabeth Rogers 104
John K. H. Miller to Sarah Gabriel 23 Nov. 1826 96
K. W. Miller to Nancy L. Parsons 14 Aug. 1844 179
Martha Miller to Samuel McMahan 3 Dec. 1833 16
Milton Miller to Lydia Caldwell 6 Jan. 1831 129
Nancy Miller to James Mahan 8 Feb. 1829 102
Peter Miller to Mary L. Ellis 10 March 1845 185
Polly Miller to James Boiles 28 Dec. 1836 57
Rebecca Miller to Strawther O'Roarke 3 Nov. 1842 151
Robert Miller to Nancy Bennett 10 Jan. 1850 26
Selvina Ardilon Miller to Eli Farris 3 Nov. 1837 55
Susan Miller to John W. Huse 8 Feb. 1848 252
T. A. Miller to Helen E. Walgenbach 7 April 1845 188
Thomas K. Miller to Mary Jane Houx 8 Jan. 1832 142
William Miller to Sally Mulky 31 Aug. 1820 16
William Miller to Polly Carpenter 14 July 1827 80
William Miller to Miss Boler 3 Nov. 1843 300
William Miller to Sarah Dodds 12 April 1846 212
William A. Miller to Agnes C. Mitchell 21 Jan. 1823 40
Young E. Miller to Emily Barnes 31 Aug. 1831 138

America Mills to Enoch McClanahan 2 Aug. 1838 85
Henry Mills to Susan Lewis 20 Aug. 1840 114
Mary S. Mills to William F. Lawrence 13 Feb. 1839 94

Barbary Millsap to Clark Johnson 1 Jan. 1826 54
Maniel Millsap to Katy Baker 25 May 1826 64
Polly Millsap to John McMahan 27 Oct. 1836 63
Riley Millsap to Nancy Jane Campbell 22 Nov. 1836 58
Robert Millsap to Zulley Moon 10 Dec. 1830 136
Mrs. Zulica Millsap to Isaac Clark 29 Dec. 1836 57

Charlotte Millum to Thomas Millum 6 Oct. 1844 170
Thomas Millum to Charlotte Millum 6 Oct. 1844 170

Rush Milman to Mary Jane Thomas 19 Sept. 1849 20

Blanche A. Minzen to U. A. Smith 29 March 1846 206

Agnes Mitchell to John Fine 30 Sept. 1826 75
Agnes C. Mitchell to William A. Miller 21 Jan. 1823 40
Charles D. Mitchell to Mary Hughes 18 Oct. 1843 162
Elizabeth Mitchell to William H. Tucker 7 Oct. 1846 220
Lucy Mitchell to Roderick Ramsey Mills 6 June 1843 156
Martha Mitchell to William Calvert, Jr. 26 July 1837 73
William Mitchell to Eliza Carrell 24 Dec. 1829 117
William Mitchell to Martha Ann Morrow 20 June 1846 260

Jeremiah Mize to Martha W. Lawlin 3 Sept. 1848 7
Nancy Mize to James Briles 7 Oct. 1849 24

Elijah Mock to Mary Shackleford 12 June 1824 46

Mary Jane Moldan to John L. Glazebrook 23 Oct. 1828 101

James L. Moody to Nancy C. James 6 Sept. 1849 18
Martha Ann Moody to Josephus Ross 29 Aug. 1849 18

Ann Moon to James W. Road 13 Dec. 1849 23
Delila Moon to Moses Heath 8 Jan. 1826 55
Elizabeth Moon to Henry C. King 13 Jan. 1846 252
Jasper Moon to Nancy Cathey 11 Sept. 1831 137
Jesse Moon to Mary Gillum 2 March 1820 89
Partheny Moon to Stephen O. Howell 23 Oct. 1836 55
Vireeaney Moon to Huston Makely 10 Oct. 1839 100
Zulley Moon to Robert Millsap 10 Dec. 1830 136

Charles Moore to Martha Ann English 27 July 1846 265
George Moore to Frances Stephens 24 May 1827
Henry E. Moore to Mariah Dunn 9 July 1836 63
Isaac Moore to Eidia White 10 Jan. 1833 19
James Moore to Ann Patrick 13 Dec. 1832 161
James Moore to Polly Deaking 24 Dec. 1832 1
Joseph Moore to Martha Ann Richie 3 Oct. 1844 26
Joseph H. Moore to Mary A. McCarty 24 Jan. 1850 26
Margaret Moore to Lawrence Stephens 24 Sept. 1820 22
Mrs. Mary Ann Moore to William Lewis 23 May 1850 32
Rachael S. Moore to Jacob E. Stafford 18 July 1843 161
Roady Ann Moore to William F. Martin 12 Aug. 1841 129
Robert C. Moore to Elizabeth R. Corum 19 Oct. 1843 166
Sarah Moore to John Johnson 24 Dec. 1820 22
Thomas Moore to Lucinda Derrill 3 July 1829 106
William Moore to Matilda Smith 30 June 1836 53

Henry Moreland to Martha Ann Ferguson 26 Nov. 1841 138
James Moreland to Katherine Smiley 7 July 1828 92
John Moreland to Ann Farris 10 Feb. 1825 72

Page 144 A2
Will of William Morgan
    To my sons: James W. and John H. ...
    To my wife, Nancy...
Written: 14 September 1854   Recorded: 30 Jan. 1855
George W. West and James D. Franklin
St. Clair Morgan to Sarah Seat, daughter of G. Seat 3 Oct. 1837
Joseph Morgan to Elvina _____ 31 Oct. 1834 23

Page 113 A2
Will of Eri Morley
    To my wife, ...
    To my daughters: Lidda Faris and Roxey Calvert...
    To my son, John...
    My son in law, Simon Calvert and son, John, Exe.
Written: 18 November 1853   Recorded: 25 November 1853
John J. Morley to Matilda Doyle 28 Oct. 1837 74
Lydia Morley to Thomas W. C. Faris 8 Oct. 1826 65
Rocksey Morley to Leonard Calvert 4 Dec. 1829 103

Page 150 A2
Will of Hammond Morris
    To my daughter, Malinda Baxter, wife of Hugh Baxter...
    To my daughter, Susannah Tevis, wife of Snoden Tevis...
    To my daughter, Charlotte White, wife of Jesse White...
    To my daughter, Lucinda Porter, wife of Green L. Porter...
    To my grand daughter, Susan Amanda Woods, daughter of John Woods...
    To my grand daughter, Darkas Pully, wife of Lorenzo D. Pully
    To my daughter, Rebecca Braly, wife of Josiah Braly...
    To my daughter, Martha Kernzy, wife of Thomas Kernzy...
    To my daughter, Elizabeth Kernzy, wife of Benjamin Kernzy..
    Charles H. Brooking, John Woods, and Jesse White, Exe.
Written: 1843   Recorded: 28 September 1859
Goolsby Woods and John Ashcraft
David Morris to Lucy Smith 16 Aug. 1835 32
Elizabeth Morris to James James 2 May 1841 127
Hugh Baxter Morris to Mary Jane Wiley 25 March 1846 207
Isabel Morris to Howard Hayes 29 Oct. 1829 110
Lotty Morris to Jesse White 29 Oct. 1833 19
Margaret Morris to Joseph Fry 4 Jan. 1849 7
Lucinda Morris to Green Porter 22 Dec. 1836 60
Martha Morris to George W. Bosley 12 July 1836 59
Nancy Morris to John McFarland 1 July 1824 48
Nancy Morris to ___ Arnold 26 Nov. 1833 19
Thomas J. Morris to Jane Scott 8 Sept. 1831 136

Page 399 A2
Will of Levi R. Morrison
    To my wife, Martha F. ...
    To my son, William L. ...
    To the heirs of my son, Aanze D., dec. ...
    To the heirs of my deceased daughter, Emily E. Harlan...
    Martha F. and William L., Exe.
Written: 6 June 1867   Recorded: 14 February 1868
Witnesses: Edward Chilton and John J. Hoge
Abby C. Morrison to Joseph B. Steel   15 Oct. 1827   83
Nathaniel Morrison to Rodo Blasgane   13 Dec. 1826   99
Stubblefield Morrison to Elizabeth Dinwiddie   12 Dec. 1830   129

Jane Morrow to Samuel McFarland   15 Sept. 1824   50
Jane Morrow to A. J. Rothrock   11 Jan. 1849   5
Margaret Morrow to Phillip Houx   14 Sept. 1824   48
Martha Ann Morrow to William Mitchell   20 June 1848   260

Page 198 A2   Will of George W. Morton
    To my wife, Emily S. ...
    To my sons: John M. and George W. ...
    To my daughters: Elizabeth S. Sloan, Jane H. Ingram,
Ann T. Stockton, Mary Redwood, Matilda J., Emily C. Morton,...
    To William W. Morris, a friend...
    To my sister, Elizabeth Morton...
    To my grandchildren: Elizabeth Mattie and Mattie S.
Phillipson...
    John McCutchen, Exe. and Washington Adams, Attorney
Written: 10 November 1855   Recorded: 17 March 1857
Witnesses: R. D. Perry, Samuel J. Tutt, and William W. Morris
Ann Thompson Morton to Richard Garnett Stockton   30 Jan. 1844
Jane H. Morton to Jacob Ingram   22 Nov. 1842   153
Mary McNair Morton to Edward Redwood   3 Jan. 1843   150

Elizabeth T. Moss to Joseph R. K. Meredith   26 June 1844   210
Nancy Moss to Absolem Meredith   2 Nov. 1843   164

Will of Mary Murphy   Page 153 A
    To my son, James H. ...
Written: 16 February 1841   Recorded: 3 Sept. 1841
Witnesses: James H. Glasgow and William Steele

Martha H. Mucker to Howard D. English   25 Dec. 1849   25

Charles R. Muggah to Sarah U. Ferriott   23 July 1846   215

Wer Muir to Thomas Talbot   23 May 1848   250

Elizabeth Mulky to Charles Howard   26 April 1820   14
Sally Mulky to William Miller   31 Aug. 1820   16

NOTES

Elizabeth Mullins to James Kelly 17 Aug. 1839 101
Frances Mullins to William D. Hampton 9 Nov. 1823 44
Luvancy Mullins to Joseph Quinn 29 March 1840 113
Mowrany Mullins to Absalom Huff 20 Jan. 1820 10
Patsy Mullins to John Backster 16 July 1820 16
Sally Mullins to John Woolf 26 Nov. 1832 165

Cumadurs Mulum to Delaney Jarvis 12 Aug. 1845 196

David C. Munday, Clark Co., Ky. to Sarah Ann Pigg 22 Nov. 1849

F. B. Murdock to Mary Ann Graham 13 Nov. 1844 185

Micajah Murphy to Jane Green 20 June 1841 129

Hiram Murray to Mary D. Puckitt 25 Feb. 1830 114
William D. Murray to Sally W. Renick 24 Oct. 1820 114

Anne Music to Jeremiah Meadows 28 June 1819 2

John Christopher Musin to Elanor McClanahan 6 Oct. 1849 21

Henry Mark Meyers to Harriet Elizabeth Hickok 2 Nov. 1842 148

Henry Nabring to Mary Biscoss 5 Aug. 1844 173

Sally Nanney to William Jolly 12 March 1826 61

John Nanson to Jane Cartner 11 June 1822 32

John W. Nash of Virginia to Mary Frances Jones 16 May 1841 126

Henry Nauman to Martha Hoffman 1 Nov. 1849 24

Henry Nave, Saline Co., Mo. to Amanda Church 30 April 1846 208
Nancy Nave to William White 5 March 1820 13

Ellen Neal to John Burk 16 July 1847 237
Malinda Neal to Benjamin Gilbert 27 June 1843 159
Mary Neal to Benjamin Gilbert 19 Dec. 1838 91
Rev. Minnor Neal to Nancy Amick 18 Aug. 1842 145
Nancy E. Neal to George W. Smith 2 Aug. 1848 264
Nathan Neal to Elizabeth Stone 23 March 1826 56
Sarah Neal to James W. Brindin 26 May 1840 111
Thomas Neal to Elizabeth H. Foster 27 Nov. 1850 35

William Neely to Mary M. McClanahan 5 Sept. 1833 8

Page 136 A2 Will of George Neff
    To my son, Jacob...
    To my son, Peter...
    To my wife, Cuaricel...
    Jacob Neff, Exe.
Written: 5 Aug. 1854   Recorded: 13 November 1854
Witnesses: Phillip H. Stahl, J. G. Roller, and C. H. Roller
Henry Jacob Neff to Elizabeth Know 15 Jan. 1850 31

Gaberelah Nelson to Anderson W. Harris 25 Jan. 1844 168
James Nelson to Margaret J. Nelson 10 Nov. 1847 246
Luraney Nelson to Joseph Williams 4 March 1847 227
Margaret J. Nelson to James Nelson 10 Nov. 1847 246
Mariah Nelson to Andrew McClanahan 26 Dec. 1839 105
Thomas H. Nelson to Mary L. Wyan 12 Dec. 1837 76

Joseph H. Nep to Parthena W. Kelly 27 Feb. 1840 107

James F. Newbold to Elizabeth Bowen 16 March 1841 125

Harrison Newkirk of Morgan Co., Mo. to Martha J. Renshaw 24 Dec. 1840 121

Jesse Newman to Elizabeth Hill 25 Feb. 1846 202

Moses Andrew Jackson Nexon to Lucinda Wooten 30 Dec. 1832 167

Mary Ann Noah to William Nelly McFarland 7 Oct. 1846 221

Page 6 A2 Will of T. W. Noel
    To the children of my brother, Dr. James H. Noel, formerly of Essex Co., Va. ...
    To my brother, Robert S. Noel, also of Va.
    To the children of my sister Fanny Macey, dec. of lately consort to Gustavus S. Macey of Franklin Co., Ky.
    To my nephew, Theodorick I. Macey...
    To my nephew, Robert Macey...
Written: 27 November 1847   Recorded: 21 Jan. 1848
Witnesses: George W. Phillips and Thomas Hanna

Henry L. Norfu to Elizabeth Eckhard 23 Dec. 1849 24

Richard A. Norman to Virginia H. Wear 19 Feb. 1846 205

Sarah Norris to James C. McCutchen 3 Oct. 1844 210
William W. Norris to Sarah E. Spenny 10 May 1846 209

Jacob Noryer to Elizabeth Snyer 3 March 1846 209

George Novel to Levisa Boyd 14 May 1839 96

Page 269 A2
Will of John Norton of Lexington, Kentucky
   To my brother in law, Jacob Updegraff,...
   To the sons and daughters of my nephew, William H. Norton towit Emma D. Norton, George D. Norton, Washington Norton, and John Norton...
   To my sister Patty Gallagher, wife of James Gallagher and to her daughter in law the widow of Augustus Gallagher...
   To my sister, Julia Ann Norton...
   To my brother, Jeshuwa Norton...
   To Elizabeth Norton, wife of George W. Norton...
   To Mary E. O'rear, daughter of Thomas C. O'rear...
   To my brother, George...
   To Mrs. Mourning Nanny, widow of my brother, Henry, my farm in Madison County, Tenn. near Jackson.
   To my nephew, George W. Norton and his wife, Elizabeth, of Lexington...
   To my friend, John Clarke and his wife my niece, Maria L. Clarke...
   To my niece, Mrs. S. G. Orear...
Written: 5 Feb. 1858   Recorded: 16 May 1860
Witnesses: F. R. Hunt, S. B. Todd, and Farius A. Grimstead

James M. Newlett to Ann Eliza S. Peyton 13 Oct. 1846 221-

James Monroe Nugent to Virginia M. James 26 Nov. 1850 35
Mary Ann Nugent to Orville Newman 14 June 1846 212
Sarah Jane Nugent to John M. Stone 5 Dec. 1850 36

Page 255 A2
Will of Turner O'Bryan
   To my wife, Elizabeth...
   To my daughter, Evaline Farris...
   To my sons: Redick, William J., Caleb H., Dixon, Turner, and Jorden...
   J. L. O'Bryan, Exe.
Written: 10 October 1859
Witnesses: Edmond P. Elliott and James T. O'Bryan
Caleb O'Brien to Catherine Robertson 16 Aug. 1849 22
Caroline F. O'Bryan to Jacob Devaul 10 Oct. 1847 241
Cornelia O'Bryan to Oscar Wright 6 May 1846 200
Emilee O'Brian to Alfred Masquierier 26 Feb. 1837 67
Evalina O'Bryan to E. Farris 21 April 1849 11
James O'Brian to Virginia Dastable 26 June 1846 212
John O'Bryan to Mary Reavis 14 Aug. 1834 23
Jorden T. O'Bryan to Amelia Reavis 1 Oct. 1835 32
Robert O'Bryan to Martha Adams 22 Feb. 1846 255
Sama O'Bryan to Henry Elliott 20 Oct. 1847 242

Emaline K. O'Dell to Thomas George 16 Dec. 1847 249

Jonathan C. Odle to Emily Boyd   21 May 1832   151

Mary Ann Odinele to Thomas Doran   22 Dec. 1843   155

Hugh O'Donnell to Eliza J. Cartey   3 May 1847   231

Dimretta Ogle to William B. Jones   11 Feb. 1841   122

Amanda Susan Oglesby to William Calbert   23 April 1843   157
Malvina Oglesby to William Knaus   26 Oct. 1843   165
Martha Ann Oglesby to Jesse Fields   14 Nov. 1833   12
Mary Ann Oglesby to Finis E. Wear   27 Nov. 1834   26
Martha Jane Oglesby to David Eller   9 Dec. 1847   245
Nimrod Oglesby to Mary Jane McClean   26 March 1839   93
Eliza Oglesby to John Marquis Henry   26 Oct. 1842   150
Pleasant G. Oglesby to Lilly Woolery   24 Jan. 1833   16

Elizabeth O'Herrel to James Lewis   16 Sept. 1848   1

Margaret O'Howell to James H. Hongerford   1 May 1843   157
Stephen O'Howell to Partheny Moon   23 Oct. 1836   55

Page 10 A2
Will of Charles O'Neal
    To my wife, Anis...
    To my children: William, Nancy, Nathan, Edward, Sally now Sally Calvert, Ellen now Kirkpatrick, and the heir James Gilbert infant heir of Mary, late Mary Gilbert, and Elijah...
    Anis O'Neal, Exe.
Written: 9 March 1841   Recorded: 15 April 1848
Witnesses: George P. Harlan and Joseph H. Harlan

Trussey O'Rear to Betsy Jane Davis   14 May 1835   29

Strawther O'Roarke to Rebecca Miller   3 Nov. 1842   151

Page 129 A2   Will of Joseph Ormrod
    I direct my personal property and interest shall first be sold at public sale, as demand most advantages to my executors with the exception of my books and manuscripts which I request may be divided among my children by my first wife as they or my two daughters may agree on bestowing them at their option upon their half brother, George such as they may think will be useful to him.
    Such other of my personal property which can not be divided among my children Mary, Amanda, and Joseph I direct to be sold in all events.
    To my son, George by my present wife $300. to be invested as my executors may see fit.
Continued--

Will of Joseph Ormrod Continued

To my children by my first wife Mary, Amanda, and Joseph...
I will only say further that it is not my wish that a son of mine should be placed behind a counter where he will be apt to become familiarized with arts of deception. With his mind intent only on frivolities and have his intellect annihilated nor is it my wish that he should become a member of any of the so called professions and left with a decided predilection for some of them. He should appear to have a mind particularly adapted to its exercise and for unswerving success in it. An unmistakable predilection and fitness for any pursuit in life should in my opinion be disregarded.

And further should my son, Joseph, when he has attained twenty one years in life have contracted habits of idleness and dissipation or either of them then I will he shall receive only one tenth of the part that might otherwise be coming to him and that the residue of his sister, Mary.

I make no provision for my present wife in this my last will and testament in consideration of her personal and other estate which would have been invested in me by our marriage having been second to her for her separate use by our marriage contract.

My friends, Washington Adams and Jordan O'Bryan, Exe.
Written: 7 ___ 1854   Recorded: 26 August 1854
Witnesses: James McCuthen and John S. C. Hogan

James Ormrod to Eliza Ann Hickman 7 Jan. 1847 226

John Otten to Joahannah Westerman 18 Jan. 1849 6

Dr. H. Pace to Lucretia Hart 11 July 1833 4

Ira Page to Susan Davis 14 Aug. 1844 179
Mary M. Page to Eli W. Hardcastle 18 Aug. 1844 176
Page 9 D   Will of Mary Palmer, of Warrenton, Fauquire Co.Va.
I bequeath a debt of $500, with the exception of the interest thereon from the fourth day of October 1821 up to the time of my death due me from Robert Brent to John Walden in trust for the sole and separate use of my daughter, Betsy Brent.

Having passed a large portion of my life in the house of Robert Brent...

I bequeath one half of the portion now due to me from the estate of my brother Septimius Norris decd to John Walden, in trust for my daughter, Betsy Brent...

I bequeath a debt of $472. from the sixth day of October 1817...due to me from Henry L. Y. Pope to John Walden in trust for the sole and separate use of my daughter,Sarah T. Pope...

To my sons in law, Robert Brent and Henry L. Y. Pope...
My friend, John Walden, Exe.
Written: 16 February 1831   Recorded: 24 January 1842
Witnesses: John Smith, Baldwin Day, and Walker M. Yeatman

James W. Palmer to Mrs. Sarah Simons 4 May 1849 24

Page 150 A   Will of Thomas Parker
    To my wife, Sarah...
    To my daughters: Martha W. and Elizabeth H. ...
    To my son, John L. ...
Written: 23 February 1837   Recorded: 5 August 1841
Witnesses: Durd Jones and William George
James Parker to Elvira Davis 24 Sept. 1837 75
John Parker to Margaret McGuire 23 Dec. 1836 47
Robert W. Parker to Margaret Wear Given 10 Sept. 1828 94
Sally Parker to Abraham McDonald 16 Aug. 1825 53
Susan Parker to Hiram McDonald 16 Aug. 1825 53
William Parker to Emily Moll 20 Aug. 1835 36

Alexander Parks to Emily M. Jones 13 July 1843 159
Bird Parks to Derindia Lee 19 March 1840 112
Catherine Parks to Labon Pigg 23 Nov. 1835 36
Catherine Parks to Joseph A. Bowles 1 Aug. 1850 32
James Parks to Elizabeth Jane Reavis 1 Jan. 1850 32
Louisa Parks to John Bebybee 30 Aug. 1839 100
Martha E. Parks to Frederick M. Duncan 10 Oct. 1839 103
Mary Parks to Jacob Bauthman 13 June 1833 10
Mary Parks to James Birdsong 1 Aug. 1839 103
Samuel Parks to Nancy Jones 16 Nov. 1826 68
Samuel Parks to Christiana Clark 7 Feb. 1833 3

Nathaniel Parrett to Mary B. Dewey 7 Oct. 1847 241
Susan Parrott to Newton Soury 28 Oct. 1847 250

Frances Parrish to John Allison 1 March 1848 252

Page 301 A2   Will of James Parsons
    To my daughters: Frances A. Glazier, Nancy S. Miller, Mary E. Wear, Martha C. Logan, Lucy C. Larry, and Louisa E. Melvin...
    To my son, William S. ...
    My son in law, Charles Glazier and William S., Exc.
Written: 24 July 1861   Recorded: 26 August 1861
Witnesses: J. M. Campbell, James P. Gabriel, Silvester Stoffler, and G. W. Logan
Frances A. Parsons to Charles Glazier 25 March 1841 136
John W. Parsons, Morgan Co., Mo. to Mildred A. Yancy
    25 Feb. 1841 124
Luny W. Parsons to Sarah Ann E. Wilkerson 2 June 1844 175
Martha C. Parsons to John W. Logan 6 May 1847 237
Mary E. Parsons to William B. Wear 22 May 1845 195
Nancy L. Parsons to K. W. Miller 14 Aug. 1844 179

William Parvy to Polly Everson 3 Jan. 1820 13

Rhodes Pascal to Mary Jane Mahan 22 Dec. 1846 225

Elicia Ann Paston to Emerson J. Stephens 1 Nov. 1847 243

Elizabeth Pate to William Stevens 9 Nov. 1846 220
Thomas Pate to Rebekah Calvert 4 April 1824 45

Page 124 B   Will of Thomas M. Patrick
    To my wife, Catharine...
    To my children...
Written: 16 April 1847   Recorded: 11 Aug. 1847
Witnesses: C. V. Gallagher and Eliza Ann Ormrod
Ann Patrick to James Moore 13 Dec. 1832 161
Arthur Patrick to Martha Cole 4 Dec. 1827 71
Elias Patrick to Susan Collins 19 Jan. 1837 61
James Patrick to Mary Jean Ponty 29 May 1826 91
Jane Patrick to Lewis Rice 29 Oct. 1833 90
Maria Patrick to John Rickets 12 Feb. 1843 154
Mary Patrick to Gravenor Lacy 24 Aug. 1837 73
Thomas Patrick to Catherine Peters 31 May 1836 53

Jane Z. Patterson to Talton T. Barnes 24 Dec. 1839 104
Nicholas Patterson to Martha Shoemaker 6 Sept. 1846 221
William I. C. Patterson to Martha Ellen Kelly 23 April 1846 207

Page 129 B   Will of David J. Patteson
    To my wife, Elizabeth H.
Written: 4 November 1843   Recorded: 6 January 1845
Witnesses: Elias E. Buckner, William P. Sterett, and Hillary Harris

A. F. Patton to Amanda Harland 16 March 1847 237

Cleveland Pain to Joel J. Conn 23 June 1835 31
James R. Payne to Lucy P. Chandler 6 Dec. 1837 76

Robert Douglas Paxton to Sydney C. Calloway 10 Nov. 1842 148

Page 437 A2 Will of Pete Peak
    To my wife, Elizabeth...
    To my daughter, Elizabeth Youngkamp...
    To my sons: Mathias, August, John, Frank, and Lawrence...
    My son in law, Bernard Young and August, Exe.
Written: 20 October 1870   Recorded: 2 November 1870
Witnesses: Henry Hews and Conrad Kirsch

Thomas H. Pearson, Howard Co., Mo. to Lucy Cartner 4 Aug. 1831 135

William Penland to Nancy Stephens 4 April 1824 71

Thomas Perry to Lerlda Reavis 23 Dec. 1846 225

Catherine Peters to Thomas T. Patrick 31 May 1836 53
David Peters to Lucy Kelly 25 July 1825 52
Priscilla Peters to Harvey Harper 8 March 1827 77
Sally Peters to Charles N. Gallagh 16 June 1840 111

William Petitt to Lucinda Cramer 8 Sept. 1839 100

Sophia Petty to John Hill 22 Sept. 1844 174

Page 182 B   Will of Ellen Peyton
    To my nieces: Caroline E. Peyton and Ann E. Bronaugh, wife of C. C. Bronaugh...
    To my nephews, William Y. Peyton and Henry E. Peyton...
    To my brother, Frederic L. Peyton...
    To my sister, Susan F. Bronaugh...
    My relation, Addison Bronaugh, Exe.
Written: 8 February 1847   Recorded: 5 August 1847
Witnesses: Barton L. Wilson and Reuben V. Harvey
Ann Eliza S. Peyton to James M. Nowlett 13 Oct. 1846 221
F. L. Peyton to Lucretia C. Ross 1841 123

Margaret Pharis to Isaac King 29 Aug. 1844 177

Willis Phips to Elizabeth Smith 28 April 1844 178

Page 80 A2   Will of George W. Phillips
    To my wife, Mary D. ...
    To my children: Lawrence Lee, Charles, William H., and Georgeann Phillips...
    To my two oldest children: Laura Lee Phillips and Charles Phillips...
    My interest of estate of Isaac Swearingen, deceased, in the county of Franklin and state of Indiana...
    Also my interest in the estate of my father, Levi Phillips, deceased of Hyattstown, Montgomery Co., state of Maryland...
    Also my interest in the estate of my mother, Elinora Phillips, wife of said Levi Phillips...
Written: 14 May 1822   Recorded: 30 October 1852
Witnesses: George S. Cockrell, Dennis McFadden, and Thomas C. Cockrell
John Phillips to Lucy Ann Tittsworth 13 June 1839 98
William Phillips to Virginia Samuel 30 March 1847 229

Page 412 A2   Will of Anthony Pierenger
    To my wife, Maria...
    To my children: Johanna, Elizabeth, Rosina, Anna, and Eva
Written: 24 September 1868   Recorded: 11 February 1869
Witnesses: F. W. Ludwig and E. Joperich M. D.

Labon Pigg to Catherine Parks 23 Nov. 1835 36
Sarah Ann Pigg to David C. Munday 22 Nov. 1849 26

John Piper to Adeline Huston 16 April 1829 103

Thomas T. Plant to Elizabeth Richie 26 Feb. 1845 188

Merrit D. Platt to Mary Margaret E. Webb 12 Dec. 1847 246

Elizabeth Flemmons to Harland Hammons 11 Nov. 1829 98
James G. Flemmons to Romea Gilbreath 10 March 1836 52
Thomas Flemmons to Polly Calvert 26 Sept. 1829 113

Page 339 A2 Will of James S. Pogue
    To my brothers: Robert C., William A., Jacob C., John, and Thomas T. ...
    To my sisters: Sarah N., Barshaba J., and Rhoda A. Pogue..
    Silas J. W. McGuire, Exe.
Written: 13 April 1859   Recorded: 8 September 1863
Witnesses: Lewis Edson and Silas M. Ross

Page 340 A2 Will of Joseph S. Poindexter
    To my wife, Martha...
    To my three sons: Thomas, John, and Shelton...
    To my daughter, Sallie Ann Wilson...
    My son, Thomas, Exe.
Witnesses: Stanard Webb and C. Breathitt
Recorded: 26 October 1863
Page 178 B Will of Peter Poindexter
    To my wife, Elizabeth...
    To my children...
Written: 10 February 1847   Recorded: 4 June 1847
Witnesses: C. W. Longan and William B. Gibbs

Mira M. Pollard to Thom McGuire 3 Nov. 1835 44

Benjamin G. Pollock to Mary Carver 18 Nov. 1841 130
Elizabeth Ann Pollock to Zechariah Green Wilson 14 June 1838 82
John Pollock to Mary Lindsay 21 July 1828 92
Louisa G. Pollock to George W. Campbell 21 Feb. 1839 93
William A. Pollock to Sarah A. Baulton 6 Aug. 1843 161

Joel Ponton to Sally Reavis 4 Jan. 1827 68

Mary Jean Ponty to James Patrick 29 May 1828 91

Ann Porter to William Flint 7 Nov. 1833 6
Green Porter to Lucinda Morris 22 Dec. 1836 60

Page 315 A2 Will of Henry S. Y. Pope
   The date of my birth as I have been informed was the 11th day of November, 1795.
   To my friend, Miss Caroline Johnson, daughter of the late C. D. W. Johnson...
   To Florida Sutherland and Sally Pope Orrick; to R. R. Thompson and Mrs. S. Y. Megginer; to Eliza Ann Bond; to Sophia Lannius; to William T. and Walker Yeatman...
   H. E. Benedict, Exe.
Written: 10 February 1862   Recorded: 12 August 1862
Witnesses: William Kinney and David Ballentine

Page 32 A Will of George Potter
   Written by Honorable Robert P. Clark, Judge of the Probate Court after verbal will had been made in presence of Justenian Williams, Joseph Ormrod, and Richard Shackleford.
   To his children: John, Samuel, Elizabeth, William, and Hannah...
   To his daughter, Mary Adison...
   To the children, Ruth Boyd, Harrison Boyd, Emily Boyd, and Serinda Boyd, children of his daughter, Frances Boyd, dec.
   To his wife, Hannah...
Recorded: 24 July 1826
Page 140 B Will of William Potter
   To my wife, Nancy...
   To my minor children...
   To my sons: James D. Potter and Abraham Potter, who has died
   To my daughter, Sarah Ann Potter...
   To my minor children: Joseph A., Mary, Major Ellen, William S., Elizabeth, John, Stephen Cole, and Thomas...
Written: 26 July 1844   Recorded: 19 Aug. 1845
Witnesses: H. L. G. Pope, Terry Rockwell, and F. R. Haydon
Abraham Potter to Betsey Bennett 10 Nov. 1842 150
Henry G. Potter to Sidney Elizabeth Kenrick 21 March 1849 12
Jane Potter to Willie P. Hamrick 8 Feb. 1844 168
Joseph A. Potter to Elizabeth Guyer 1 Sept. 1825 55
Mary Potter to John Brownfield 10 Dec. 1840 at the residence of John Potter 120
Sarah A. Potter to Peter McNicle 20 Feb. 1844 171
William Potter to Nancy Dillard 19 Nov. 1819 7
William Potter to Hannah Dewitt 14 May 1843 157

Henry P. Potts to Lucy Jane Smith 9 Jan. 1840 104
Susan C. Potts to Joseph Cline 16 April 1846 212
William Potts to Judith C. Smith 29 Sept. 1847 240

George Powell to Jerard Roberson 27 March 1849 14
Mary A. Powell to Benjamin P. Caldwell 2 March 1847 228

William Powers to Susanna Edwards 4 May 1823 42

Thomas A. Poyer to Adaline A. Ross 18 Aug. 1849 22

John H. Price to Hannah Harris 14 May 1848 259
Thomas W. F. Price to Frances N. Campbell 24 Nov. 1841 139

Tipton Prior to Susan Simmons 11 May 1847 235

Benjamin Proctor to _____ _____ 1831 139
John Proctor to Lidy Westbrook 5 Nov. 1820 19
Mary Proctor to James Hook 12 Dec. 1833 13

Isham R. Puckett to Rebecca W. Smith 25 Feb. 1844 170
Mary D. Puckett to Hiram Murray 28 Feb. 1830 114

Lorenzo D. Pulley to Demonas Cruse 22 April 1834 19

Caleb B. Purdin to Eliza Ann Rector 22 June 1831 134

Caroline Pusely to John Lamm 26 May 1836 82

Darius E. Putnam to Miss Jeffries 7 May 1849 24

George Washington Quick to Bernitte Reece 23 Jan. 1838 76
Jacob Quick to Polly Puckett 1 Jan. 1828 86
Thomas Quick to Rachel Johsnon 8 Nov. 1827 86

Hodge Raburn to Sarah Reid 22 Nov. 1822 39

Penelope Rail to John C. Whitters 4 Oct. 1842 149

Mary Raiter to George Long 7 Sept. 1842 145

Mathew H. Ralston to Elizabeth Jennings 18 Oct. 1849 21

Daniel L. Ramy, Pettis Co., Mo. to Eliza G. Rice 28 Sept. 1836

Maria Ramsey to Jesse Bigs 29 Aug. 1830 123

Margaret Randle to James Jones 1 June 1848 263

Polly Randolph to Lewis Lundford Longan 20 Dec. 1835 42

Page 171 B Will of Mathew Rankin
    To my daughters: Ann Seat and Elizabeth Scott...
    To my sons: James William and Smith...
Written: 9 Oct. 1845   Recorded: 25 August 1846
Witnesses: Henry Bear and James F. Reid
Mary S. Rankin to James Amos 27 April 1848 256
William Rankin to Elizabeth Ann McFarland 4 April 1844 172

Nancy Ransberger to Phillip Shoemaker 27 Sept. 1842 146

Page 369 A2 Will of N. J. Ransom
    To my wife, Camelia...
Written: 25 November 1865   Recorded: 14 February 1866
Witnesses: A. J. Lacy to Rufus H. Scott

Patrick Rathburn to Margaret Jane Wilkerson 9 May 1849 13

Annjalenah Ray to Arrey B. Howard 6 Jan. 1831 129
Jesse Ray to Mary Smith 219 8 Sept. 1846
John Rea to Sarah Conner 22 Feb. 1842 140

William Rayle to Sarah McCullouch 15 Dec. 1835 40

Page 358 A2
Will of Samuel Read
    To my daughter, Milly A. Mundall...
    To my son, James Thomas Read...
Written: 21 August 1865   Recorded: 23 October 1865
Gilbert Apperson, William York, Thomas A. Harris, and William H. Ellis, witnesses
Mrs. Caroline A. Read to Ewing E. Woolery 18 Oct. 1847 246
James W. Read to Ardell J. Moon 13 Dec. 1849 23
Martha C. Read to Andrew M. Moon 1 April 1841 125
Mary Read to Jeptha Duncan 31 Dec. 1834 24
Nancy B. Read to R. L. S. Bradley 22 June 1848 260
Pamelia I. Read to Horsley Red Given 15 Jan. 1831 131
Sarah F. Read to Henry R. Walker 18 March 1829 100

Mary Roanspeacher to Francis Crouse 7 Jan. 1844 166

Page 143 A Will of Andrew A. Reavis
    To my wife and children...
Written: 7 February 1841   Recorded: 8 May 1841
Witnesses: James and Abraham Jones
Page 35 A Will of David Reavis
    To my ten children: Samuel D., Rhoda Russell, William, Edward, Andrew A., Hannah Doyle, Joseph, James, Elizabeth, and Sarah...
Written: 17 Sept. 1826   Recorded: 5 October 1826
Attest: Abram Jones and William Johnson
Will of Lewis D. Reavis Page 406 A2
    To my wife, Polly...to my Brothers, Henry J. and Wm. T.
    To my sister, Mary J. O'Bryan...
Written: 20 June 1868   Recorded: 15 October 1868
Witnesses: Jacob Baughman Pisgah and William York Disgah
Page 289 Will of Susan B. Reavis
    To my daughter, Maria Louise Reavis
Written: 24 December 1860   Recorded: 18 January 1861
Witnesses: A. B. Boy, M. E. O'Bryan, and James F. Conner

Amelia Reavis to Jorden T. O'Bryan 1 Oct. 1835 32
Anderson Reavis to Sarah Berkley 4 Aug. 1836 53
Anderson W. Reavis to Susannah Conner 5 March 1844 171
Ashley L. Reavis to Catherine Bowles 20 Oct. 1835 36
Catherine Reavis to William H. Dandridge 1 May 1845 188
Elizabeth Reavis to John D. Longan 2 Sept. 1827 84
Elizabeth Reavis to John Williams 25 Oct. 1842 84
Elizabeth Jane Reavis to James Parks 1 Jan. 1850 25
Emilee Reavis to Frederick Longan 6 May 1849 13
Fenton G. Reavis to Mary Isabel Dickson 18 April 1839 98
Harriet Reavis to Ransom P. Dowman 4 Aug. 1836 63
Henry I. Reavis to Sally McCullough 6 Nov. 1831 142
Jackson J. Reavis to Zerilda H. Levins 24 May 1838 83
Joseph P. Reaves to Frances W. Briscoe 3 Jan. 1839 91
Larelda Reavis to Thomas Perry 23 Dec. 1846 225
Lewis D. Reavis to Mary Hunt 23 June 1836 52
Martha Reavis to John R. French 25 April 1843 129
Mary Reavis to John O'Bryan 14 Aug. 1834 23
Mary Catherine Reavis to William Edmons 4 Nov. 1845 197
Sally Reavis to Joel Ponton 4 Jan. 1827 68

Eliza Ann Rector to Caleb B. Purdin 22 June 1831 134
Enoch J. Rector to Parthena Jones 14 Feb. 1839 96
Lewallen Rector to Amanda Mattingly 18 Oct. 1838 90
Mary Rector to Isiah Hannah 22 Nov. 1827 87
Mary Rector to Woodson Bagwell 14 April 1847 238

Horsley Red to Pamelia I. Read Given 15 Jan. 1831 131

Edward Redwood to Mary McMair Morton 3 Jan. 1843 150

Page 361 A2 Will of Lydia R. Reece
    To my nephew, James R. Stultz...
    To my niece, Elizabeth Lydia Margaret Stultz...
    Samuel Read, Exe.
Written 22 Nov. 1865
Bernitte Reece to George Washing Quick 23 Jan. 1838 76

Page 195 A2
Will of Molly C. Reed
    To my grandson, Anthony Reed Bradley...
    To my grandsons and daughters who are the children of my
second son, William E. as follows: John Foster, Henry Walker,
and Medora Ellen Reed...
    To my sister, Nancy W. Dunn...
    To my grandson, Anthony Winston Walker...
    To my children: Anthony, James and Mary E. Walker
    My son, Anthony J., Exe.
Written: 28 Dec. 1855   Recorded: 6 March 1857
Witnesses: H. L. Walker and James M. Walker

Elizabeth Reed to Elijah Kincheloe 26 May 1840 110
Grezel Reed to Samuel Reed 13 Jan. 1825 51
James Reed to Sarah M. Jones 11 Aug. 1850 33
Jesse Reed to Margaret Henchlow 13 Aug. 1833 7
John Reed to Sarah Kirkpatrick 20 March 1823 41
Margaret J. Reed to Major J. Wilkerson 18 July 1832 153
Mary Elizabeth Reed to Anthony Smith 13 April 1831 133
Samuel Reed to Grezel Reed 13 Jan. 1825 51
Samuel Reed to Elizabeth Harris 26 April 1840 109
Sarah Reid to Hodge Raburn 22 Nov. 1822 39
William A Reed to Mahala Collier 22 Jan. 1833 163
Soloman Reed to Elizabeth Fuller 12 March 1826 62

Deahy Rees to John Graves 4 Feb. 1834 15
Betsy Rees to James Hubbard Given 17 Nov. 1831 137
Catherine Rees to Thomas Turner Given 1 July 1830 122

Margaret Reeves to Abraham Job 13 Oct. 1822 36

Magdalene Reiler to Franklin Streg 24 Nov. 1845 196

Charles Reinhard to Frederiche Tottle 23 Sept. 1841 13

Gilbert S. Rence to Mary Jane Stokeley 15 Feb. 1848 258

James H. Renfro, Henry Co., Mo. to Eliza Ann Dickson
    27 Oct. 1841 135

Sally W. Renick to William D. Murray 24 Oct. 1820 19

Benjamin Rennison to Mary Rice 1 July 1844 175
Catherine Rennison to James C. Seat 25 Sept. 1848 1
George Rennison to Sally Stow 2 Jan. 1834 13
James Rennison to Sarah Robinson 26 May 1842 143
Joseph Rennison to Aristine Seat 15 Dec. 1836 56
Joseph Rennison to Sary Yarnall 10 Jan. 1850 29
Mary Rennison to James Gartner 14 Jan. 1830 120
Sarah Rennison to Abel G. Hampton 27 Jan. 1832 143
William Rennison to Mary Yarnall 20 June 1844 176

Elijah Renshaw to Winiford Stephens, daughter of William
    Stephens, dec. 3 March 1842 149
John W. Renshaw to Margaret A. Martin 12 Oct. 1835 41
Martha J. Renshaw to Harrison Newkirk 24 Dec. 1840 121

John G. Ressler to Sarah Ann Walker 13 March 1845 184

John Retherford to Jane Shackleford 24 July 1842 145

John Row to Jane Hughes 9 Jan. 1831 128

Whitfield Reynolds to Laminda Turley 30 Dec. 1838 92
William Reynolds to Martha Dixon 9 Sept. 1843 175
William Reynolds to Jane Howard 10 Aug. 1848 263

Eliza G. Rice to Daniel L. Ramy 28 Sept. 1836 55
Jacob Rice to Polly Weeden 2 Nov. 1834 25
Julia Ann Rice to Smith Gillum 18 Aug. 1842 147
Lewis Rice to Jane Patrick 29 Oct. 1838 90
Lucy Jane Rice to Richard Brannum 23 Nov. 1837 76
Mary Rice to Benjamin Rennison 18 July 1844 175
Mary E. Rice to Charles M. Scroggin 16 Jan. 1850 26
Richard Rice to Sarah Caroline Kirkpatrick 5 Sept. 1844 175
Samuel F. Rice to Margaret Robinson 19 July 1845 192

Maria S. Richards to Wesley H. Wickersham 25 Feb. 1849 8

John C. Richardson to Mary E. Lionberger 16 Feb. 1847 226
Mary Richardson to John K. Allison __ Jan. 1832 144
Sary Richardson to Benjamin F. McFarland Given 3 Dec. 1830 132
Susan T. Richardson to Joseph L. Davis 14 Jan. 1836 43

Cynthia L. Richeson to Joel S. Sheppard 17 Nov. 1839 101

Page 184 A2 Will of Andrew Richey, Hickory County, Mo.
   To my wife, Nancy...
   To my grandson, James William Bradley, son of my deceased daughter, Rachel Matilda Bradley...
   To my children: John Dennis, Nancy Caroline, wife of John W. Ritchey, Polly Ann Hazle, wife of Ignacious Hazle, James Sumerell, Andrew Caldwell, William Simpson, and Thomas Marion...
Written : 28 September 1853   Recorded: 5 May 1856
Witnesses: A. M. Foster, Thomas Davis, and Mark S. Means
Elizabeth Richie to Thomas T. Plant 26 Feb. 1845 188
Martha Ann Richie to Joseph Moore 3 Oct. 1844 178
Samuel Richey to Nancy McCarty 19 Dec. 1824 49

John Ricketts to Maria Patrick 12 Feb. 1843 154

Henry Rickman to Mary Ann Dorsey 1 Dec. 1850 36
James Rickman to Sally Mayfield 21 Dec. 1844 183
Matilda Rickman to Isaac P. Stover 1 Feb. 1844 173
William Rickman to Lidy Drils 8 May 1842 144

Louisa Ricks to William S. Turley 17 May 1840 113

Crecience Rida to Mike Shadring 4 Feb. 1847 225

Harriett Riddle to Samuel W. McMahan 17 March 1833 2
Jutitia Riddle to Jesse Turley 14 Feb. 1822 34
Lucy Riddle to Thomas McMahan, Jr. 25 March 1830 115
Samuel Riddle to Mary Kencheloe 24 Dec. 1839 104

Benjamin Ridgway, Howard Co., Mo. to Manerva Simmons
    Recorded 5 Oct. 1833 6

Lucinda Riggs to William McFarland 3 Jan. 1830 112
Margaret Riggs to Edward Houx 3 Feb. 1847 228
Rachel Riggs to Thompson B. Corum 7 Oct. 1834 23

Alexander H. Reads to Dollie Maria Tutt 7 Feb. 1837 65

Sarah Robard to Hugh Allison 39 Jan. 1844 166

Jerard Roberson to George Powell 27 March 1849 14
John Roberson to Phamy Catron 12 June 1820 20
Prudence Roberson to John Stock 23 July 1849 17
William N. Roberson to Rhoda Stevens, daughter of William
    Stevens, dec. 26 Feb. 1841 130

Jenac Roberts to Jerry W. Miller 7 Jan. 1832 140
Joy Roberts to Stephen K. Hancock Given 3 Feb. 1830 112
Nancy Roberts to Henry Middleton, both of Simeon Co., Ky.
    8 April 1848 255
Susan Roberts to Nathan Perry 28 Feb. 1843 155

Page 102 A2 Will of Catherine Robertson...
    Son, Edward, deceased; son, Charles, dec.; son William, dec.
son, John, deceased
    Daughters Margaret Deakins, deceased, Catherine Hurley,
and Mary Howard, deceased...bequeath each of them if they are
living 25¢ each and to the children of these that are dead
10¢ each. This provision is made to prevent legalitation and
to show they have not escaped my mind in making my will.
    Son, Andrew, Exe.
Written: 8 November 1844 Recorded: 20 June 1853
Witnesses: John Wilson, Jesse L. Shirley, and Charles T. Lewis
Page 14 A2 Will of Edward Robertson
    To my wife, Catherine...
    To the children of my deceased daughter, Margaret Deakins.
to the children of my deceased daughter, Catharine Hurley..
to the children of my deceased daughter, Mary Howard...
    To the children of my son, Edward, deceased...
    To my sons: John, Andrew, and Charles...
    Andrew and Charles, my sons, Exe.
Written: 28 May 1847   Recorded: 11 May 1848
Witnesses: John Garnett, I. C. Bullock, Peter B. Harris, and
Abram Trigg
Andrew Robertson to Katharine Shirley __ Dec. 1829 115
Catharine Robertson to William Hurt 12 Sept. 1837 71
Catherine Robertson to Caleb O'Bryan 18 Aug. 1849 22
Charles Robertson to Lucinda Fort 7 Nov. 1822 39
Dolly Robertson to William Goodman 19 Feb. 1826 56

Elizabeth Robertson to Joseph Tucker 28 Feb. 1837 65
Elizabeth Ann Robertson to John B. T. Johnson 17 Dec. 1835 42
George Robertson to Renizah Hurt 23 Aug. 1844 173
George Robertson to Peggy Rowe 25 Oct. 1830 124
George N. Robertson to Mary Angeline Mann 29 Aug. 1845 193
John Robertson to Mary McClure 22 July 1821 22
John Robertson, Morgan Co. to Emily Davis, daughter of Phillip
    E. Davis, dec. 14 April 1842
Joseph Robertson to Lucinda Green 11 June 1846 214
Julia A. Robertson to Alexander Shannaon 29 Nov. 1849 22
Katherine Robertson to Robert McCulloch, Jr. 27 July 1837 69
    Miss Robertson, daughter of Edward Robertson
Martha Robertson to Mansfield Burnard 4 Aug. 1842 146
Mary Ann Robertson to Phillip Barner 21 Feb. 1839 94
Mary Ann Robertson to Cyrus Shirley 10 March 1841 119
William Robertson to Caroline Masters 22 March 1832 146

Ann J. Robinson to William R. Brown 26 Oct. 1831 140
Edetha Robinson to John I. Meyer 24 Dec. 1846 227
Edward Robinson to Lydia M. Coy 20 Feb. 1827 76
George Robinson to Lorenly Stinson 20 July 1837 73
Hardy Robinson to Mary Frances Strite 28 March 1847 231
James Robinson to Sinthy Deakin 15 Jan. 1829 101
John Robinson to Luella Wolf 26 July 1840 113
Kisjiah Robinson to William Cartner 28 July 1842 147
Margaret Robinson to Samuel F. Rich 10 July 1845 192
Mathew Robinson to Mary E. Collins 7 Jan. 1846 202
Mary Robinson to Felix Corum 25 Feb. 1836 51
Mary A. O. Robinson to Andrew J. Sharp 6 April 1843 154
Polly Robinson to Edmond Howard 10 June 1824 46
Sally Robinson to Thomas Densman 18 Feb. 1827 69
Sarah Robinson to James Rennison 26 May 1842 143
Sarah I. Robinson to O. P. Davis 12 Sept. 1843 160

Ann Eliza Robison to James Cordry 15 Jan. 1850 26
Catherine Robison to Wilson Sam 20 Dec. 1849 29
Parthena Robeson to James Broyles 22 Sept. 1839 99

John C. Rochester to Nancy Kelley 28 Feb. 1821 19
Sophia E. Rochester to James F. Lear 14 April 1842 143
Thomas Rochester to Malinda Ross 18 Jan. 1849 9

Page 92 B Will of Julius Rodgers
    To my wife, Calley...
    To my children: Edward, Carry Ann, John, and William...
    Calley, Exe.
Written: 4 August 1844   Recorded: 24 September 1844
Witnesses: Henry Bausfield and Robert B. Bacon

Page 213 A2 Will of James Roe
    To my wife, Martha Jane...
    To my sister, Elizabeth...
Written: 13 July 1858   Recorded: 30 July 1858
Witnesses: Peter Wilson, Henry S. Wilhelm, and S. A. Summers
Page 290 A2 Will of Lewis Roe
    To my wife, Jane...
    To my minor heirs: James Henry, Nancy Jane, Rhoda Frances, and Elizabeth Adaline...
    To my daughter, Ann...
    Samuel Hughes, Exe.
Written: 1 March 1853   Recorded: 22 January 1861
Witnesses: A. J. Elliott and T. I. Hughes
Alexander Roe to Louiza Casady 13 Aug. 1832 154
Alexander Roe to Nancy Ann Walton 26 Sept. 1844 210
Ann M. Roe to Starlin R. Wooldridge 19 Dec. 1838 93
Peggy Rowe to George Robertson 25 Oct. 1830 124
James Roe to Martha Rosser 14 May 1835 29

Page 283 A2 Will of Hugh Rogers
    To my daughter, Ann E. Lintz, and her son, William P. Whitaker, my grandson...
    To my children: Ferdinand A., Hugh, John F., Alfreel S. and Mary L. Rogers and to my said grandson, W. P. Whittaker...
    Joseph S. Stephens, Exe.
Written: 24 September 1860   Recorded: 24 October 1860
Witnesses: Edward Chilton and J. A. Tutt
Elizabeth Rogers to John Miller 7 May 1829 104
William M. Rogers to Polly Lillard 1 May 1820 12

Robert Rollins to Mrs. Nancy Kells 24 Sept. 1846 217

Ann Ron to Holbert Cole 20 Dec. 1819 22

John Coleman Ronald to Sarah Barton Merrill at the residence of
    Wilson Merrill 24 Jan. 1843 151

Page 86 A2 Will of Lewis Rose
    To my wife, Martha S. ...
    To my grandchildren: Mary Catherine McKenzie, Louis William McKenzie, Josha Granville McKenzie, Martha Eliza McKenzie, children of Susannah McKenzie, dec. ...
    John Calhoun and James Terarly, Exe.
Written: 7 November 1852   Recorded: 12 November 1852
Elenora Rose to Enoch H. Gatewood 28 Nov. 1850 35

Adaline A. Ross to Thomas A. Peyer 10 Aug. 1849 22
Alexander Ross to Manerva Campbell 24 March 1835 28
Clolum Ross to Hannah Fawbush 6 Dec. 1820 18
Daniel Ross to Lucy Frances Shackleford 25 July 1844 173
David Ross to Polly Houx 1 Nov. 1832 157

David Ross to Elizabeth Weeden 15 Feb. 1835 27
Elizabeth Ross to Edmond Wooldridge 4 Dec. 1834 24
James Ross to Mrs. Deborah Kelly 20 June 1847 236
James C. Ross to Joanna Lowery 5 June 1839 98
Jane Ross to Andrew Cathey 22 June 1832 150
Josephus Ross to Martha Ann Moody 29 Aug. 1849 18
Lucretia C. Ross to F. L. Peyton ____ 1841 123
Lucy Ross to Bolin Savage __ July 1830 143
Lucy Ross to James Fields 22 Dec. 1831 139
Malinda Ross to Thomas Rochester 18 Jan. 1849 9
Peter Ross to Susan Ann Duncan 14 May 1836 51
Rhoda Ross to Samuel S. Coulburn 8 Oct. 1846 222
Robert Ross to Minerva Potter 15 April 1832 150
Sary Ann Ross to Dealo F. Forbus 17 Aug. 1848 1
Susan Ross to David McFarland 28 Jan. 1828 87

Martha Rosser to James Roe 14 May 1835 '29

A. J. Rothrock to Jane Morrow 11 Jan. 1849 5

Mary Ann Rousfield to James F. Conner 15 Oct. 1843 163

Louisa Rowles, daughter of William and Sarah Rowles, to
    William J. Campbell 4 Jan. 1844 169

Joseph C. Roy to N. A. How 17 April 1845 188

Henry Rubey to Winifred W. Ewing 2? Feb. 1822 30
Henry N. Rubey, Pettis Co., Mo. to Mary A. Carson 15 Oct. 1839
Lucinda Rubey to George N. Ewing 27 May 1824 50
Malinda Rubey to John T. A. Henderson 25 March 1830 114
Urban B. Rubey to Catherine Cockrel 18 Feb. 1830 113
William Rubey to June J. Ewing 6 Sept. 1821 20

George T. Rucker to Eliza C. Howe 20 Oct. 1849 20
John L. Rucker to Mary ?. Hurbard 2 Jan. 1845 182

Eliza J. Ruley to John Walton 1 Jan. 1835 26

Frances Runal to Wiatt Jones ____ 1849 11

Page 132 A2 Will of Thomas Russell
    To my wife, Eliza E. ...
    To my children and grandchildren, viz Thomas Wind Russell,
James Hughes Russell and the heirs of my son, James H. Russell..
    To my sons: Thomas T., Albert, Alexander B., William H.,
Joseph D., Samuel B., and John N. ... To my daughters: Eliza M.
Ann T., and Angeletta...
    Elizabeth, my wife, Exe.
Written: 9 May 184?   Recorded: 18 September 1854
Witnesses: Joseph A. Potter and William Nicholson

Andrew Russell to Norman Martin 3 Aug. 1819 10
James H. Russell to Margaret J. Wyan 2 April 1840 110
John Russell to Nancy Allee 2 Sept. 1830 125

Page 191 A2 Will of Charles Rutherford
 To Jesse Ogden; to Elizabeth Edwards; $10. to Prince, a slave belonging to Elizabeth Caldwell; $5. to a slave belonging to Robert Givens.
 I give and bequeath the remaining balance if any to Witty Davis and Anna Davis my two daughters who is the children of Jane Davis.
 Jesse Odgen, Exe.
Written: 30 October 1854   Recorded: 10 February 1857
Witnesses: Alexander Givens and Preston Norman
William P. Rutherford to Phoebe Dillard 29 Dec. 1835 37

Eleinor Rymal to David McClanahan 26 June 1837 68
Elizabeth Rimal to Michael Capp 1 Sept. 1844 178
Kiciah Rymal to James M. McClanahan 28 Dec. 1837 77
Nancy Rymel to William Giles 14 Oct. 1840 115
Newton Rimel to Lyda Ann McClanahan 11 Aug. 1850 33

William Saling to Mary Williams 3 May 1824 52

Robert Salmons to Rhoda Kelly 8 Jan. 1850 30

Wilson Sam to Catherine Robison 20 Dec. 1849 29

Nancy Samuel to William C. Batchelor 22 March 1838 78
Virginia Samuel to William Phillips 30 March 1847 229

Elizabeth Sanders to James Smithey 1 June 1849 15

Richard Sanford to Nancy Aramer 9 March 1848 254

Henry S. Sarters to Nancy Bass 12 June 1835 29

Samuel W. Saunders to Ann Kennedy 18 June 1844 176

Bolin Savage to Lucy Ross __ July 1830 143
John Savage to Casander Stephens 29 Jan. 1825 72
John H. Savage to Cinthy Jane Crawford 2 April 1830 120
Polly Savage to James Williams 23 Feb. 1826 60

Thelida Saw to Joseph Forsyth 16 Feb. 1841 122

Page 188 A2 Will of Jacob Schieb
 To my wife, Margaret...
 To my sons: Jacob and Frederick... to my grandson, Edmond Myers... Frederick, Exe.
Written: 18 September 1855   Recorded: 13 August 1856
Witnesses: Leroy Chandler and Henderson Talley

Christopher Schlolyhaner to Dorothea Schnerdir 9 March 1848 257

Christine Schlotzhauer to Diedrick Karstens 20 Nov. 1850 34

Henry Schmidt to Theresa Spieler 29 July 1847 239

Odela Schmultz to Anthony Ganter 4 Oct. 1842 145

Dorothea Schnerdir to Christopher Schlolyhaner 9 March 1848 257

Page 59 A Will of James Scritchfield
   To my wife, Elizabeth...
   To my sons: Garland Mary and John Murphy ...
   To my daughters: Lucy Boyd, Prudence Story, and Betsey Ann...
   To my son, James Berry...
   Elizabeth and Alexandriah Johnson, Exe.
Written: 19 December 1832   Recorded: 16 January 1833
Witnesses: John Smith and Thomas Smith
E.alias Scritchfield to James Hornback 27 July 1831 136
Lucinda Schritchfield to Robert Boyd 18 Sept. 1829 97
Prudence Schritchfield to Cornelius Story 8 Feb. 1829 98
Garlan Lee Scritchfield to Permalia Boyd 22 Aug. 1833 9

Ann Elizabeth Scott to William J. Woolery 10 March 1847 233
Emily Scott to Edward H. Hubbard 26 Aug. 1847 244
Euphemia Scott to Emanuel Drinkwater 4 Feb. 1821 19
James Scott to Artemisia Johnson 28 June 1849 19
Jane Scott to Thomas J. Morris Sept. 1831 136
Jane Scott to Alvin George 11 April 1839 4
Malinda Scott to William Anderson 18 April 1830 119
Mary A. Scott to Cornelius Edwards 21 April 1849 11
H. W. Scott to Susan Townsend 28 Oct. 1849 21 Scott of Pettis
Peter Scott to Lucinda Martin 30 June 1846 218
William Scott to Caroline Berry 7 Dec. 1843
Winney Scott to Hardy Midlin 27 Nov. 1833 17

Hank Scragg, Cole Co., Mo. to Louisa Mahan 20 March 1834 18

Charles M. Scroggin to Mary B. Rice 16 Jan. 1850 26

John S. Scruggs to Dianna Tobin 9 Nov. 1848 2

Nicholas J. Scrugm to Susan Job 8 July 1849 17

John Seaber, Howard Co., Mo. to Charlotte E. Steiner
   23 May 1844 170

Cristine Seat to Joseph Rennison 15 Dec. 1836 56
Clarinda Seat to William W. Calvert 3 Oct. 1849 19
James C. Seat to Catherine Rennison 25 Sept. 1848 1

Jane Seat to Valentine Martin 11 July 1848 266
Marion Seat to Frances Massey 4 June 1845 169
Martha M. Seat to Oliver R. Howe at the residence of John B.
      Seat 21 Dec. 1848 5
Sarah Seat, daughter of G. Seat to St. Clair Morgan 3 Oct. 1837
Saritha Seat to John Dunham 21 June 1832 153

John Seeth to Polly Walker 2 April 1829 101
V. Elizabeth Seivers to Benjamin Sombart 23 April 1850 30

John Self to Polly Travis 17 Jan. 1827 74

Custis Segraves to Emily Ferbes 6 Sept. 1837 72

John A. Seltyne to Nancy George 19 Feb. 1846 256

Page 343 A 2 Will of William M. Settle
      To my wife, Sarah...
      To my only surviving child, Levenia Settle...
      Augustus S. Pullim, Exe.
Written: 24 February 1864   Recorded: 26 April 1864
Witnesses: W. D. Minor and W. J. Woolery

Page 93 A2 Will of Reuben S. Severidge
      To my wife, Rebecca,..
      To my daughter, Jerusha Ann...
      B. S. Wilson, Exe.
Written: 16 February 1853   Recorded: 15 March 1853
Witnesses: F. W. G. Thomas and S. Houck

Page 352 A2 Will of Benjamin Seward
      To my wife, Catharine M. ...
      To our children, Horace H. and Margaret Seaward...
      My wife and my brother, Charles E., Exe.
Written: June 1864   Recorded: 21 September 1865
Witnesses: Emmett R. Hayden and Benjamin Tompkins

Eliza Shackleford to Nicholas Dillard 7 March 1839 95
Elizabeth Shackleford to Sudwill A. Cramer 16 Feb. 1843 153
Jane Shackleford to John Rutherford 24 July 1842 145
Lucy Frances Shackleford to Daniel Ross 25 July 1844 173
Mary Shackleford to Elijah Hock 12 June 1824 46
Nancy Shackleford to Andrew Cramer 27 Oct. 1850 36

Mike Shadring to Crecience Rida 4 Feb. 1847 225

Jefferson Shanklin to Zanippa Lampton 6 April 1837 22

Alexander Shannon to Julia A. Robertson 29 Nov. 1849 22

Andrew Sharp to Sarah Calvert 3 Sept. 1835 33
Andrew J. Sharp to Mary A. G. Robinson 6 April 1843 154

John Shaw to Jane Hood 14 Feb. 1832 144

Peter Shelby to Adaline H. Adams 25 Feb. 1839 92

Page 29A Will of John Sheppard
    To my cousins, Thomas Farris and Senthy Westbrook...
Written: 14 March 1826   Recorded: 24 April 1826
Witnesses: Joseph Westbrook, Allen Wallis, and Drury Wallace
Belsam Shepherd to Bernet Furnish 23 May 1842 142
Joel S. Sheppard to Cynthia L. Richeson 17 Nov. 1839 101
Mary Shepphard to Crud Taylor 17 Aug. 1848 7

William S. Sherman to Eliza Heath 1836 '52

Thomas Shernwell to Nancy Beon 6 Jan. 1835 30

William C. Shields to Frances Goodman 17 Sept. 1848 266

Page 359 A2 Will of William Shipley
    To my wife, Sophia E. ...
    To my son, William W. ...
    To my daughters: Martha Ann Shipley, Mary Catharine
Shipley, Maria J. Wilcox, and Sophia E. Crun...
Written: 11 October 1865   Recorded: 2 November 1865
George Shipley to Elizabeth Ellice 25 March 1830 113
Margaret Shipley to Jonathan P. Martin 6 April 1827 90
Rachael Shipley to Levi Woods 22 Jan. 1826 61

Page 187 A2 Will of Jesse S. Shirley
    To my nephew, Jesse Dodd...To my sister, Marthan Jane Dodd;
To my nieces: Elizabeth Catharine Shirley and Mary E. Gardner;
to my step-daughter, Mary Durncil; to my son, Robert Miller;
and to my daughter, Elizabeth Smith...
Written: 9 June 1856   Recorded: 26 May 1856
Witnesses: Benjamin Rogers and S. S. Seat
Cynthia Jane Shirley to James A. Gardner 19 Nov. 1835 40
Cyrus Shirley to Mary Ann Robertson 10 March 1841 119
Elizabeth Shirley to Willoughby Maddox at the house of Frederick
Shirley 11 Nov. 1847 243
Jesse Shirley to Elizabeth Miller 17 Dec. 1835 40
Katharine Shirley to Andrew Robertson _ Dec. 1829 115
Matilda Shirley to Samuel Gilmore 16 May 1830 120
Polly Shirley to Stepen Woolery 3 Oct. 1839 100
William Shirley to Ann Hoof 17 Dec. 1829 103

Joseph G. Shobernell to Nancy Kirk 17 Dec. 1840 119

Sally Shockley to John Hammons 5 July 1829 105

Page 49 A2 Will of Rufus Shoemaker
  To my wife, Angeline...
  To my oldest daughter who married Peter Cole and my second who married Andrew McBroom...
  Angline, Peter Cole and Andrew McBroom, Exe.
Written: 29 July 1850   Recorded: 21 April 1851
Witnesses: Jonatius Hazell and P. Shoemaker

Charles Shoemaker to Hariot Humphreys 1 Feb. 1827 73
Elener W. Shoemaker to Justinian W. Shoemaker 5 April 1846 200
Hannah Shoemaker to Elijah Hook 20 Aug. 1839 99
Helen Shoemaker to Andrew McBrown 5 April 1840 255
Horace Shoemaker to Mary Ann Son 30 Oct. 1850 34
Justinian W. Shoemaker to Elenor W. Shoemaker 5 April 1846 200
Lidia Shoemaker to Timothy McGuire 20 March 1845 190
Lucinda Shoemaker to Peter Cole 6 March 1845 183
Martha Shoemaker to Nicholas Patterson 6 Sept. 1846 221
Mary Shoemaker to E. Hook 15 July 1849 15
Mary Ann Shoemaker to Joseph Story 14 May 1844 172
Oliver H. Shoemaker to Phealena Simmons 3 May 1844 170
Phillip Shoemaker to Nancy Ransberger 27 Sept. 1842 146
Phillip Shoemaker to Lemember Gurgess 18 July 1850 31
Phillip W. Shoemaker to Susan E. Johnston 24 Feb. 1850 29
Rufus Shoemaker to Eliza Ann Hungerford 28 Aug. 1823 43
Susan Shoemaker to Samuel Hickman 1 June 1848 259

Irene Short to Rudolphus D. Wells 8 Nov. 1849 27
James C. Short to Susan Mary Carpenter 27 Oct. 1844 179

John Christian Shupp to Mary Ann Massel 31 Oct. 1846 2

_____ Sidebottom to Louisa Dodds 7 Jan. 1846 199

Samuel Simmerrill to Matilda Wood 11 Feb. 1836 50

Elizabeth Simmonds to Charles James Sturd 16 Oct. 1832 159
George W. Simmons to Cynthia S. Mahan 25 Oct. 1838 88
Manerva Simmons to Benjamin Ridgway Rec. 5 Oct. 1833 6
Mary E. Simmons to Franklin W. Hickocks 25 Oct. 1841 138
Phealena Simons to Oliver H. Shoemaker 3 May 1844 170
Mrs. Sarah Simons to James W. Palmer 4 May 1849 24
Susan Simmons to Tipton Prior 11 May 1847 235
William Simons to Koren Jeringen 1 July 1838 86

Adam Simonton to Cynthia Cropper 30 Oct. 1828 93
Adam Simonton to Rebecca Clarke 12 Dec. 1839 105

Francis Simpson to Mary Jane Corum 6 Oct. 1840 115

Samuel A. Sitter to Malinda Fisher 8 Dec. 1836 57

Louisa Skidmore to David Given 4 Feb. 1847 228

119

James Slenslan to Martha Martin 30 July 1837 72
See Appenda for Will of William Sloan
Miss A. A. Sloan to A. McCutchen 27 Nov. 1848 3
Betsey Sloan to William Bryant 17 Aug. 1824 50
Catharine Sloan to Gustavious Smiley 25 Feb. 1845 184
Patsy Ewing Sloan to Dean McCutchen Given 27 Oct. 1829 109
Phebe M. Sloan to Benjamin Cooper 18 March 1831 131
Robert Sloan to Margaret D. Ewing 13 Dec. 1826 67
Eliza Sloss to George Houx 16 Jan. 1834 14

Carry Slutchour to Conrad Cash 20 March 1841 127
Rudalf Slutchower to Catharine Young 3 March 1847 226

Isabella Small to George W. Smiley 17 Aug. 1826 64

Russell Smallwood to Peggy Briscoe __ June 1820 16

Page 201 A2   Will of Dujeselin Smiley
  To my brothers: Lycurgus, G. A., and Samuel Peters, my brother in law...
  I have disposed of my estate according to my feelings, there is William Cole and Rhoda his wife; Hugh Galbraith and Jerusha his wife; Stephen D. Smileys Heirs; Elvira Smiley; John Ingram; Elvira Ingrahams heirs; George Vinson Ingram; Thomas S. Ingram; Nancy Ingram; and John W. Ingram; Decalb Smiley; and Thomas B. Smiley...
  My friend Joseph J. Stephens, adm.
Written: 6 February 1857   Recorded: 4 May 1857
Witnesses: Miles Allen, Kinsey H. Wood, and Joseph Hill
Page 170 A2 Will of Nancy Smiley
  To my sons: Thomas D., Decalb, and Dujeselin...
  I leave my worthy friend whom I shall hereafter appoint my Executor to sell my Negro, Flora at private sale and after paying the debts of administration and all other just debts to divide the remainder of the money amongest my children whom I shall name equally, viz William Cole and Rhoda his wife; Hugh Galbreath and Jarusha his wife; Samuel Peters and Artimacy his wife; Gustavis Smiley; J. F. Smiley, Lycurgus Smiley, Thomas D. Smiley; Dugustin Smiley, and Decalb Smiley. My son, Decature who died about nine years ago he heft one heir named Alvira. I have given her all I entend to give her of my estate. Elvira Ingram her heirs, George V. Ingram, Thomas S. Ingram, Nancy A. Ingram, and J. W. Ingram I have given them all I intend to give them.   S. C. Stephens, Exe.
Written: 19 November 1853   Recorded: 25 January 1856
Elvira Smiley to John Ingram 23 Aug. 1827 30
George W. Smiley to Isabella Small 17 Aug. 1826 64
Geruna Smiley to Hugh Gilbreath 30 April 1833 20
Gustavious Smiley to Catharine Sloan 25 Feb. 1845 184
Katherine Smiley to James Marland 7 July 1828 92
Redah Smiley to William Cool 12 May 1822 35
Sikugust Smiley to Parmelia Jane Brown 30 May 1848 262

Page 148 B Will of Daniel Smith
　　To my sons: James D., Thomas B., and to my daughter, Unity Talbot, Polly Martin, and Dradoni Chism...
　　To Nancy Ogle and her husband, David Ogle...
　　To my grandson, Daniel A. Ogle and my grand-daughter, Zuliana Ogle, now the wife of Nathan J. Dunn who are the children of my deceased daughter, Betsy Ogle who was the first wife of David Ogle...
　　To my son in law, Isaac Martin...
Written: 19 May 1843　　Recorded: 3 December 1845
Witnesses: Bennett C. Clark and William Gibson

Page 74 B Will of John Smith
　　To my son, Vanburen...
Written: 20 March 1844　　Recorded: 9 May 1844
Witnesses: C. L. and R. E. Bell

Page 64 A2 Will of Mary E. Smith
　　To my son, Charles Edward...
　　To the daughter of my sister, Susan Turner...
　　To my brothers: James A. Tutt, Lewis C. Tutt, and Henry Tutt and to my sister, Sarah Hill...
　　James A. Tutt, Exe.
Written: _ December 1851　　Recorded: 13 February 1852
Witnesses: Henry Withers and Isaac Lionberger

Page 179 A2 Will of William J. Smith
　　To my wife, Mary...
　　My friend, Joseph G. Steele, Exe.
Written: 17 October 1855　　Recorded: 12 March 1856
Witnesses: Green, William, and Joseph G. Steele and William H. Shanklin

Anthony Smith to Mary Elizabeth Reed 13 April 1831 133
Charles H. Smith to Rebecca Hood 27 Oct. 1829 144
Diadian Smith to Mikel Chism 4 Feb. 1830 118
Dinna Smith to Amos McDaniel 2 March 1845 187
Eliza Smith to William Fisher 25 Dec. 1827 86
Eliza Smith to Kenneth McKensey 13 Jan. 1828 98
Elizabeth Smith to Alexander Hatfield 20 Aug. 1826 76
Elizabeth Smith to John McCaleb 15 Aug. 1839 99
Elizabeth Smith to Willis Phips 28 April 1844 170
Emily Smith to John Campbell 14 June 1846 215
George W. Smith to Nancy E. Neal C Aug. 1848 264
Isaac Smith to Sabria Fisher 6 Jan. 1822 29
Jefferson Smith, Morgan Co., Mo. to Mary Ann Kealen 10 Mar. 1841
John Smith to Sally McMahan 3 May 1819 1
Judith C. Smith to William Potts 29 Sept. 1847 240
Lucy Smith to David Morris 16 Aug. 1835 32
Malvina L. Smith to Andrew Collins 25 Feb. 1845 184
Maria Smith to Peter Harmon Rec. 7 April 1828 90
Mariah Smith to Pleasant Dankston 21 Nov. 1833 9
Martha Smith to John Woolery 16 Oct. 1845 196
Mrs. Marthy Ann Smith to James A. Gardner 10 Nov. 1847 243

Matilda Smith to William Moore   30 June 1836   53
Mary Smith to Isaac Martin   22 Feb. 1827   78
Mary Smith to Alexander Wilson   1 Jan. 1828   89
Mary Ann Smith to George Leonard Khoehn   6 Nov. 1848   2
Melinda Smith to James Evans   4 June 1844   171
Nancy Smith to Jacob Calahan   4 Dec. 1843   167
Rebecca W. Smith to Isham R. Pucket   25 Feb. 1844   170
Reuben Smith to Giddida Hall   4 Jan. 1829   97
Sally Smith to Harvey Durch   9 March 1826   59
Sidney Smith to Mary A. McDaniel   30 Aug. 1848   265
Thomas B. Smith to Elizabeth M. Massey   10 July 1842   144
Thomas R. Smith to Mary Ann Hutchinson   25 July 1839   99
U. A. Smith to Blanche A. Menzen   29 March 1846   206
William A. D. Smith to Melinda Hoozer   24 Sept. 1835   46

Isiah P. Smithers to Margaret L. McFarland   21 Oct. 1841   133
Isiah P. Smithers to Julia McFarland   31 Dec. 1845   199
Nancy Ann Smithers to Peter S. Boatman   8 March 1849   12

James Smithey to Elizabeth Sanders   1 June 1849   15

Page 329 A2   Will of Eleven H. Smoot
    To my wife, Rebecca Ann...
Written: 26 January 1856   Recorded: 9 April 1863
Witnesses: James C. Wilson and John Murphy

Mary Snigan to Stephen Whitman   31 May 1848   258

Andrew I. Snodgrass to Salina Burgher   22 July 1834   22
Edward Snodgrass to Nancy Harris   19 Dec. 1830   128
Edward Snodgrass to Lucy Harris   21 Feb. 1836   50
Elizabeth Snodgrass to Allen Conner   24 July 1827   83
James Snodgrass to Marthy Hunter   15 Jan. 1846   199
John Snodgrass to Rebecca Huff   6 April 1845   187
Joseph Snodgrass to Sally Hooser   1 Dec. 1825   62
Reuben Snodgrass to Nancy Martin   61   5 Oct. 1826
William Snodgrass to Dorcas Huff   29 Dec. 1836   58

Elizabeth Snyder to Jacob Noryer   3 March 1846   209

Hogan Soloman to Jane Drinkwater   26 March 1845   189
Nicholas B. Soloman to Margaret A. Decker   23 July 1846   216

Benjamin Sombart to V. Elizabeth Seivers   23 April 1850   30
Eliza W. Sumbart to Charles Force   7 April 1845   188
Emilee Sembart to Andrew Haas   1 Feb. 1849   6
Julia Sombart to Stephen Weaver   1 Nov. 1841   137

Page 419 A2   Will of Lorenz Somner
    To my wife; to my sons: Austin P. and James D. ...
    To my brother Joshua F.
Written: 29 May 1855   Recorded: 13 July 1863

George W. Son to Martha Jane Howard 8 Aug. 1850 34
James Son to Margaret Trotter 26 July 1829 100
John Son to Isabel McClure 20 July 1821 22
Mary Ann Son to Horace Shoemaker 30 Oct. 1850 34
William Son to Lavanna Burger 7 Dec. 1826 66

Job Sorgrass to Sarah Ann Martin 18 June 1846 216

Newton Soury to Susan Parrott 28 Oct. 1847 250

Polly Sparks to Jacob Waggoner 26 Sept. 1830 124
Richard M. Sparks to Mary C. Duncan 3 Jan. 1850 29

William S. Speed to Sarah Ardell Hutchinson 15 June 1846 216

Elija Spence to Nancy Estus 29 Nov. 1830 128

John B. Spencer to Margaret B. Whitman 29 Aug. 1850 32

George Speebu to Catharine Donhouser 17 Nov. 1848 3

Page 240 A2 Will of Weeden Spenny
    To my grand-daughter, Mary Elizabeth Norris...
    To my sister, Mary Parrets' heirs now living in the state of Kentucky...
Written: 8 Jan. 1858   Recorded: 12 March 1859
Witnesses: James M. Stephens and Charles K. Cullers
Elizabeth Spenny to William Haggans 20 Sept. 1839 100
Sarah E. Spenny to William W. Norris 10 May 1846 209

John Guthridge Spieler to Eleanor Kemper 25 March 1843 154
Theresa Spieler to Henry Schmidt 29 July 1847 239

Elisha Spivey to Alhay Guyn 28 Aug. 1822 37

William Sponhimore to Polly Green 22 April 1824 47

Louisa Springfield to John Higginbotham 21 Jan. 1841 121

Jacob E. Stafford to Rachael S. Moore 18 July 1843 161
Mrs. Rachel Stafford to Robert S. Lewis 29 June 1848 266

Augustina Henrietta Stahl to Francis Marvin Caldwell
    19 April 1842 141

Louisa H. Stahr to John G. Encke 9 May 1850 31

Lucy C. Standley to Benjamin A. Ferrell 13 Feb. 1829 99
Jonathan M. Stanley to Mrs. Jane Bighan 30 Nov. 1828 95
William Stanly to Polly Burris 13 Aug. 1838 88

Page 245 A2 Will of Joseph Staples
    To my wife, Elizabeth E. ...
    To my children: William E., John M., Susan A. Parberry, Martha T. Poindexter, George, James, and Thomas...
    William E. Staples, John M. Staples, and William S. Poindexter, Exs.
Written: 12 May 1859   Recorded: 2 June 1859
Witnesses: Samuel Hughes, Jesse O'Neal, and Richard Wells

Thomas I. Stark to Amanda Hannon 3 March 1847 236

John Stean to Rachel McGee 4 May 1826 61
John B. Stean, Saline Co., Mo. to Eliza Huston 11 Aug. 1836

Page 259 A2 Will of Steele: Joshua D.
    To my wife, Ally C. ...
    John N. Steele and Robert G. Steele, Exe.
Witnesses: J. N. Steel, Emanuel Shanbuger, Joseph Feland, and William Steele
Written: 24 January 1860   Recorded: 2 March 1860
Clamentina Steel to Nathaniel Garten 15 Feb. 1831 131
Daniel C. Steel to Elizabeth Tucker 10 July 1847 234
Eliza Jane Steel to Green Rayburn Cordry 11 Aug. 1839 105
Florinda Steel to Granville Erevin 10 Jan. 1843 153
Greene Steele to Margaret Kiveet 17 March 1845 186
Jane Steel to Hiram C. Lowry 30 Aug. 1838 84
Joseph D. Steel to Abby C. Morrison 15 Oct. 1827 83
Margaret Steel to Robert Wallace 24 June 1824 50
Margaret Steel to Jenkins Withers 2 April 1839 96
Martha Ellen Steel to Benjamin F. Koontz 23 May 1846 210
Nancy M. Steel to Andrew P. Forbes 23 Feb. 1831 132
Rachel Steel to Harvey Howe 4 Dec. 1830 126
Rachel Steel to Alexander S. Wear 19 Feb. 1833 165
Robert Steel to Eliza Burrus 30 Aug. 1848 264
Sally Steel to Peter B. Cockrell Given 25 Dec. 1828 100
William W. B. Steel to Sarah Hedrick 18 Feb. 1836 49
William I. Steel to Martha Finch 26 Sept. 1830 86

Page 135 B Will of Nancy Steger, of the County of Powhatan, State of Virginia
    To my sons: Wade M. and Jefferson...
    To my daughters: Elizabeth M., Susan H., wife of William H. Palmore...
    To my other children: Charles Scott, Thomas Jefferson Giles, Wade M. Anne, and William Francis...
    My friend, John W. Nash, Exe.
Written: 26 August 1843   Recorded: 1 May 1845
Witnesses: Samuel Steger and Z. J. Stokes

NOTES

Will of Jacob Steinbeck Page 416 A2
    To my wife, Louisa...
    To my sons: Gustau and William...
    To my daughters: Johanna and Conradine
Written: 24 September 1869   Recorded: 10 September 1869
Witnesses: Hermann Storm and Joseph Mueller

Page 426 A2 Will of Jacob D. Steiner
    To my eldest daughter: Chicotta Seibel; to my daughter, Agnes Hannaca; to my daughter, Ananda E. Rentschler...
    To my son, Jacob...
    To my wife, Sibnia...
Written: 6 May 1868   Recorded: 25 November 1869
Charlotte E. Steiner to John Seaber 23 May 1844 170

Page 211 A2 Will of Peter Stephens
    To my wife, Elizabeth...
    To my son, Joseph S....
Written: 11 November 1857   Recorded: 23 April 1858
Witnesses: Robert P. Richardson and Lawrence C. Stephens
Absalom Stephens to Elizabeth Haney 20 Feb. 1833 166
Casander Stephens to John Savage 29 Jan. 1825 72
Dodge Stephens to Mary Cropper 4 Sept. 1834 23
Emerson J. Stephens to Elicia Ann Paston 18 Nov. 1847 243
Frances Stephens to George Moore 24 May 1827 70
George H. Stephens to Sarah Ann Hickman 9 March 1848 254
Jacob Stephens to Rody Levens 24 July 1848 262
Jaily Ann Stephens to David W. McClain 4 Dec. 1845 200
John A. Stephens to Surilda Daxter 6 Feb. 1845 186
Page 1023 Will of Joseph Stephens, Senior
    To my wife, Catherine...
    To my sons: Andrew Jackson and Thomas H. Benton Stephens..
    To my other children: Margaret M. E., John D., George D., Alpha Ann, Susan, and Hannah Isabella...
Written: 7 March 1836   Recorded: 2 August 1836
Witnesses: John Briscoe, James Cole, and Nancy Cole
Joseph Stephens to Ann McNee 17 Feb. 1825 72
Joseph Jefferson Stephens to Katherine Kavanaugh Woods,
    daughter of General Charles Woods 29 Nov. 1832 158
Joseph L. Stephens to Margaret Lydia Corum 12 Nov. 1850 37
Lawrence Stephens to Margaret Moore 24 Sept. 1820 37
Levin Stephens to Eliza Jane Allison 19 May 1846 209
Louiza Stephens to Jacob Byler 20 Jan. 1831 126
Mary Stephens to John Davis 11 June 1835 45
Mary L. Stephens to Samuel P. McFarland 19 Oct. 1841 134
Nancy Stephens to William Penland 4 April 1824 71
Peter Stephens to Elizabeth H. Dollis 14 March 1839 96
Rhody Ann Stephens to William Yarnill 16 Dec. 1841 137
Thomas Stephens to Jane Hoozer 11 Aug. 1839 103
Wineford Stepons, daughter of William Stephens, deceased, to
    Elijah Renshaw 3 March 1842 149

William Stephens to Major Dillard 22 May 1845 192
William H. Stephens to Maria Adams 9 Nov. 1847 242
William Stephens to Sarah Jane Armstrong 25 Oct. 1849 20
Zilphy Stephens to Pemberton Cason 22 July 1825 72

J. A. Sterret to Simpson Beck 18 July 1843 165

Lucinda Stevens to George Holt 24 Nov. 1833 10
Margaret Elizabeth Stevens to Reuben Bowles 1840 114
Rhoda Stevens, daughter of William Stevens to William M.
    Roberson 26 Feb. 1841 130
William Stevens to Elizabeth Pate 9 Nov. 1846 220

Page 84 B Will of Thomas Stevenson
    To my wife,
    To my sons: Andrew H. and Hugh A. ..
    To my daughters: Eliza Byres and Mary Jane Dupuy...
    My son in law, Samuel W. Dupuy, Exe.
Written: 9 March 1844   Recorded: 13 August 1844
Witnesses: A. H. Neal and Samuel Barr

Page 96 A2 Will of James Stinson
    To the heirs of Elizabeth Fisher and Stephen Stinson...
    To Mary White, Horace W. Robertson...
    To my sons: John H., Joseph H., and Edmund...
    Edmund and John H., Exe.
Written: 28 February 1853   Recorded: 17 March 1853
Witnesses: Stephen and William S. Howard, Moniteau Co., Mo.
Elizabeth Stinson to John Fisher 28 Dec. 1825 62
Joseph W. Stinson to Mary Ann Alexander 15 May 1845 191
Lorenly Stinson to George Robinson 20 July 1837 73
Polly Stinson to John White 23 July 1831 157
Stephen Stinson to Nancy Martin 2 Feb. 1832 156

John Stock to Prudence Roberson 23 July 1849 17

Mary Stocknill to R. Givney 4 Jan. 1831 140

Thomas Stockstill to Nancy Jones 11 June 1832 2

Richard Garnett Stockton to Ann Thompson Horton 30 Jan. 1844

Wesley Stoffle to Ritty Campbell 29 March 1849 9

Mary Jane Stokeley to Gilbert S. Ronce 15 Feb. 1848 258

Alexander Stone to Nancy McFarland 1 Dec. 1829 111
Deborah Stone to Stephen Dial 27 Aug. 1820 16
Dicy Stone to Joshua Lewis 8 Feb. 1823 41
Elizabeth Stone to Nathan Neel 23 March 1826 58

Granderson Stone to Mary Ann Campbell 21 Dec. 1848 7
Jane Stone to Wiette Kirkindall 24 April 1832 152
John M. Stone to Sarah Jane Nugent 5 Dec. 1850 38
Martha E. Stone to John Bell 12 Nov. 1840 117

Page 108 A Will of James Story
    To my sons: William C., Thomas, Cornelius, Elizabeth Allen, Prudence Johnson, and Mary Ann Story..., my daughters.
    To my son, James E.
Written: 16 February 1833   Recorded: 8 December 1836
Witnesses: Jacob and Allen I. Gabriel
Catherine Story to Samuel Hammond 19 March 1822 30
Cornelius Story to Prudence Schrichfield 8 Feb. 1829 172
Prudence Story to Jacob Johnston, 23 Dec. 1825 55

Isaac P. Stover, Platte Co., Mo. to Matilda Rickman 1 Feb. 1844 173
Mary Stover to New Britten 23 Dec. 1821 23

Sally Stow to George Rennison 2 Jan. 1834 13

Mary or Polly Strain to James Hampton 17 Aug. 1828 93

Gideon E. M. Strange, Howard Co., Mo. to Clara Flournoy 13 Jan. 1846 204

Franklin Streg to Magdalene Reiller 24 Nov. 1845 196

Mary Frances Strite to Hardy Robinson 20 March 1847 231

Page 389 A2 Will of Betthaser Stuckert

Charles James Sturd to Elizabeth Simmonds 16 Oct. 1832 159

Johnston Stutts to Elizabeth Williams 20 Oct. 1849 22

Samuel P. Sueringer to Jennett Thomas 12 June 1845 191

Amelia Sullivan to William C. McClain 27 May 1842 143
Janey Sullivan to William T. Cole 11 Feb. 1840 100

John Fenton Summers to Virginia Coleman 3 Jan. 1847 223
Narcissa Summers to Nathaniel L. Ford 1 Sept. 1844 178

Page 401 A2   Will of Thomas P. Sutherland
    To my wife, Lydia P.
    P. C. Blakslee, adm.
Written: Recorded: 16 April 1869
Witnesses: A. B. Stevenson and William Keener

Benjamin Sutherland to Susan Clark 18 Feb. 1841 126
John H. Sutherland to Craminta McMahan 22 March 1838 78
Huckleberry Southerland to Sarah Bridgewater 5 March 1835 26
Nathaniel Sutherland to Mary Dix 21 Dec. 1847 251

David P. Swearingen to Lydia Margaret Woolery 20 June 1839 97
Martha Swearingen to Joshua T. Williams 13 June 1839 108
Samuel S. Swearingen to Elizabeth J. Garrett 28 Nov. 1844 183
William Swearingen to Polly Hinley 2 Sept. 1819 7
William Swearingen to Rebecca Johnson 29 March 1832 146

Willis M. Tackett to Sidney Ann Harrison 23 Dec. 1847 249

Levi Talbot to Mary Dunn 19 Feb. 1843 152
Thomas Talbot to Wer Muir 23 May 1848 258

Lucy Ann Taliafur to James M. Baker 14 March 1848 259
Mary Talliaferro to Thomas Tucker 21 Oct. 1847 246

Henderson Tally to Mary Ann Osburn Taylor 15 Dec. 1836 61

Pheby Talytell to Wiley Jones 10 Oct. 1847 246

James Tankersly to Agnes Calloway 23 May 1838 81
James Tankersly to Agnes Calloway 23 May 1838 81

Nancy Tarwater to Renfrelour Clark 27 Jan. 1820 8

Elijah Tawler to Nancy Drinkwater 8 Nov. 1846 225

Agnes Jane Taylor to Jesse Jones 2 March 1837 66
Arabella C. Taylor to J. H. Maxon 16 Sept. 1841 132
Celia Taylor to Hugh Brown 7 Feb. 1836 50
Crud Taylor to Mary Sheppard 17 Aug. 1848 7
Hannah B. Taylor to Frederick Arrent, Andrew Co., Mo.
 14 June 1846 211
James Taylor to Louisa Farris 22 May 1834 21
James H. Taylor to Harding Douglas 15 Aug. 1843 21
John Taylor to Elizabeth Calvert 12 April 1832 148
John H. Taylor to Meranda A. Hunt 10 Aug. 1845 193
John Taylor to Elizabeth Cockrill 27 June 1844 172
Julain Taylor to Ignatius Adams 26 Feb. 1833 3
Levy Taylor to Menerva Bone 20 June 1831 126

Page 126 B Will of Jacob Thomas
 To my wife, Jane...
 To my sons and daughter: James, Andrew, Jonas, Thomas, and Margaret
Written: 21 October 1844 Recorded: 11 February 1845
Witnesses: George Crawford and Henry Dear

Page 1 B Will of Silas Thomas
   To my wife, Elizabeth...
   William Wheeler, my son in law and my wife, Exe.
Written: 4 September 1841   Recorded: 4 November 1841
Witnesses: William Steele and Nathan Neel
Page 79 B Will of William Thomas
   To my eldest son, William, Jr.
   To my children: Tabitha Maltby, Patsy Henry, Nancy Hoover, Susan Givens, Mary Bird, Elizabeth Foster, William, and Benjamin...
   To my grandson, William Henry...
Written: 19 April 1844   Recorded: 20 May 1844
Witnesses: Jordan and T. S. O'Bryan and Eri Morley

Adam Thomas to Harriet Thomas 21 Feb. 1836 46
Catharine Thomas to Andrew W. Woolery 28 Nov. 1844 180
Elizabeth Thomas to Thomas Foster 4 Nov. 1835 35
Harriet Thomas to Adam Thomas 21 Feb. 1836 46
Isaac Thomas to Harriet Goodno 9 April 1829 102
Jacob Thomas to Catharine Woolsey 27 April 1820 22
James Thomas to Nancy Woolery 4 Jan. 1846 201
Jennett Thomas to Samuel P. Lueringen 12 June 1845 191
Jesse Thoms to Mary Ann James 12 June 1845
Jonas Thomas to Isella Woolery 8 Feb. 1835 25
Dr. J. P. Thomas to Lucy Wallace 27 Aug. 1846 219
Malinda Thomas to John Newman 30 April 1833 1
Margaret Thomas to William Woolery 1 Jan. 1835 25
Mary Jane Thomas to Rush Hilman 19 Sept. 1849 20
Mary Thomas to James Boll 29 May 1823 42
Polly Thomas to Andrew T. Meredith 16 June 1846 213
Samuel Thomas to Malinda J. Lilly 4 July 1849 15
Sarah Thomas to Herman E. Bidstreep 12 Dec. 1823 45
Sarah Thomas to Harris Horns Furgarson 4 June 1850 32
Tabitha Thomas to Peter Mautthy 17 Nov. 1842 149
Thomas Thomas to Mrs. Elizabeth Lawrence 4 April 1841 125
William H. Thomas to Cindrilla Tevis 29 Jan. 1836 49

Page 62 B Will of Richard Thompson
   To my sons: Richard R., Thomas Edward and his wife Margaret, William Henry, and Harrison...
   To my daughters: Charlotte, Ann Bond, and Louisa T. Megguier...
Written: 4 November 1838   Recorded: 10 May 1844
P. R. Hayden and David Andrews

Alexander H. Thompson to Lucy H. Collins 7 May 1844 170
Mrs. Catharine Ann Thompson to William Anderson 18 Sept. 1842
Ellen Thompson to William Graves 16 Feb. 1843 152
James Thompson to Judy Ann Buckner 16 Jan. 1840 106
Leonard Thompson to Elizabeth Hog 15 March 1832 147
Hiram Thompson to Stephen Mayfield 29 April 1846 210
Phillip W. Thompson to Penelope Alexander 21 Feb. 1850 29

Richard R. Thompson to Mary Elizabeth Kelly 11 Jan. 1848 255

Hiram Thornton to Sophia Turley 16 April 1835 29
James Thornton to Amanda M. Bridgewater 21 Nov. 1844 181
John Thornton to Katherine House 7 Dec. 1820 17

Page 414 A2   Will of Benjamin F. Thorp
    To my wife, Eliza J. ...
    Eli P. Adams, Exe.
Written: 24 April 1869   Recorded: 28 May 1869
Witnesses: Samuel Maxwell, James F. Adams, and Urban E. Davis

Page 165 B Casper Thro
    To my wife, Catharine...
    To my three children: Pauline, John Edward, and William..
    David Andrews and Catharine Thro, Exe.
Written: 29 April 1846   Recorded: 19 August 1846
Witnesses: Reinhard Hidrick and Alfred L. Townsley

William D. Tiler to Edmonia M. Turley 14 Dec. 1843 166

David Tittsworth to Lavinia May 14 July 1831 135
Elizabeth Tittsworth to George W. Embree 19 Jan. 1848 251
Jail W. Tittsworth to Pike M. Bradley 5 Sept. 1849 18
Lucy Ann Tittsworth to John Phillips 13 June 1839 90
Nancy Tittsworth to Joseph Woolery 17 Aug. 1828 94
Nancy Tittsworth to James Forsythe 5 Oct. 1841 135
Polly Titsworth to Henry Berger 23 June 1833 12
Priscilla Tittsworth to William W. Calvert 31 Dec. 1839 105

John Titus to Nancy Jane Tool 23 Sept. 1841 136

Page 68 A2   Will of Jeremiah Tivis
    To my wife, Mixey...
    To the heirs of my daughter, Emeline Fowler: Franklin and Elizabeth Fowler...
    To the heirs of my daughter, Dulcenda Corum: Cleopatra, James Crow, Nancy, and William...
    To my daughter, Cindrilla Thomas...
    To my sons: Thomas, Simon, John Wesley, and Perry...
    To my daughter, Julian
Written: 8 March 1852 Lawrence Stephens, Exe. Rec. 3 Sept. 1844
Witnesses: John A. A. Tutt and William R. Gibbs

Dianna Tobin to John W. Scruggs 9 Nov. 1848 2

Robert L. Todd to Sally W. Hall 31 Oct. 1850 33
William H. Todd to Elizabeth Apperson 19 Sept. 1850 36

Richard Tolbert to Lucetta Howard 29 Sept. 1846 223

Thomas T. Toler to Martha Drinkwater 3 June 1846   214

Nancy Tomlin to John F. Clark 9 Nov. 1843   164

Page 25 A2 Will of Mary Tompkins
    To my nephew, Benjamin White, Boon Co., Mo. ...
    I have resided with my nephew and family, viz Albert G. Tompkins...
    To my brother, George Tompkins, Cole Co., Mo., now deceased
Written: 8 Aug. 1846   Recorded: 12 April 1849
Witnesses: William A. Lacey and William N. McClanahan

Catharine Tompkins to George Logan 19 Nov. 1846   224

Page 161 A2 Will of Sally Tompkins
    To my daughter, Mary Ann Powell, six large silver spoons
    To my daughter, Catharine Y. Tracy, one silver tumbler marked J. R. T.
    To my daughter, Theodocia Harrison, one silver tumbler marked R. T.
    To my son, William M., $200.
    To my son, Benjamin, the house and lot and all the improvements that I purchased from Jesse Homan.
    Buy Nancy Tompkins, my son Gwyns' daughter a ring.
    Every thing else of mine I wish my son, Benjamin to have to do as he pleases, it being a poor compensation of his care for me ever since he was a boy.
Written: 26 October 1854   Recorded: 6 August 1855
Witnesses: T. W. G. Thomas and C. L. Loomis

Nancy Jane Tool to John Titus 23 Sept. 1841   136

Fredriche Tottle to Charles Reinhard 23 Sept. 1841   132

Elizabeth F. Townsend to Benjamin Lawless 29 Feb. 1844   170
Lucy Ann Townsend to James N. Jamison 10 March 1846   208
Susan Townsend to N. W. Scott 28 Oct. 1849   21

S. L. Townsley to Eliza Ann Dow 12 May 1844   171

Martha Ann L. Townson to David N. Jones 30 March 1837   66

Elizabeth Travilian to Jonathan Hedrick 23 Dec. 1824   51

Elizabeth Travis to Ettel Johnson 23 Dec. 1821   24
Polly Travis to John Self 17 Jan. 1827   74
William Travis to Polly Drinkwater 27 Dec. 1821   24

Absolom H. Trion to Elizabeth McCullough 25 April 1838   81

William H. Trigg to Sarah Wyan 17 March 1835   42

John Trotter to Lucinda Cannada Given 10 May 1827 82
Margaret Trotter to James Son 26 July 1829 108

Katherine Truce to Green P. Allison 10 Jan. 1841 122

Page 319 A2 Will of Jane Tucker
    To my sons: Alexander, William, Walter, James, Joseph, Samuel F., and Robert...
    To my daughter, Eliza Glenn...
    To my grand daughter, Susan McMillen...
    Isaac Lionberger, Exe.
Written: 26 December 1860   Recorded: 15 September 1862
Witnesses: George Stucker and Washington Adams

Page 215 A2 Will of Matthew James Tucker
    To my daughters: Mary Elizabeth Tucker and Ann O. Seat...
    To my sons: Robert and James W. Tucker...
    My son, James W. and Alexander Givens, Exe.
Written: 14 February 1857   Recorded: 9 August 1858
Witnesses: S. J. W. McGuire, James Rankin, and Alex. Givens

Amanda M. Tucker to Josiah D. Adams 9 Oct. 1838 87
Douglas A. Tucker to Maria E. Bronaugh 14 May 1846 209
Elizabeth Tucker to Daniel C. Steel 10 July 1847 234
Jacob H. Tucker to Catherine P. Bronaugh 21 Nov. 1848 4
Joseph Tucker to Elizabeth Robertson 28 Feb. 1837 65
John Wesley Tucker, Livingston Co., Mo. to Nancy Jane Tucker 11 May 1841 127
Nancy Jane Tucker to John Wesley Tucker 11 May 1841 127
Robert Tucker to Margaret Adams 10 Jan. 1839 91
Thomas Tucker to Mary Talliaferro 21 Oct. 1847 246
William Tucker to Elly McFarland 31 Aug. 1826 66
William M. Tucker to Elizabeth Mitchell 7 Oct. 1846 220

Eleanor J. Turbin to Benton C. Blades 18 May 1848 259

Page 438 A2 Will of Samuel Turley
    To my wife, Mary...
    To my two son in laws: John W. McMahan and William P. Walton...
    To my sons: Federal W. and James...
    To my daughters: Eliza McMahan, Matilda Woolridge, Louisa Jane Walton, and Nancy Ann Woolridge...
Written: 4 February 1860   Recorded: 3 November 1870
Witnesses: Milton Turley and David Castleman

Edmonia M. Turley to William D. Tiler 14 Dec. 1843 166
Elzira Turley to John M. McMahan 19 April 1832 151
Jane Turley to John Baker 5 Nov. 1846 219
Jesse Turley to Jutitia Riddle 14 Feb. 1822 34
Jesse L. Turley to Lucy Herndon 12 Sept. 1833 7
Laminda Turley to Whitfield Reynolds 30 Dec. 1838 92
Louisa Jane Turley to William P. Walton 7 May 1839 112

Matilda Turley to Samuel Wooldridge 19 Dec. 1840 121
Mildred Turley to Henry C. McMahan 23 Nov. 1848 3
Odelia M. Turley to William Harris 4 May 1843 158
Salinda Turley to Henry Harvey 4 Dec. 1832 166
Sophia Turley to Hiram Thornton 16 April 1835 29
William S. Turley to Louisa Ricks 17 May 1840 113

James Turner to Tabitha Billingsley 4 Jan. 1822 32
John Turner to Nancy Campbell 11 Feb. 1819 1
Mrs. Mary Turner to Thomas Driskill 28 Aug. 1839 101
Moses Turner to Eliza McClanahan 30 July 1828 91
Sophia Turner to Moses Driskill 20 Nov. 184 2
Thomas Turner, late of Virginia, now of Saline Co., Mo. to
    Catherine Rees Given 1 July 1830 122

Page 116 A2 Will of Gabriel Tutt
    To my wife, Jane C. ...
    To my three sons: William I., Samuel I., and Thomas E. ...
Written: 24 September 1850   Recorded: 14 December 1853
Witnesses: Phillip A. Tutt, Robert H. Talferro, and Thomas Tucker
Page 136 A Will of Richard J. Tutt
    To my son, Henry...
    To my daughter, Mary Ellen Tutt...
    To my other children: Susan Turner, Elizabeth Walden, dec.
Sally Hill, John L. C., and James A. ...
    Heirs of my late daughter, Robert Berryman, Thomas Edward, and Charles Conner, of my late daughter, Elizabeth Walden...
Written: 22 May 1840   Recorded: 4 November 1840
Witnesses: Robert Hill, Allen S. Nance, and Jeptha V. Boone
Dollie Marie Tutt to Alexander M. Roads 7 Feb. 1837 65
Fannie W. Tutt to John S. McCutchen 17 Aug. 1847 239
Martha V. Tutt to James Hutchinson 18 Dec. 1845 190
Samuel J. Tutt to Elizabeth Hutchinson 2 Feb. 1843 153

Mary F. Tyler to George W. Harris 9 Nov. 1841 136

Mary N. Ulesse to Uriah Jolly 9 Sept. 1847 241

George Ulever to Margaret Hasel 6 Oct. 1847 242

William J. Underwood to Nancy Ann Carry 27 Aug. 1848 1

Eliza Vandaver to Joshua Gay 24 Jan. 1850 27

Page 343 A2 Will of Martin Vanderpool
    To my wife, Mary Elizabeth... To my adopted daughter, Albertine Bull, wife of George J. Bull...To my sister, Therisea Vinleman...
Written: 6 September 1858   Recorded: 3 February 1865
Witnesses: John S. Stephens, J. S. Weeden, and Thomas N. Oglesby

NOTES

Amanda Vanplank to William Lamont 15 Dec. 1844 180

Page 435 A2 Will of Elizabeth Varner
   To Mary Clay, Hiram and Joseph Gray, Wesley Gray, and Henrietta Gray...
     James H. Walker and William S. Cordry, Exe.
Written: 17 May 1870 Recorded: 5 October 1870
Witnesses: John D. Cordry, J. M. Daniel, and Henry H. Smith
Daniel Varner to Stacy Ann Cordry 1 Feb. 1844 166

Aaron Vaughn to Maria Terrill 22 Sept. 1836 63
Becky Von to Jesse Johnson 18 Nov. 1827 84
Catharine Vaughn to Ira E. Barnes 12 April 1846 205
Dorothy Ana Vaughn to Andrew T. Barnes 2 Sept. 1845 193
Joseph Vaugn to Elvira Hill 29 July 1835 37
James Vaughn to Charity Hill 4 Nov. 1837 77
John Vaughn to Nancy Han 15 May 1826 64
John Vaughn to Mahala Johnson 24 July 1828 93
Joshua Vaughn to Betsey Birdsong 2 Aug. 1827 79
Mary Vaughn to John Gabriel, Jr. 14 Feb. 1827 73
Patsy Vaughn to Peter Calvert 26 Nov. 1835 40
Letta Vaughan to John Allen 27 Feb. 1849 6
Thomas Vaughn to Sarah Hammons 14 Oct. 1829 110

Page 90 A2 Will of Ivannus F. Vaulemans
   To my wife, Thursday...
   To my children: John, Alterene, Dominick, Josephine, Carolina, and Mary...
Written: 26 January 1851 Recorded: 3 February 1853
Witnesses: Charles N. Brooking, John Valemans, and Polydone Wees

Drury Venable to Shaney Fry 2 July 1837 69

Page 363 A2 Will of George Vollrath
   To my wife, Resina...
   To my brother, Nicholas...
Written: 27 April 1861 Recorded: 30 November 1865
Witnesses: Washington Adams, Veit Eppstein, and N. Vollrath

Matilda T. Volwaer to Thomas Waters 24 Sept. 1849 19

Page 127 A Will of Moses Wadley
   To my brother, Francis L. Wadley...
   To my sister, Elizabeth, wife of James E. Woolery...
Written: 15 August 1839 Recorded: 7 November 1839
Witnesses: F. M. G. Thomas and Samuel L. Briscoe
David Wadley to Jane Conner 27 Jan. 1825 51
Elizabeth Wadley to James Woolery 11 April 1839 95
Francis S. Wadley to Jain Davis 14 Jan. 1844 167

Jacob Waggoner to Polly Sparks 26 Sept. 1830 124

Helen E. Walgenbach to T. A. Miller 7 April 1845 188

Henry R. Walker to Sarah F. Read 18 March 1829 100
Polly Walker to John Soeth 2 April 1829 101
Sarah Ann Walker to John G. Ressler 13 March 1845 184

Page 217 A2 Will of Robert Wallace, Senior
    To my sons: George W., Robert, Jr., William B., Addison, Joseph D., and Newton...
    To my daughters: Margaret H. Jamison, Mary S. Finley, Sarah E. Cooper, Catharine Jane Wallace, and Ann Eliza Wallace..
    To my wife, Margaret...
    William B., Joseph B., and Margaret, Exe.
Written: 11 January 1854   Recorded: 27 August 1856
Witnesses: Washington Adams, John S. Stephens, and H. A. Hutchinson
George W. Wallace to Lucinda Jamison 1 May 1838 80
Harvey B. Wallace to Mahala Houx 16 Nov. 1840 117
Lucy Wallace to Dr. J. P. Thomas 27 Aug. 1846 219
Margaret Wallace to Ephraim Jamison 21 July 1841 131
Mary Wallace to Wilker H. Finley 26 Feb. 1840 109
Robert Wallace to Margaret Steel 24 June 1824 50
Sarah E. Wallace to Dudley Cooper 1 May 1850 31
Thomas B. Wallace to Rose A. Elliott 3 April 1838 80

Mrs. Mary Jane Waller to Martillus Ferrill 7 March 1837 65

Harriet J. Walls to George C. Dugan 7 Jan. 1849 5
Hosea Walls to Elizabeth Whitney 20 July 1836 54

Page 260 A2 Will of James Walter
    To my mother, Sarah...
    To my brothers: Charles P. and George...
    To my sisters: Caroline Sarah Haywood, Cornelia Louisa Zeigler, and Sarah A. Foster...
    To my wife, Martha C. ...
Written: 13 August 1859   Recorded: 3 March 1860
Witnesses: G. G. Vest and H. A. Hutchinson
James Walter to Martha C. Kenney 28 Nov. 1842

Drunett Walton to Benjamin Bell 3 Oct. 1844 210
John Walton to Eliza J. Ruley 1 Jan. 1835 26
Nancy Ann Walton to Alexander Roe 26 Sept. 1844 210
William P. Walton to Louisa Jane Turley 7 May 1839 112

Alexander S. Wear to Rachel Steel 19 Feb. 1833 165
Catharine Wear to John Caloway 21 Dec. 1842 167
Cinthy F. Wear to James M. Allcorn, Jr. 14 Feb. 1833 163

Page 49 A Will of Hugh Wear
   To Mary Burns, Elizabeth L. McCorkle, James Wear, William
B. Wear, and Margaret Stephens, my lawful heirs...
   My son, William D., special guardian for my son, James
   John Miller, Exo.
Written: 11 October 1830   Recorded: 26 October 1830
John Wear, John Miller, James L. Wear, witnesses
Eleanor I. Wear to K. A. B. Johnston 19 March 1845 185
Elizabeth Ware to Charles Calloway 15 April 1846 214
Finis E. Wear to Mary Ann Oglesby 27 Nov. 1834 26
George D. Wear to Mary Ann Cordry 27 Sept. 1838 87
Rev. Hugh W. Wear, Pettis Co., Mo. to Harriett E. Eller
   15 April 1847 230
John T. Ware to Sarah Maria Calloway 20 Oct. 1843 162
Jonathan W. Wear, Dade Co., Mo. to Cathren E. Cordry
   12 Jan. 1843 151
Mary Wear to Milton Finley 15 Aug. 1833 6
Mary Wear to William L. Cordray 29 March 1837 79
M. Wear to Barnet Johnson 7 Dec. 1848 3
Macoline B. Wear to John Anthony 20 Nov. 1845 201
Margaret Wear to Robert W. Parker Given 10 Sept. 1828 94
Malinda Wear to Wilson C. Foster 16 Feb. 1841 122
Mary D. Weir to Alfred McCutchen 26 Aug. 1832 158
Mary E. Wear to John B. Cordry 4 July 1838 84
Mary Katherine Wear to Andrew A. Foster 16 Nov. 1841 135
Nancy Wear, aged about 27 years to Achilles Eubank, aged about
   79 years 13 Aug. 1837 70
Samuel Wear to Orbany C. Cline 20 Dec. 1848 11
S. K. Wear to Nancy L. Wood 3 April 1849 9
Virginia M. Wear to Richard A. Norman 19 Feb. 1846 205
William B. Wear, Pettis Co., Mo. to Mary E. Parsons
   22 May 1845 195
William G. Wear to Sarah A. Yancy 2 Nov. 1837 75

Henry Webster to Amanda McFarland 20 April 1835 28

Adam Weaver to Nancy Gabriel 1 Nov. 1827 85
Elizabeth Weaver to Major Adier 8 July 1827 79
Sally Ann Weaver to Samuel Coffman 10 May 1848 261
Sebela Weaver to George W. Helmreich 12 Oct. 1843 163
Stephen Weaver, Chariton Co., Mo. to Julia Sombart
   1 Nov. 1841 137

Archibald Weatherford to Ellena Campbell 22 Oct. 1845 196

Page 68 B Will of Cuthbert Webb
   To my sister, Mary, wife of William P. Nicholson...
   Isaac W. Scott, Exe.
Written: 20 March 1839   Recorded: 7 May 1844
Witnesses: W. T. Scott and C. B. Henry

John S. Webb to Susannah Zilhart   23 Nov. 1843   163
Leonard Webb to Jane P. Wells   17 May 1849   13
Mary Margaret E. Webb to Merrit D. Platt   12 Dec. 1847   246

Benjamin Weeden to Eliza Berry   3 Jan. 1828   90
Benjamin Weeden to Jane P. Wells   17 May 1849   13
Mary Margaret E. Webb to Merrit D. Platt   12 Dec. 1847   246

Benjamin Weeden to Eliza Berry   3 Jan. 1828   90
Benjamin Weeden to Catherine A. Fitten   27 March 1837   68
Elizabeth Weeden to David Ross   15 Feb. 1835   27
Daniel Weeden to Mary J. Fitten   19 Oct. 1842   148
Mathew Weeden to Margaret Kirkpatrick   15 Jan. 1837   62
Polly Weeden to Jacob Rice   2 Nov. 1834   25
Sarah A. Weeden, daughter of Benjamin Weeden to Jacob Teeter
    23 April 1848   257

Anthony Welch to Margaret J. Anderson   21 May 1843   158

Jane P. Wells to Leonard Webb   17 May 1849   13
Joseph Wells to Sally Bradley   28 March 1820   13
Mary Jane Wells to Benjamin F. Berkley   21 June 1849   14
Mathew Wells to Elizabeth Wood   22 Sept. 1847   247
Rebecca Wells to Thurman Harris   12 Feb. 1849   10
Page 395 A2   Will of John Wells
    To my sons: Wilson, Eli, Rufus R., John, Sidwell, and James...
    To my daughters: Martha, wife of Edward Harris; Deborah Ann, wife of Isaac M. Dickey; Cina, wife of John Homan
Written: 14 October 1867   Recorded: 6 February 1868
Witnesses: Soloman Shinn, Henry Loew, and S. A. Summers
Rudolphus D. Wells to Irene Short   8 Nov. 1849   27

Johun Wemple to Barbara Martin   9 Dec. 1849   22

Charles West to Mary Hanna Merrill at the residence of Wilson Merrill   10 Aug. 1841   129

Page 69 A   Will of Joseph Westbrook
    To my wife, Hannah...
    To my daughter, Polly Farris...
    To my sons: Joseph, Caldwell, and Richard...
Written: 2 Feb. 1830   Recorded: 10 June 1833
Witnesses: John Smith, John Wilkinson, Andrew Robertson, and Lendezy Burk
Page 76 A   Will of Richard Westbrook
    To my wife, Lydia...to my sons: Joseph and William...
to my daughters: Sarah Farris, Deborah Kary, Polly Caldwell, Lydia Procter of Jackson Co., Mo., Modest Farris, and Margaret Farris
Written: 22 October 1832   Recorded: 30 September 1833

Ann E. Westbrook to Michael Hornbeck 18 June 1846 217
Elizabeth Westbrook to John Hastey 18 Dec. 1838 91
Elverton Caldwell Westbrook to Larry M. Fields 11 Jan. 1849 6
Hannah Westbrook to Daniel Bankston, Morgan Co., Mo.
   3 March 1842 142
Joseph Westbrook to Mary Givens 12 Aug. 1841 133
Lidy Westbrook to John Proctor 5 Nov. 1820 19
Mary Westbrook to John Faris 17 Dec. 1826 67
Midist Westbrook to Sampson Harris 24 Dec. 1829 116
William Westbrook to Cynthia Jones 28 March 1822 31
Johannah Westerman to John Otten 18 Jan. 1849 6

Enoch Wethers to Sarah Hughes 15 March 1838 62

Page 446 A2 Will of Susan G. White
   To my nephew, Samuel Rice, of Indiana...
   To my brother William White's daughter, Susan G. Logan...
   To my brother, James A. White
Written: 4 May 1870   Recorded: 27 July 1870
Witnesses: J. W. Drafflin and William D. Adams
Anna White to Edmond Baxter 27 Dec. 1849 25
Daniel Milton White to Mary Jane Davis 1 Jan. 1841 124
Eidia White to Isaac Moore 10 Jan. 1833 19
Elizabeth White to Howard Gist 10 Oct. 1839 101
Fielden White to Harriett Dush 29 Feb. 1848 257
Hartley White to Nancy Ests 31 March 1833 1
James H. White, Chariton Co., Mo. to Margaret Allison
   17 July 1838 91
Jesse White to Lotty Morris 29 Oct. 1833 19
John White to Polly Stinson 2? July 1831 157
Lucinda White to Gabriel W. Gaugh 20 Jan. 1839 92
Nancy White to William Drinkwater 24 May 1836 60
William White to Nancy Mave 5 March 1820 13

Andrew Whitlow to Susan Harvey 3 Feb. 1842 139

Christian Whitman to Barbara Zimmerman 13 April 1849 10
Margaret P. Whitman to John B. Spencer 29 Aug. 1850 32
Stephen Whitman to Mary Snigan 31 May 1848 258

Elizabeth Whitney to Hosea Wall 20 July 1836 54

Thompson Whitson to Hannah Har 26 March 1820 11

John C. Whitters to Penelope Rail 4 Oct. 1842 149

Wesley H. Wickersham to Maria S. Richards 25 Feb. 1849 6

Delitha Wiley to Isaac Duncan 5 May 1834 21
Mary Jane Wiley to Hugh Baxter Morris 26 March 1846 207

Page 16 A2 Will of James G. Wilkerson
    To my wife, Elizabeth...
    To my three oldest children: John S., Sarah A. E. Parsons and William C. ...
    To each of my other children: Eliza E. Wilkerson, James C. Wilkerson, Elizabeth R. Wilkerson, Zippora U. Wilkerson, Rebecca D. Wilkerson, Hannah A. Wilkerson, and Charity M. Wilkerson...
    Elizabeth, my wife, Exe.
Written: 4 December 1846   Recorded: 1 June 1848
Witnesses: William Steele and Thomas T. McCulloch
John Wilkerson to Mary Koontz 2 March 1848 254
Major J. Wilkerson to Margaret J. Reed 16 July 1832 153
Margaret Jane Wilkerson to Patrick Rathburn 9 May 1849 13
Sarah Ann E. Wilkerson to Luny W. Parsons 2 June 1844 175

Page 158 A2 Will of Joseph Wilkins, city of Baltimore and state of Maryland
    To my sons: Doct. Joseph and John...
    And the remaining three parts among my three daughters: Sarah E. Cooch, Ellen Tompkins, and Caroline Wilkins...
    To my wife, Mary C. ...
    Mary C., John Glenn, and Dr. Joseph Wilkins, Exe.
Written: 18 July 1847 in the City of Baltimore
Witnesses: J. J. Atkinson, Caleb B. Moore, and John T. Woodside
Recorded: 12 June 1855

Page 23 A Will of Luke Williams
    To my wife, Mary...
    To my children...
Written: 20 August 1824   Recorded: 25 February 1825
Witnesses: James Williams and Jesse Parsons
Page 23 A2 Will of Richard Williams
    To my sons and daughters:...
    To my wife, Tabitha...
Written: 23 November 1846   Recorded: 5 April 1849
Witnesses: David and John S. Jones
Benjamin Williams to Catharine Wright 25 Oct. 1843 162
Mrs. Catharine Williams to Thomas Drinkwater 28 May 1846 232
Elizabeth Williams to Absolem Woods 16 March 1827 77
Elizabeth Williams to Johnston Stults 28 Oct. 1849 22
James Williams to Polly Savage 23 Feb. 1826 60
James Williams to Camilla Hill 31 Aug. 1848 264
John Williams to Emilee Bruffee 25 May 1837 68
John Williams to Elizabeth Reavis 25 Oct. 1842 150
Joseph Williams to Luraney Nelson 4 March 1847 227
Joshua Williams to Martha Swearingen 13 June 1839 108
Lousanna Williams to William Cox 30 Nov. 1834 25
Luke Williams to Louisa Baty 14 July 1833 12
Manerva Williams to Levy Holt 10 Jan. 1839 95

Marcus Williams, Jr. to Mary Jane Littlepage   14 March 1839   95
Martha Williams to William Ellison   31 Dec. 1823   44
Mary Williams to Willing Saling   3 May 1824   52
Morgan Williams to Bartholmew Job   21 Nov. 1833   12
Nancy Williams to James Henry   23 Feb. 1840   109
Prudence E. Williams to John Woolery   9 April 1840   115
Richard Williams, Jackson Co., Mo. to Mrs. Emily Harris
   26 June 1841   130
Robert M. Williams to Sophia McCulloch   30 Dec. 1840   120
Rox Ann Williams to Robert C. Bell   8 Oct. 1843   164
Sandy J. Williams to Jane Logan   18 June 1846   211
Sarah Ann Williams to James E. McCutchen   4 Oct. 1832   160
Sarah Williams to Benoni Berkly   10 Oct. 1838   89
Susan Williams to William Driskell   27 Jan. 1839   95
William Williams to Winniford Hill   19 Dec. 1850   38
Page 76 A2   Will of John Williamson
   To my sons: Joseph and John, Jr. ...
   To my daughters: Sarah E. McClanahan and Mary Bruce...
   To my grand-daughter, Polly S. McClanahan
   William N. McClanahan, Exe.
Written: 16 April 1849   Recorded: 21 August 1852
Witnesses: S. W. Robinson and William Henshaw
Page 424 A2   Will of Thomas W. Williamson, Moniteau Co., Mo.
   To my wife, Rebecca...
   To my children: Washington H., Isaac M., Nancy, Mary J.,
James F., Williamson, and Martha Bradley...
   William Henshaw, Exe.
Written: 22 August 1864   Recorded: 26 September 1869
Witnesses: William Snodgrass and Washington C. P. Taylor
Cintha Williamson to James Hampton   9 April 1846   206

Page 164 A2   Will of Alfred T. Wilson
   To my son, George G. ...
   My estate to be equally divided among my children, share
and share alike.
   To my wife, Sophronia M. ...
   From my father in laws estate, Isaac Herrel...
   To my son, George G., guardian of my minor children...
Written: July 1855   Recorded: 20 August 1855
Witnesses: H. J. Lacy and Samuel Drousius
Alexander Wilson to Mary Smith   1 Jan. 1828   89
Ann Wilson to L. A. Pollock   7 Feb. 1841   126
Harriett E. Wilson to John R. Bagwell   9 Sept. 1847   255
Jane Wilson to Isaac Barton   17 March 1840   107
John Wilson to Mary Jane Johnson   30 Oct. 1843   163
Joseph W. Wilson to Mary A. Wilson   12 May 1842   144
Mary Wilson to Joseph Byler   10 Aug. 1835   31
Mary A. Wilson to Joseph W. Wilson   12 May 1842   144
Peter Wilson to Henrietta Bartlett   13 Dec. 1849   23
Robert A. Wilson to Mary A. Davis   8 Dec. 1839   108
Zachariah Green Wilson to Elizabeth Ann Pollock   14 June 1838   82

Page 148 A2 Will of Edward Winders
    To my wife, Nancy...
    To my daughters: Susan Potter and Lucinda Yarnall...
    To my son, William N. ...
    Nancy and William N., Exe.
Written: 10 December 1851   Recorded: 30 April 1855
Witnesses: E. Patrick, James Cole, and Charles G. Rose
John W. Winders to Sarah S. Miles 2 Sept. 1847 239
Susannah Winders to John Hubbard Potter 11 Jan. 1844 168

Nancy Wingate to James McClanahan 20 June 1847 236

Page 422 A2 Will of Elisha F. Winsor
    To my mother, Marinda Robertson...
    My brother, Thomas A. Winsor, Exe.
Written: 12 June 1869   Recorded: 22 October 1869
Witnesses: Samuel Maxwell and Joseph R. Johnston

Margaret Wisdom to Greenville J. Harvey 13 Jan. 1850 30
Suda Wisdom to Wyal Zimmerman 25 Jan. 1849 14

Jenkins Withers to Margaret Steel 2 April 1839 96

Finis Anderson Witherspoon to America Missouri McCuthchon
    19 Sept. 1850 33

Safurny Witt to Calvin Huff 6 April 1847 235

Delila Wolf to William Conner 19 July 1830 122
Luella Wolf to John Robinson 26 July 1840 113
John Woolf to Sally Mullins 26 Nov. 1832 165

Alexander Wood to Louisa J. Driskill 31 Jan. 1850 29
Elizabeth Wood to Andrew Hornback 30 July 1846 222
Elizabeth Wood to Mathew Wells 22 Sept. 1847 247
Jeriah Wood to Ann Miller 21 Oct. 1824 49
Matilda Wood to Samuel Simmerrill 11 Feb. 1836 50
Nancy Wood to James Mason 12 Sept. 1830 123
Nancy L. Wood to S. K. Wear 3 April 1849 9
Penelopy Wood to Leroy Howard 27 Dec. 1833 16
Presley Wood to Sarah Burress 13 April 1843 155
Sally Wood to Andrew Hornback 12 Jan. 1837 61
Sarah Ann Wood to Alford Carey 3 April 1849 10

Page 27 A Will of Peter Woods
    To my wife, Jail...
    To my son, William M. and my daughter, Saryann...
Written: 30 June 1825   Recorded: 17 November 1825
Witnesses: Charles Woods and John Hix
Absolem Woods to Elizabeth Williams 18 March 1827 77
Archibald Woods to Elizabeth Kelly 12 Sept. 1822 36

Elizabeth Woods to Daniel G. Hughes 13 Jan. 1825 52
Green Woods to Mary Estes 30 Nov. 1821 28
Jail C. Woods to John G. Collins 5 March 1849 13
John Woods to Nancy McClure 6 Sept. 1821 26
Katherine Kavanaugh Woods, daughter of General Charles Woods,
    to Joseph Jefferson Stephens 29 Nov. 1832 158
Levi Woods to Rachael Shipley 22 Jan. 1826 61
Levi Woods to Mariah Campbell 6 Oct. 1833 9
Mary Ann Woods to Mark Cole 27 May 1834 21
Nancy Woods to William Cole Given 10 Oct. 1828 95
Polly Woods to Joshua Dolls 10 May 1821 21
Sally Woods to Martin Kidwell 16 April 1848 259
Sarah Woods to Archibald McDuffin 17 Jan. 1850 30
Sarah Ann Woods to Benjamin McPherson 8 Dec. 1839 105
    Sarah Ann, daughter of Green Woods
Sarah D. Woods, daughter of Gen. Woods to Amos Ashcraft
    11 March 1841 130
Susan N. Woods to John E. Ashcraft 19 Sept. 1844 180
William Woods to Sarah McGuier Given 10 Oct. 1828 96

Page 98 A2 Will of Margaret Woolridge
    To my sons: David, Edmund, and Starling R. ...
    To my daughters: Nancy Winders, Charlotte Kirkman,
Margaret Fisher, and Susan Meredith...
    To my grand-children: Elizabeth T. Meredith, William
McKinsey Moss, children of my deceased daughter, Polly Moss...
    To my son, Samuel...
Written: 11 August 1849   Recorded: 16 April 1853
Witnesses: Elias Patrick, William J. White, and Charles G. Rose
Page 27 A2 Will of Samuel Woolridge
    To my wife, Margaret...
    To each of my grand-children towit William McKensey Moss,
Elizabeth T. Meredith, and Nancy N. Meredith, heirs of my
daughter, Polly Moss, dec. ...
    To my children: David, Nancy Winders, Lotty Kirkman,
Edmond, Starlin R., Margaret Fisher, Susan Meredith, and Samuel.
    My son, Samuel, Exe.
Written: 29 July 1842   Recorded: 24 May 1849
Witnesses: Nathaniel T. Allison and Freeman Wing
Edmond Woolridge to Elizabeth Ross 4 Dec. 1834 24
John W. H. Woolridge to Sarah Lacy 12 Oct. 1848 4
Margaret Woolridge to Joseph Fisher 1 Aug. 1842 146
Samuel Woolridge to Matilda Turley 19 Dec. 1840 121
Starlin Woolridge to Ann M. Roe 19 Dec. 1838 93
Susanna Woolridge to Thomas Meredith 23 Aug. 1832 155

Page 15 B Will of Henry Woolery
   To my wife, Nancy...
   To my daughter, Cornely Berkley, wife of Jesse G. Berkley..
   To my daughter, Milly Oglesby, wife of Pleasant B. Oglesby.
   To my daughter, Lydia Margaret Swearengen, wife of
David P. Swearengen...
   To my sons: Herrod C. and John...
   To my other children: Andrew W., Henry C., Molinda, and
William...
   My friend, William C. Lowry, Exc.
Written: 9 June 1841   Recorded: 6 May 1842
Witnesses: Anthony F. Read, Nicholas Swearengen, Pleasant W.
Sullivan, and Henry Duncan
A. B. Woolery to Emilee Corrory 14 March 1849 8
Abner Albert Woolery to Nancy A. Taylor 10 Nov. 1850 35
Andrew W. Woolery to Catherine Thomas 28 Nov. 1844 180
Abraham Woolery to Emily Branaum 7 Sept. 1845 98
Enoch Francis Woolery to Francis Jones 12 March 1846 204
Ewing E. Woolery to Mrs. Caroline A. Read 18 Oct. 1847 246
Henry Woolery, Jr. to Litvitia Beaty 31 Dec. 1829 116
Henry C. Woolery to Amanda Johnson 3 Feb. 1850 28
Isella Woolery to Jonas Thomas 8 Feb. 1835 25
James E. Woolery to Elizabeth Wadley 11 April 1839 95
John Woolery to Prudence E. Williams 9 April 1840 115
John Woolery to Martha Smith 16 Oct. 1845 196
Joseph Woolery to Nancy Tittsworth 17 Aug. 1828 94
Lydia Margaret Woolery to David P. Swearengen 20 June 1839 97
Malinda Woolery to John J. Cole 27 Dec. 1850 36
Mary Woolery to Isaac Henderson 6 July 1839 98
Nancy Woolery to James Thomas 4 Jan. 1846 201
Stephen Woolery to Polly Shirley 3 Oct. 1839 100
William Woolery to Margaret Thomas 1 Jan. 1835 25
William J. Woolery to Ann Elizabeth Scott 10 March 1847 233

Catharine Woolsey to Jacob Thomas 27 April 1820 22
Cornelia Woolsey to Jesse G. Berkley 9 Nov. 1826 60

Cynthia Wooten to John Hatfield 30 Aug. 1829 109
Lucinda Wooten to Moses Andrew Jackson Nexon 30 Dec. 1832 167

Page 193 A2 Will of George W. Wright
   To my grand-children: Mary Louisa and George Edward,
children of my son Edward Wright, deceased...
   To my sons: Oscar, Abram I., and George...
   To my daughters: Catharine and Louisa...
   Oscar and Abram I., Exe.
Written: 9 December 1851   Recorded: 4 March 1857
Witnesses: James H. and George W. Baker
A. N. Wright to Kypasia Ann Isball 7 Sept. 1841 133
Catharine Wright to Benjamin Williams 25 Oct. 1843 162

Edward Wright to Emily Bradley 20 July 1842 147
Emilee N. Wright to Robert S. Austin 20 Dec. 1848 5
Mary H. Wright to Moses D. Hogan 12 June 1849 18
Nancy Wright to Moses Allen 30 April 1838 79
Oscar Wright to Cornelia O'Bryan 6 May 1846 208
Synthey Wright to Stephen Combs 27 July 1822 35

Wesley John Wunylan to Catharine Johnson Menifee 17 Aug. 1847 248

Page 20 B Will of Jacob Wyan
    To my daughters: Sarah L. Trigg; Mary G. Nelson; Nancy S. Myers, late Nancy S. Whitley, of the state of Kentucky; Margaret J. Russell and her husband, James Russell; and Paulina E. Wyan...
    To my son, Wesley J. Wyan...
    To my son in law, William H. Trigg...
    To my wife...
    My friend, Jordan O'Bryan and my son in laws, Thomas W. Nelson and William H. Trigg, Exe.
Written: 5 April 1842 Recorded: 2 May 1842
Witnesses: J. Collins, John G. Miller, and J. N. Laine
Margaret J. Wyan to James H. Russell 2 April 1840 110
Mary L. Wyan to Thomas H. Nelson 12 Dec. 1837 76
Sarah Wyan to William H. Trigg 17 March 1835 42

Charles H. Wyseng to Sarah M. Foster 1 June 1847 235

Page 107 A2 Will of Lucy Zachary
    To Columbus Higgerson, William Morten, Angeline Morton, Benjamin Herndons bond of $25.: Lucy Higgerson, Jane T. Turley, and Lucy Stephens...
    To my sister, Julia Stephens, my Negro boy Dangerfield who goes to James H. Higgerson at her death for his freedom.
Written: 6 Nov. 1851 Recorded: 14 September 1853
Witnesses: Daniel Bigger and James Higgerson

Page 420 A2 Will of Joseph Zeringer
    To my wife, Elnora...
    To my sons: Frank H., Otho Sigle...
    To my daughter, Christianna...

Peter Zey to Catharine Zimmerman 11 Jan. 1846 211

Susannah Zilhart to John S. Webb 23 Nov. 1843 164

Barbara Zimmerman to Christina Whitman 13 April 1849 10
Catharine Zimmerman to Peter Zey 11 Jan. 1846 211
Wyal Zimmerman to Suda Wisdom 25 Jan. 1849 14

ADDENDA

Names not given:
_____ _____ to Christopher Johns 6 Dec. 1832 160
_____ _____ to Benjamin Proctor _____ 1831 139
Elvira _____ to Joseph Morgan 31 Oct. 1834 23

Sarah Ann Ward Branch to John E. Cowan 1 May 1845 186
James Campbell to Elizene Ann Jennings 19
Elvira Hill to Joseph Vaughn 29 July 1835 37
George Kautz to Mary H. Houghton 2 Jan. 1871 228
David L. Mathews to Margaret S. Wear 7 Dec. 1848 3
Sally McMahan to John Smith 3 May 1819 1
Benjamin Middaugh to Lurella A. Stafford 29 Sept. 1870
Roderick Ramsey Mills to Lucy Mitchell 6 June 1843 156
Andrew B. Moon to Martha C. Read 1 April 1841 125
Seaburn G. Nazel to Nancy A. Jolly 4 Dec. 1845 198
Thomas Parks to Sally Hart Given 2 July 1830 121
Stephen Fisher Peterson to Gertrude Wattuscherd 20 Aug. 1849 20
John Hubbard Potter to Susannah Winders 11 Jan. 1844 168
Page 416 A2 Will of William Sloan
    To my sons: James A. and William T. ...
    Amongst my heirs: James A.; William T.; Elizabeth A. McCutchen, formerly Elizabeth A. Sloan, Catharine Smiley or her heirs; Mary McFarland, formerly Mary Sloan; Virginia A. Sloan and Archibald R. C. Sloan...
Written: 10 May 1869   Recorded: 30 July 1869
Witnesses: Samuel Wear, J. D. McCutchen, and R. L. Reed
Eliza Stone to David Colter 13 April 1820 5
James Tankersly to Agnes Galloway 23 May 1838 81
George Tennille to Sally Davis 21 Nov. 1819 6
George Volrath to Rosanna Fouch 18 April 1844 169

www.ingramcontent.com/pod-product-compliance
Lightning Source LLC
Chambersburg PA
CBHW020654300426
44112CB00007B/381